Chineseness and Modernity in a Changing China

Essays in Honour of Professor Wang Gungwu

EAI Series on East Asia

Series Editors: WANG Gungwu
(East Asian Institute, National University of Singapore)

ZHENG Yongnian
(East Asian Institute, National University of Singapore)

About the Series

EAI Series on East Asia was initiated by the East Asian Institute (EAI) (http://www.eai.nus.edu.sg). EAI was set up in April 1997 as an autonomous research organisation under a statute of the National University of Singapore. The analyses in this series are by scholars who have spent years researching on their areas of interest in East Asia, primarily, China, Japan and South Korea, and in the realms of politics, economy, society and international relations.

Published:

Chineseness and Modernity in a Changing China:
Essays in Honour of Professor Wang Gungwu
 edited by ZHENG Yongnian and ZHAO Litao

China and East Asian Economic Integration
 edited by Sarah Y TONG and KONG Tuan Yuen

Suzhou Industrial Park: Achievements, Challenges and Prospects
 by John WONG and LYE Liang Fook

Chinese Society in the Xi Jinping Era
 edited by ZHAO Litao and QI Dongtao

China's Economic Modernisation and Structural Changes:
Essays in Honour of John Wong
 edited by ZHENG Yongnian and Sarah Y TONG

Politics, Culture and Identities in East Asia: Integration and Division
 edited by LAM Peng Er and LIM Tai Wei

China's Development: Social Investment and Challenges
 by ZHAO Litao

*The complete list of the published volumes in the series can also be found at
http://www.worldscientific.com/series/eaisea

EAI Series on
East Asia

Chineseness and Modernity in a Changing China

Essays in Honour of Professor Wang Gungwu

Editors

ZHENG Yongnian

East Asian Institute
National University of Singapore
Singapore

ZHAO Litao

East Asian Institute
National University of Singapore
Singapore

World Scientific

NEW JERSEY · LONDON · SINGAPORE · BEIJING · SHANGHAI · HONG KONG · TAIPEI · CHENNAI · TOKYO

Published by

World Scientific Publishing Co. Pte. Ltd.

5 Toh Tuck Link, Singapore 596224

USA office: 27 Warren Street, Suite 401-402, Hackensack, NJ 07601

UK office: 57 Shelton Street, Covent Garden, London WC2H 9HE

Library of Congress Cataloging-in-Publication Data

Names: Zheng, Yongnian, editor. | Zhao, Litao, 1972–   editor.
Title: Chineseness and modernity in a changing China : essays in honour of
    Professor Wang Gungwu / editors Zheng Yongnian, East Asia Institute,
    National University of Singapore, Singapore, Zhao Litao, East Asia Institute,
    National University of Singapore, Singapore.
Other titles: Essays in honour of Professor Wang Gungwu
Description: First edition. | New Jersey : World Scientific, [2020] |
    Series: EAI series on East Asia | Includes bibliographical references. |
Identifiers: LCCN 2019034326 | ISBN 9789811210785 (hardback)
Subjects: LCSH: National characteristics, Chinese. | China--Civilization--1949- |
    Chinese--Ethnic identity. | Wang, Gungwu.
Classification: LCC DS779.23 .C478 2020 | DDC 951.05--dc23
LC record available at https://lccn.loc.gov/2019034326

British Library Cataloguing-in-Publication Data
A catalogue record for this book is available from the British Library.

For any available supplementary material, please visit
https://www.worldscientific.com/worldscibooks/10.1142/11565#t=suppl

Desk Editor: Lixi Dong

Typeset by Stallion Press
Email: enquiries@stallionpress.com

Printed in Singapore

Contents

About the Editors

ZHENG Yongnian is Professor of Political Science at the East Asian Institute, National University of Singapore. He is Editor of Series on *Contemporary China* (World Scientific Publishing) and Editor of *China Policy Series* (Routledge). He is also the Editor of *China: An International Journal* and the co-editor of *East Asian Policy*. He has studied both China's transformation and its external relations. His papers have appeared in journals such as *Comparative Political Studies, Political Science Quarterly, Third World Quarterly* and *China Quarterly*. He is the author of numerous books, including *Market in State, The Chinese Communist Party as Organizational Emperor, Technological Empowerment, De Facto Federalism in China, Discovering Chinese Nationalism in China* and *Globalization and State Transformation in China*, and coeditor of dozens of books on China's domestic development and international relations including the latest volumes *China Entering the Xi Era* and *China and International Relations: The Chinese View and the Contribution of Wang Gungwu*. Besides his research work, Professor Zheng has also been an academic activist. He served as a consultant to United Nations Development Programme on China's rural development and democracy. In addition, he has been a columnist for *Xinbao* (Hong Kong) and *Zaobao* (Singapore) for many years, writing numerous commentaries on China's domestic and international affairs. Professor Zheng received his BA and MA degrees from Beijing University, and his PhD at Princeton University. He was a recipient of Social Science Research Council-MacArthur Foundation Fellowship (1995–1997) and John D and Catherine T MacArthur Foundation Fellowship (2003–2004). He was Professor and founding Research Director of the China Policy Institute, the University of Nottingham, United Kingdom (2005–2008).

ZHAO Litao is Senior Research Fellow at the East Asian Institute, National University of Singapore. He obtained his PhD degree in sociology from Stanford University. His research interests include social stratification and mobility, sociology of education, social policy, technology and innovation, with a regional focus on China. His research has appeared in *China Quarterly, Research in Social Stratification and Mobility, Journal of Contemporary China, International Journal of Educational Development, Built Environment, Social Sciences in China, Copenhagen Journal of Asian Studies, China: An International Journal, Frontiers of Education in China, Issues and Studies,* and so on. He has authored, edited or co-edited many books, including *China's Development: Social Investment and Challenges* (2017), *China's Social Development and Policy* (2013) and *China's Great Urbanization* (2013). He is an associated editor of *China: An International Journal* and also serves on the editorial board of *East Asian Policy*.

About the Contributors

Kjeld Erik BRØDSGAARD is Professor at the Department of International Economics, Government and Business and Director of the China Studies programme at the Copenhagen Business School. His most recent books include *From Accelerated Accumulation to Socialist Market Economy in China* (2017); *Critical Readings on the Chinese Communist Party*, four volumes (2017); *Chinese Politics as Fragmented Authoritarianism: Earthquakes, Energy and Environment* (2016); *Hainan — State, Society, and Business in a Chinese Province* (*2012*); *The Chinese Communist Party in Reform* (with Zheng Yongnian, 2006). Professor Brødsgaard has held visiting research appointments in China, Hong Kong, Singapore, Taiwan and the USA. He is, among others, member of the International Advisory Board of the East Asian Institute, National University of Singapore; member of the Board of Sino-Danish University Centre for Education and Research; and a trustee of the Cambridge China Development Trust. He is also a Non-resident Senior Fellow at the Nordic Institute of Asian Studies and an Honorary Research Fellow at the Research Centre for Contemporary China, School of Government, Peking University. His current research covers state-Party-business relations in China; the nomenklatura system and cadre management; SOE reform; and the rise of Chinese supermanagers.

CHEN Juan is a Research Assistant at the East Asian Institute, National University of Singapore. She graduated with a Bachelor's degree in International Politics from Peking University, China. Her research interests include political development of China, state-social relations and mass political behaviour; she has written on topics including Chinese cyber nationalism, Chinese Communist Youth League and neo-nationalism in Japan.

John F COPPER is the Stanley J Buckman Distinguished Professor of International Studies (emeritus) at Rhodes College in Memphis, Tennessee. He is the author of more than 35 books on China, Taiwan and US China policy. His book *China's Global Role* (1980) won the Clarence Day Foundation Award for outstanding research and creative activity. Professor Copper has also contributed to more than 40 other books and published over 150 articles in scholarly journals, magazines and newspapers. His recent books include the three volume work titled *China's Foreign Aid and Foreign Investment Diplomacy* (2016), *Taiwan at a Tipping Point* (2018), *Donald J. Trump and China* (2019) and *Taiwan: Nation State or Province?*, seventh edition (2019). Professor Copper has testified before several US Congressional committees, including the Senate Foreign Relations Committee and the House Foreign Affairs Committee. In 1997, he was the recipient of the International Communications Award for promoting global understanding. Professor Copper has lived in Asia for 15 years.

Paul EVANS is Professor of Asian and trans-Pacific international relations in the School of Public Policy and Global Affairs at the University of British Columbia (UBC). Before going to UBC in 1999 he taught and directed research centres and programmes at York University, the University of Toronto and Harvard University. In addition to serving as the Director of UBC's Institute of Asian Research and Liu Institute for Global Issues, he served as Co-CEO of the Asia Pacific Foundation of Canada from 2005 to 2008. He has held visiting appointments at several universities in Australia, Asia and North America and helped found the Council for Security Cooperation in Asia Pacific. The author or editor of eight books, his first was a biography of John Fairbank and his most recent a history of the idea of engagement in Canadian China policy.

Ryan HO Qixu is Research Assistant at the East Asian Institute, National University of Singapore. He graduated with a Bachelor of Arts (with Honours) from the Faculty of Arts and Social Science (Department of History), National University of Singapore in 2017. His research interests include the use of history as propaganda in China and Taiwan, and the personality cult of Chiang Kai-shek in Taiwan. He has previously written on topics related to the history of Taiwan's constitutional reforms, the status of Uighur and Hui Muslims, and Islamophobia in China.

HUANG Jianli is Associate Professor at the Department of History of the National University of Singapore and concurrently Research Associate at the university's East Asian Institute. His research straddles two related fields — the history of Republican China from the 1910s to 1940s and Chinese diaspora studies. His book, *The Politics of Depoliticization in Republican China* (1996, second edition 1999), was translated into Chinese in 2010. He is also the author of *The Scripting of a National History: Singapore and Its Pasts* (2008, with Hong Lysa). His co-edited volumes include *Power and Identity in the Chinese World Order* (2003) and *Macro Perspectives and New Directions in the Studies of Chinese Overseas* (Chinese, 2002). He has also published in a broad range of international-refereed journals, such as *Frontiers of History in China, Modern Asian Studies, Inter-Asia Cultural Studies, Journal of Chinese Overseas* and *Journal of Southeast Asian Studies*.

QI Dongtao is Research Fellow at the East Asian Institute, National University of Singapore. He obtained his PhD in Sociology from Stanford University and conducts research in the field of political sociology, especially on state-society relation, nationalism, social movement and higher education in Taiwan and mainland China. His publications have appeared in *China Quarterly, Journal of Contemporary China, China: An International Journal, International Journal of China Studies, East Asian Policy* and so on. He also published a book *The Taiwan Independence Movement in and out of Power* (World Scientific

Publishing, 2016), some book chapters on Chinese working class and trade unions, Chinese think tanks, electoral politics, social movement and social welfare system in Taiwan, and co-edited three books on China's social policies and social transformation. He has also published over 30 commentaries on Taiwan's politics and cross-Strait relations in *Lianhe Zaobao* and some online media. He is completing a book manuscript tentatively titled, *Taiwan Independence Movement Returns to Power*, which uses three analytical frameworks to respectively summarise the new developments and challenges in Taiwan's politics, China's Taiwan polices and China-Taiwan-US triangular relations in the era of great power competition since 2016.

QIAN Jiwei is Senior Research Fellow at the East Asian Institute, National University of Singapore. He is also the co-editor of the book series, *Social Policy and Development Studies in East Asia* (Palgrave Macmillan). He obtained his BSc in computer science from Fudan University, China and PhD degree in Economics from the National University of Singapore. His research has appeared in publications such as *The China Quarterly, Health Economics, Policy and Law, Health Policy and Planning, Journal of European Social Policy, Journal of Mental Health Policy and Economics, Journal of Social Policy, Land Use Policy, Public Administration and Development, Public Choice, Singapore Economic Review* and *Social Policy & Administration*. He is also on the editorial board *of China: An International Journal* and *East Asian Policy.* His current research interests include political economy, development economics and health economics. His recent co-authored paper on the informal sector in China was awarded the best conference paper 2019 at the 32nd Annual Meeting of Association of Chinese Political Studies.

Anthony REID is a Southeast Asian historian who began his career in Wang Gungwu's History Department at the University of Malaya (1965–70). He is again based as Emeritus Professor at the Australian National University where he served as Professor of Southeast Asian History before 1999. In between he was founding director of the

Centre for Southeast Asian Studies at UCLA, Los Angeles (1999–2002) and of the Asia Research Institute, National University of Singapore (2002–2007). His books include *Southeast Asia in the Age of Commerce, c.1450–1680* (2 vols,1988–93); *Imperial Alchemy: Nationalism and Political Identity in Southeast Asia* (2010); *A History of Southeast Asia: Critical Crossroads* (2015); and as editor, *Negotiating Asymmetry: China's Place in Asia* (2009); *Asian Freedoms: The Idea of Freedom in East and Southeast Asia* (1998); and *Essential Outsiders: Chinese and Jews in the Modern Transformation of Southeast Asia and Central Europe* (1997). He recently experimented with a novel, *Mataram* (2018), as Tony Reid.

Leo SURYADINATA is currently Visiting Senior Fellow, ISEAS-Yusof Ishak Institute (Singapore) and Professor (Adj) with S Rajaratnam School of International Studies, Nanyang Technological University (NTU). He served as Director of the Chinese Heritage Centre (Singapore, 2006–2013, NTU) and was a Professor in the Department of Political Science, National University of Singapore (NUS) before joining NTU. He was also President of the International Society for the Study of Chinese Overseas (2007–2013). He has published extensively on Southeast Asian Politics, ethnic Chinese in Southeast Asia and China-ASEAN relations. His latest books are *The Making of Southeast Asian Nations* (2015) and *The Rise of China and the Chinese Overseas: Beijing's Policy in Southeast Asia and Beyond* (2017). He was awarded the 2018 Cultural Award by the Indonesian government for his contribution to the Studies of Chinese Indonesians.

LIM Guanie is Research Fellow at the Nanyang Centre for Public Administration, Nanyang Technological University, Singapore. His main research interests are public policy, value chain analysis, and the Belt and Road Initiative in Southeast Asia. Dr Lim is also interested in broader political economic issues within Asia, especially those of China, Vietnam and Malaysia. He is currently working on his monograph, which details the economic catching-up process of key Southeast Asian economies.

LIU Hong's areas of expertise include Asian governance from a transnational perspective, China's interactions with Southeast Asia, global talent management, and Chinese social and business networks. He has published 15 books and more than 100 articles in the English, Chinese, Japanese and Indonesian languages, including in leading international journals such as *World Politics, Journal of Asian Studies, The China Quarterly, Journal of Contemporary China, Journal of Southeast Asian Studies, International Journal of Comparative Sociology, Ethnic and Racial Studies, Journal of Ethnic and Migration Studies, Asian Journal of Public Policy,* and *Nature and Culture.* He is the Editor-in-chief of Public Governance in Asia monograph series (published by Routledge) and the *Journal of Chinese Overseas* (published by Brill).

SHAN Wei is Research Fellow at the East Asian Institute, National University of Singapore. He received his bachelor's and master's degrees in International Studies from Peking University and PhD in Political Science from Texas A&M University. His research focuses on the political behaviour of citizens and state responses in the context of political and economic development. He covers topics such as Chinese citizens' political participation, political culture, ethnic politics and regime stability. He is the author of two monographs, *Political Leadership and Political Change in Rural China* and *Political Stability in China's Changing Social Landscape* (forthcoming). His articles have been published in *China Quarterly* and other journals.

WANG Huiyao (Henry) is the founder and President of the Centre for China and Globalisation, China's leading non-government think tank that ranked among the top 100 think tanks in the world. China's Premier has appointed Dr Wang as a Counsellor of the State Council, China's cabinet. Dr Wang is also Vice Chairman of China Association for International Economic Cooperation Association of the Ministry of Commerce and Chairman of China Global Talent Society under the Ministry of Human Resources and Social Security. In addition, Dr Wang is Dean of the Institute of Development Studies of China

Southwestern University of Finance and Economics and a Vice Chairman of China Western (Overseas) Returned Scholars Association. He also sits on the Migration Advisory Board of the International Organisation of Migration of the United Nations. Dr Wang pursued his PhD studies in international business at the University of Western Ontario and University of Manchester. He was a Senior Fellow at the Harvard Kennedy School and a Visiting Fellow at Brookings Institution. Dr Wang has written and edited over 70 books in both Chinese and English on global trade, global governance, global migration, China outbound and inbound investment, Chinese diasporas and Chinese think tanks.

Introduction

ZHENG Yongnian and ZHAO Litao

That the East Asian Institute (EAI) is synonymous with Wang Gungwu is not an overstatement. Since day one of the institute's inception, Wang has left his mark on what makes EAI today.

At EAI, we have never ceased to be amazed by Wang's wealth of experience and deep knowledge of history. Like our colleagues, we look forward to his every presence at our conferences, seminars, Tuesday discussions, annual retreats and other activities. Very often, we would adjust the dates of our formal and informal events so that Wang could grace the occasions with his presence. However, he is highly sought after both within EAI and without. We do not always manage to secure his presence, certainly much less than what we would have hoped. However, whenever he is with us, he has the ability to make it a memorable, joyful and fulfilling moment.

Amazingly, his attraction does not diminish with time. He is an exception to the general rule that growing acquaintance leads to redundant information and declining appeal. No matter how long or how well we have known him, Wang seems to be a fast-moving intellectual who always has something new to offer when it comes to understanding China, Asia and the world. For this reason, he never bores us whether it is a five-minute talk or a one-hour long seminar. Indeed, it is the expectation of something new that sustains his attraction to us.

Dr Goh Keng Swee, former Singapore deputy prime minister, invited Wang to take up the position of executive chairman of the Institute of East Asian Political Economy (IEAPE) in early 1996. After it became EAI in 1997, an autonomous research centre of the National University of Singapore (NUS), Wang headed the institute as the director until 2007 and then chairman of its Board of Directors from 2007 to 2018. He remains a valuable member of EAI after his retirement from the position of chairman of EAI. No one notices that he has retired since he comes to the office regularly.

As we know from him, he and his wife Margaret had not expected or planned such a long stay prior to their departure from Hong Kong to Singapore. Indeed, this is the longest stay in his career, longer than his stint as vice chancellor (president) of the University of Hong Kong from 1986 to 1995, or a professor and head of the Department of Far Eastern History and director of Research School of Pacific Studies at the Australian National University from 1968 to 1986. It was also longer than his early career with the University of Malaya in Singapore and Kuala Lumpur from 1957 to 1968 where he started as an assistant lecturer but became a full professor in 1963.

This unexpected and unplanned long stay in Singapore is a blessing for EAI. Starting from scratch and on a new premise, EAI is lucky to have Wang in the steering position to adequately build a strong in-house research team, establish links with research institutions and think tanks in China and other parts of the world, and define EAI's mission and make EAI useful to both the NUS and the Singapore government. Together with the late John Wong, who passed away in June 2018 and is remembered as a caring yet demanding and down-to-earth economist, Wang has nurtured and grown EAI into an internationally renowned research institute on East Asia, particularly contemporary China.

Wang is a historian. To our EAI colleagues who are trained in economics, political science, sociology and other disciplines, historian Wang is a strength rather than a mismatch. In fact, his ability to connect the past with the present often makes us forget that he is a historian. If he is present at our weekly seminars or informal discussions, we never miss the chance to ask him for comments and opinions. Not surprisingly, we would get what we expect, namely, his deep and broad knowledge as well as sharp and to-the-point analysis. At that moment, he is a political economist, political scientist or sociologist, depending on the specific topic under discussion. Eventually, we come to see Wang as a scholar who is higher and broader than a historian, an economist, a political scientist or a sociologist, and not confined by any disciplinary bounds.

Equally appealing to us is Wang's cosmopolitan approach to cultures, values and identities. To us, Wang is an educator-scholar who conforms to the ideal of a Confucian "*junzi*". We believe that Confucius' humane ideas have profoundly shaped Wang's personality and thinking. This intellectual background is evidently a source of strength for his scholarship, enabling him to present the Chinese perspective that is entirely missing or misrepresented in US- or Western-centric views such as the "clash of civilisations" or the "Thucydides's trap". Yet he is cosmopolitan enough to avoid the trap of Sino-centrism as he navigates through multiple cultures and identities.

China's rise and transformations have presented opportunities, challenges and puzzles for us, particularly because analysing China is a central task for EAI. Wang's ability to draw insights from history, articulate a perspective beyond the confines of economics, political science and sociology, and navigate through multiple cultures and identities with considerable ease is both inspiring and assuring. As an institution, EAI aspires to hold a "neutral" position — neither pro-West nor pro-China — when it comes to understanding China's internal dynamics and external relations. Through his scholarship, Wang shows that it is not only desirable but also possible to have alternative perspectives for smaller states living in international space shaped by great powers. Moreover, he demonstrates that for scholars and research institutions to attract international attention, it is important to produce relevant and useful analyses for a wide and varied audience.

To us, Wang best exemplifies EAI's approach to developing useful and practical scholarship on China and East Asia for our stakeholders and international audience. He is highly sought after in different parts of the world precisely for the fact that people find his views on a wide range of issues illuminating and his insights rarely available elsewhere. We are amazed how busy he still is in his 80s. In short, Wang's ability to inform contemporaries make him a constant magnet to not only us at EAI, but also the audience in Singapore, elsewhere in Southeast Asia and other parts of the world.

In late May 2018, when Wang was about to pass the baton of EAI chairmanship to Dr Teh Kok Peng within the month, EAI organised a conference to show our appreciation for his two decades-long leadership of EAI. We invited his former colleagues, students and scholars who are also close friends of EAI to share their thoughts about him, and/or write on topics that have long been informed by his scholarship. The invitees are eminent scholars in their own fields. They work on topics that Wang's scholarship remains an important source of inspiration, from the Chinese Communist Party (CCP) to its evolving policy towards Chinese overseas, to cross-strait relations, China-US relationship and the changing world order. This book is a collection of their papers and presentations at the conference.

To our delight, chapter authors reconfirm our view that Wang's scholarship is highly relevant and useful for understanding some of the most pressing and complex issues in our times. As Paul Evans highlights in his chapter, the question of China and the world order has come to the fore as a headline issue. If the first decade of the 21st century was preoccupied with positive externalities as well as challenges brought about by China's rapid rise, the second decade has seen a decisive shift towards the concern about the "Thucydides's trap" involving China as the challenger and the United States as the challenged. Scholars are divided between those who see a war as inevitable and those advocating for extraordinary measures of restraint and diplomacy for mutual accommodation.

Wang's perception differs from either group of scholars. He questions the assumption that the Chinese have a concept of "world order" akin to that of the Americans. To him, the concept is a Western one. As quoted by Evans in his chapter, Wang commented in an extended interview in 2010: "The Chinese did have an idea of order that was hierarchical, one in which they saw themselves as the most civilized and the most developed. But theirs was not a concept of world order that led them to justify any kind of military intervention or the expansion of Chinese territory".

From Wang's perspective, much of the discussion on the "Thucydides's trap" is misinformed. In this light, if Chinese scholars and policymakers come to see the "Thucydides's trap" in the same way as the Americans, without realising that this type of worldview is a Western one rather than a Chinese one, there is a real danger of both sides falling into the trap. By comparison, Wang sees an alternative that is deeply rooted in the traditional Chinese worldview. In Evans' words, "the prospect of accommodation or co-evolution depend precisely on the maintenance of difference rather than convergence in the spheres of what Thucydides identified as honour, fear and interest". By connecting the past to the present, Wang continues to draw our attention away from Western-centric discourses on issues of global significance.

Meanwhile, we are also delighted and intrigued by Anthony Reid's emphasis on Wang's "Southeast Asian-ness". Like Reid, we value Wang's cosmopolitan approach to cultures and identities and his contribution to pioneering research that features neither western centrism nor Sino-centrism. Reid however surprises us with an even bolder statement. While acknowledging Wang as a "card-carrying China scholar", Reid goes on to argue that "he has had an even greater impact on Southeast Asian history". This new characterisation is a good surprise to us as it adds another dimension to the importance of Wang's contribution.

Reid notes that scholarship on Southeast Asia is moving into a new stage, with China-educated scholars entering in large numbers. The abundant Chinese sources on Southeast Asia can enrich Southeast Asian studies long dominated by European sources. However, as Reid points out, if the earlier generation of scholars had learnt how to combat Euro-centrism, the new generation has to be aware of the problems of Sino-centrism. As Reid notes, Wang is a role model in this regard: "He has shown how to recognize and celebrate the Chinese threads in the rich tapestry of Southeast Asia, not as part of anybody's nationalist project, but as the essence of the hybrid, cosmopolitan crossroads the region represents".

Reid's focus is on Southeast Asian studies. If we extend his analysis further, Wang's scholarship has even broader relevance. As several chapters in this book show, China has been modifying its policies towards overseas Chinese as it seeks to build closer ties through greater outreach efforts. The new approach obscures the decades-old distinction between *huaqiao* and *huaren*, thereby creating a more unified attitude towards the Chinese overseas. However, as Wang's scholarship has convincingly shown, overseas Chinese are highly heterogenous in terms of migration history, identity, language, occupation and aspiration. In regions such as Southeast Asia, the issue of Chinese identity is extremely sensitive. Wang's scholarship serves as a useful reminder that as China grows in regional and international influence, it has to take local sensitivity into account.

In Huang Jianli's chapter, he provides a much needed, and by far the most comprehensive, review of Wang's scholarship. Huang, a historian himself, firmly positions Wang as a historian, noting that Wang contributes "significantly not only towards Chinese history in general but also pioneered a new sub-field on ethnic Chinese communities located outside of China and scattered all over the world". Such contributions place Wang among the few in his generation by the highest academic standards of knowledge production.

To us at EAI, Wang is more than a historian. Indeed, Huang goes on with an enlightening analysis of Wang's domain crossing in four major different ways, namely, spatial crossing characterised by geographical straddling between inside and outside of China, temporal crossing from the ancient past to the contemporary, inter-disciplinary crossing from history to the social sciences, and intellectual crossing from the academia to public activism. Huang's detailed analysis helps explain Wang's attraction to our EAI colleagues who are economists, sociologists and legal scholars, and trained in politics.

Needless to say, Wang's influence has gone far beyond his own domains. Scholars from different disciplines always find his approaches relevant and effective in dealing with their own subjects. For example, in his chapter on the Chinese-ness of modern China, Zheng Yongnian directly borrowed Wang's concept of "Chinese-ness" to analyse how Confucianism has survived different regimes and different leadership. Zheng used three cases to demonstrate this quality of Confucianism, namely, the New Life Movement under Chiang Kai-shek, the Learning From Lei Feng Movement under Mao Zedong and the Rule by Virtue under Jiang Zemim. Equally important, in his chapter on the logic of political reform in contemporary China, Zheng also found that when analysing changes in contemporary China, problem-solving oriented techniques are often more important than grand ideologies such as communism, socialism, liberalism and democracy. When leaders and civil society tend to justify their action by an ideology, the ultimate goal is to find a solution to the problems they encounter in their daily life. Notably, Wang has emphasised this point repeatedly when he talks about research in the institute. Indeed, conducting facts-based analysis has been the tradition of EAI since Dr Goh Keng Swee's time.

Like Zheng, other colleagues at EAI have also benefitted tremendously from Wang's writings, speeches and comments. In this book, Qian Jiwei and Ryan Ho analyse Chineseness as presented in history textbooks; Shan Wei and Chen Juan document the decline and repositioning of Chinese Communist League; Zhao Litao writes on indigenous technology as Chinese modernity; Qi Dongtao and Ryan Ho focus on the diverging reappraisal of the KMT's (Kuomintang) history in mainland China and in Taiwan. They have acknowledged Wang's books as a key source of inspiration and guidance for their research, including *The Use of History* (1968), *China and the World since 1949* (1977), *The Chineseness of China* (1991), *Divided China: Preparing for Reunification 883–947* (2007) and so on.

Wang paid much attention to China's role in the world decades before its rise to become the world's second largest economy. Combining the perspectives from within and outside China, Wang revealed the importance of domestic as well as externally determined factors in shaping China's international relations. His analysis of the Chinese overseas followed the same approach. Decades thereafter, his perspective and foresight still have strong resonance, which is evident throughout this volume. Kjeld Erik Brødsgaard notes that the Chinese Communist Party continues to adapt for better internal governance rather than greater political pluralism. John F Copper analyses the current state of cross-strait relations with an assessment of the divergent sources of increased tension in the wake of Taiwan's January 2016 election. Liu Hong and Lim Guanie use Malaysia's responses to China's Belt and Road Initiative to show that China's relationship with Southeast Asia is being updated. Leo Suryadinata describes the evolution of China's policy towards Chinese overseas from the late Qing period to the current Xi Jinping era, reminding that ethnic Chinese issues are still sensitive in certain countries. Last but not least, Wang Huiyao's focus on China's participation in global governance anticipates a greater role for China in future globalisation and global politics. Taken together, these eminent scholars shed light on the behaviours of an increasingly powerful China in the international context shaped by history as well as other powers, big or small.

In a nutshell, this book reveals Wang as a still highly active and productive scholar who has achieved the highest academic standards as well as far-reaching influence beyond the research community. We thank chapter contributors for presenting at our 2018 conference and making this book possible. We also thank Chen Juan, research assistant at EAI, who has coordinated the conference and the book project. We are grateful to Jessica Loon for copyediting the book chapters. Last but not least, our thanks go to Dong Lixi from World Scientific, who has coordinated the publication of this book.

Chapter 1

Approaches to History and Domain Crossings of a Pioneering Scholar: Wang Gungwu and His Scholarship

HUANG Jianli*

Introduction

Professor Wang Gungwu landed in Singapore in 1996 after holding numerous key academic appointments across the world. He became the East Asian Institute's founding director and later held other positions in leading and nurturing it. Wang has spent a substantial part of his academic time and energy in search of an appropriate terminology to dissect the phenomena he is analysing; hence a useful starting point here would be to identify a suitable adjectival term to characterise him and his scholarship.[1] There is a variety of offerings. Southeast Asian

---

* HUANG Jianli is Associate Professor in the Department of History, National University of Singapore. He can be contacted via email at huang.jianli@nus.edu.sg.
[1] Wang's long and passionate engagement with finding the right terms and with imposing some degree of scholarly precision on their usage is worthy of charting an epistemic understanding of knowledge production in the academic world as well as for a precious insight into the persona of the scholar. See Huang Jianli, "Conceptualizing Chinese Migration and Chinese Overseas: The Contribution of Wang Gungwu", in *Journal of Chinese Overseas*, vol. 6, Issue 1, 2010, pp. 1–21; republished as a book chapter in Zheng

historian Anthony Reid of the Australian National University chose the angle of "the Southeast Asianness of a China Scholar" to highlight the local attributes of the environment which has nurtured Wang in his primary positioning as that of a "China Scholar".[2] Venturing into the realm of morality and high praise, journalist Asad-Ul Iqbal Latif published a 2010 volume on *Wang Gungwu: Junzi* 君子, *Scholar-Gentlemen* which was launched for Wang's 70th birthday celebration.[3] *Junzi* is one of the highest honours to be endowed upon a scholar of the traditional Chinese Confucian world. There is also the 2013 edited publication of Zheng Yongnian and Phua Kok Khoo on *Wang Gungwu: Educator and Scholar*, drawing attention to Wang's contribution to the two interrelated realms of teaching and research.[4] Wang has also been termed as a "doyen" or senior member of the profession. Ien Ang, for instance, referenced Wang as being "the great doyen of overseas Chinese historical scholarship".[5]

This chapter chooses to characterise Wang as a "pioneering scholar". Although it is commonly expected that all scholars are committed to the spirit and goal of originality and expanding the frontiers of knowledge, only an exceptional few could succeed in pioneering paradigm shifts and leaving behind classics which could withstand the test of time. He is one such worthy pioneer who could be regarded as the founding father of the sub-field of "Overseas Chinese Studies" or

---

Yongnian (ed.), *China and International Relations: The Chinese View and the Contribution of Wang Gungwu*, New York, Routledge, 2010, pp. 139–157. Some parts of these previous works have been recast and incorporated into this chapter.

[2] Anthony Reid, "The Southeast Asianness of a China Scholar", paper presented at the conference on "China and the World: History and International Relations: A Conference in Honour of Prof Wang Gungwu", organised by the East Asian Institute, National University of Singapore, 25 May 2018.

[3] Asad-Ul Iqbal Latif (ed.), *Wang Gungwu: Junzi* 君子, *Scholar-Gentlemen*, Singapore, Institute of Southeast Asian Studies, 2010.

[4] Zheng Yongnian and Phua Kok Khoo (eds.), *Wang Gungwu: Educator and Scholar*, Singapore, World Scientific Press, Singapore, 2013.

[5] Ien Ang, *On Not Speaking Chinese: Living Between Asia and the West*, London, Routledge, 2001, pp. 81–82.

"Chinese Diaspora Studies". This is attained through his large body of original and insightful writings as well as keynote speeches. It is reinforced by his founding directorship of the East Asian Institute at the National University of Singapore and his overseeing of the Chinese Heritage Centre located at the Nanyang Technological University. Established in 1995, the centre is one of the leading research and resource centres on all Chinese outside of China and the editor of the regular academic publication *Journal of Chinese Overseas*.[6] His active leadership of the international academic community in this sub-field has also led him earlier to co-found the International Society for the Study of Chinese Overseas in 1992. The society has remained a lively, scholarly and non-profit professional grouping of individuals and institutions interested in and committed to advancing research and scholarly exchange in the study of Chinese overseas, providing a means for research and publications, and organising and supporting national and international conferences.[7]

However, exactly what kind of "pioneering scholar" was Wang? To ascertain this, it is necessary to further explore his approaches to history learning and writing as well as his noteworthy domain crossings across multiple platforms.

History as his Academic Discipline Home-Base

Despite being notable for his border crossing of varying forms, Wang Gungwu began his academic career as a professional historian, a path he took after an initial tussle-of-heart during his young undergraduate years between the two disciplines of English literature and history. Through a twist of fate, it was the scholarly reputation, demeanour and wisdom of his history professor, C N Parkinson (of Parkinson Law fame on the growth of bureaucracy in an organisation, in that "work will expand to fill the time available for its completion"), that had tilted

---

[6] <https://chc.ntu.edu.sg> (accessed 12 March 2019).
[7] <http://www.issco.info> (accessed 12 March 2019).

and locked Wang into this orbit of history.[8] It is therefore not surprising that Wang has later peppered some of his history essays with references to great literary works such as those of T S Eliot and E M Forster which left a lasting impression on him.[9]

Wang's initial stint in history was with the University of Malaya (then located in Singapore) where he obtained his Bachelor of Arts (Honours) (1953) and Master of Arts (1955), before advancing to the University of London for his Doctor of Philosophy in Chinese History at the School of Oriental and African Studies (1957). With that doctoral credential, he returned to the University of Malaya (with a new campus in Kuala Lumpur) as a junior faculty member, before rising to become its full professor in history with a strong portfolio of publications and administrative services. In 1968, he made the big decision of departing to head the Department of Far Eastern History at the Research School of Pacific Studies of the Australian National University. In 1986, he made another professional leap in accepting the vice-chancellorship of the Hong Kong University. Ten years thereafter, he chose to return to Southeast Asia to set up the East Asian Institute of the National University of Singapore and to guide the history fraternity on campus and other history-related projects in the island city-state.

The best singular account pointing directly to Wang's approaches to history is his 1967 inaugural professorial speech on "The Use of

---

[8] Liu Hong and Gregor Benton, "Introduction" and Liu Hong, "Looking Forward, Looking Back: An Interview with Wang Gungwu", in Gregor Benton and Liu Hong (eds.), *Diasporic Chinese Ventures: The Life and Works of Wang Gungwu*, London, RoutledgeCurzon, 2004, pp. 2 and 15; Wang recalled, "I was studying three subjects: English literature, history, and economics. I was offered the chance of doing honours in all three. My actual interest was literature but I decided to do history, because it seemed to me that the history professor [Parkinson] was a good scholar".

[9] Wang Gungwu quoted T S Eliot's *The Waste Land* in "Mixing Memory and Desire: Tracking the Migrant Cycle", in Gregor Benton and Liu Hong, *Diasporic Chinese Ventures*, pp. 140 and 150. He quoted E M Foster's *Howard's End* in Wang Gungwu, *Only Connect! Sino-Malay Encounters*, Singapore, Times Academic Press, 2003, dedication page.

History".[10] He did not subscribe to the antiquarian school of studying history just for an intrinsic interest in the past. Embracing utilitarianism, he delineated three specific uses of history: the forging of group identity, the learning of practical and moral lessons from the past and the wider search for the meaning of life and death. Wang listed three major methods to presenting history: the narrative-story format, the academic channel of critical scholarship and the platform of propaganda. With the politically turbulent 1950s and 1960s as background, his exposition carried a strong anti-colonial undertone, in favour of local nationalistic nation-building. Indeed, he spelled out his opposition to the Euro-centric, colonial framework of history and argued for an Asian-centric narrative which would emphasise indigenous sources and local agency. His summary judgment of history and critical scholarship was that "[t]he study of history is not for the faint-hearted because he will be frightened by the amount there is to know. … History is only worth studying if the historian is skeptical, curious, or a man of faith. If he is all three, he will have much to contribute".

Spatial Crossing: Geographical Straddling between inside and outside of China

Wang is a man of multiple border crossings. He was born in Surabaya of the Dutch East Indies (present-day Indonesia), grew up in Malaya, and went to universities in China, Singapore and the United Kingdom. His academic career has stretched over Malaysia, Australia, Hong Kong and Singapore, with shorter periods of academic sojourn in Europe, the United States and many other parts of the world. He could be regarded as an "international citizen" with vast experience in moving across physical territorial borders. However, it is his other forms of domain crossing that have defined his scholarship more directly and which deserve our closer attention. The first of which is spatial crossing in

---

[10] Wang Gungwu, *The Use of History*, Athens, Ohio University, Centre for International Studies, 1968, republished in other platforms in 1981 and 1992.

terms of his scholarly works that geographically straddle the line between inside and outside of China.

Notably, Wang's anchorage on the discipline of history is initially tied primarily to Chinese history, proclaiming that his "first love" and "starting point" is the history of China *per se*.[11] As Wang has confessed, "I did not set out to study the Chinese overseas. My interest was always in Chinese history. This is partly because I started life as a Chinese sojourner, a *huaqiao* 华侨, someone temporarily resident abroad. If circumstances permitted it, such a person would look foremost to China. I was no exception".[12] His pursuit of Chinese history began early with informal childhood lessons from his father who was a leading Chinese educator.[13]

However, along the way and in terms of formal university history training, Wang began to veer towards a strategy of straddling over both inside and outside of China. This has enabled him to fulfil his first love and yet take advantage of his native Southeast Asia background. It is this straddling strategy that eventually provided him with the breadth and depth of knowledge to create and lead the new sub-field of Chinese Diaspora Studies within the main general field of Chinese History.

His graduation thesis for his Bachelor of Arts (Honours) (1953) focused on the turn-of-20th century anti-Qing Dynasty activities of the Chinese reformists and revolutionaries within and outside of

---

[11] "First love" from Wang Gungwu, "A Single Chinese Diaspora?" in Gregor Benton and Liu Hong (eds.), *Diasporic Chinese Ventures*, pp. 160–162 [Speech delivered in February 1999, first published twice in 1999 and again in 2000]; "Starting point" from Liu Hong, "Looking Forward, Looking Back" (interview in 2000 in Chinese, translated by Gregor Benton in *Diasporic Chinese Ventures*, p. 17).

[12] Wang Gungwu, "A Single Chinese Diaspora?" pp. 160–162.

[13] Wang regarded his father as a true-blue *huaqiao*: "As something of a 'Chinese expatriate', my father kept his conscience clear by giving his first loyalty to the cause of Chinese education and teaching his only child that China was his country. He was truly a *huaqiao*, a Chinese sojourner or 'Overseas Chinese'". See Wang Gungwu. *Anglo-Chinese Encounters since 1800: War, Trade, Science, and Governance*, New York, Cambridge University Press, 2003, p. 151, fn 3 (based on a keynote speech delivered in 2000). See also his recent memoir *Home is Not Here*, Singapore, NUS Press, 2018.

China. His Master of Arts degree (1955) from the University of Malaya examined the ancient South Seas trade between China and its southern maritime neighbours from the foundational Qin-Han era to the golden age of Tang Dynasty. For his PhD training, Wang has made a conscious decision to focus on China *per se*: "I turned totally towards Sinology and the history of China. This gave prominence to one of my desires, to be the Chinese scholar that my parents would be proud of".[14] His doctoral dissertation (1957) with The School of Oriental and African Studies, University of London, analysed the 50 years of turmoil after the fall of the Tang Dynasty. This thesis won him the professional credential as a Chinese historian and was subsequently published as *The Structure of Power in North China during the Five Dynasties*.[15]

After Wang's return in the late 1950s to Singapore-Malaya to be "a local university man", he was stirred by the indigenous socio-political environment and attracted by the politics of new nationhood in Malaya. He joined his university colleagues in actively encouraging research on Malayan history. Based on the foundation laid in his earlier Master thesis work on the ancient Nanhai maritime trade, he followed up on the story and pushed it into a new direction when he gave a series of radio talks in 1958 which was published in the following year as *A Short Story of the Nanyang Chinese*.[16] To Wang, this piece of work represents "one of my earliest efforts to understand the Chinese of Southeast Asia" and has been in heavy demand and "out of print for a very long time", with two translated versions in Chinese (1969 and 1988) and one in Japanese (1972). He republished it in the English language in 1991 the way it is because it has become "something of a historical document

---

[14] Wang Gungwu, "Mixing Memory and Desire: Tracking the Migrant Cycles", in Gregor Benton and Liu Hong, (eds.), *Diasporic Chinese Ventures*, pp. 148–149 (speech delivered in 2003).

[15] Wang Gungwu, *The Structure of Power in North China during the Five Dynasties*, Kuala Lumpur, University of Malaya Press, 1963; republished by Stanford University Press in 1967.

[16] Wang Gungwu, "Mixing Memory and Desire", pp. 148–149; Wang Gungwu, "A Single Chinese Diaspora?" pp. 160–162; Wang Gungwu, *A Short History of the Nanyang Chinese*, Singapore, Donald Moore/Eastern Universities Press, 1959.

representing the point of view of Southeast Asian Chinese over a generation ago, in the 1950s. … I have let it stand as a record of an important
transitional period in Southeast Asian history".[17] In retrospect, this
short but incisive account of Chinese abroad in Nanyang can be taken
as the defining moment of a "take-off" in terms of Wang's crafting a new
sub-field of research and teaching centring on Chinese migration and
settlements abroad, as well as of his rising academic fame.

When Wang left the University of Malaya (and Malaysia's sensitive
racialised environment) for a new appointment with the Australian
National University in 1968, the first leg of his straddling on "inside
China" was reinvigorated by the vibrant climate of China studies and
open accessibility of source materials in Canberra. More importantly,
President Nixon's announcement of his China visit in June 1971
and China's re-admission into the international fraternity of United
Nations by October had fanned a new wave of interest around the
world in scrutinising China.[18] Wang too was caught up in this tide and
published a series of major works focusing on China in the early
1970s.[19] However, the tectonic shift in international relations also

---

[17] "Preface", in Wang Gungwu, *Community and Nation: China, Southeast Asia and
Australia*, St Leonard, Allen & Unwin for Asian Studies Association of Australia, 1992,
p. vii. This piece was left out of the earlier 1981 edition of this collection of essays originally selected by Anthony Reid; Wang's own reprint inclusion in 1992 signals the
importance he has accorded to this "take-off" moment.

[18] For the scholarly impact of these 1971 diplomatic shockwaves (which eventually led to
Malaysia establishing diplomatic ties with the PRC on 31 May 1974, Philippines on
9 June 1975 and Thailand 1 July 1975), see Wang Gungwu, "The Question of the
'Overseas Chinese'", in Wang Gungwu, *Community and Nation: Essays on Southeast Asia
and the Chinese* (selected by Anthony Reid) Singapore, Heinemann Educational Books,
1981, p. 249; Wang Gungwu, "The Chinese: What Kind of Minority", in Wang Gungwu,
China and the Chinese Overseas, Singapore, Times Academic Press, 1991, pp. 286–287
(paper first published in 1976).

[19] The reinvigoration of his interest in China is noted in the acknowledgment pages of
Wang Gungwu, *To Act is to Know: Chinese Dilemmas*, Singapore, Times Academic Press,
2003, pp. ix–xi. The volume includes essays on "The Inside and Outside of Chinese
History" (1972), "The Re-emergence of China" (1973), "Chinese Society and Chinese
Foreign Policy" (1973), "Imperial and Modern Bureaucracy" (1973) and "New Verdict on
Qin Shihuang" (1974).

revived traditional concerns about China's complicated bilateral and regional ties with Chinese "outside of China" and this in turn spurred fresh scholarly inquiries into the latter. Hence, Wang in his early years at Canberra simultaneously continued to research and publish works relating to the Chinese in Malaysia and other parts of Southeast Asia.[20]

In his spatial crossing and delicate geographical straddling between the inside and outside of China, Wang eventually reached a stage of academic journey or moment of equilibrium where "one's point of departure cannot be reduced either to a pure China or to a pure Southeast Asia", declaring that "I have feelings for both, but neither gets the upper hand".[21] Indeed, he settled by the mid-1970s into an academic strategy of standing simultaneously over the two boats of China and Chinese Overseas, and of trying to create a synergy out of this combination by focusing on "the interplay between China's view of those communities and the view of themselves by the Chinese outside" and "this interplay has guided my main writings till this day".[22]

Temporal Crossing: From the Ancient Past to the Contemporary

Another form of crossing discernable from Wang Gungwu's pool of scholarly writings is that of leaping across time scale, from the ancient

---

[20] Wang Gungwu, "Political Chinese: Their Contribution to Modern Southeast Asian History", in Wang Gungwu, *China and the Chinese Overseas*, pp. 130–146 (paper first published in 1972); Wang Gungwu, "Chinese Politics in Malaya", in Wang Gungwu, *Only Connect! Sino-Malay Encounters*, pp. 111–148 (paper first published in 1970).

[21] Liu Hong, "Looking Forward, Looking Back", p. 17.

[22] Wang Gungwu, "A Single Chinese Diaspora?" p. 163. This positive strategic interplay had been misunderstood as an issue of "bi-focalism with distraction" and a lack of depth, during a roundtable on Wang's scholarship in the East Asian Institute at the National University of Singapore on 20 September 2002 (with Liu Hong, Cui Zhiyuan and He Baogang as speakers, and Huang Jianli as moderator). The discussion was captured in an email dated 11 October 2002 from Wang to the above four and later in Liu Hong, "Zhanhou xinjiapo huaren shehui de shanbian: bentu qinghuai-quyu wangluo-quanqiu shiye" (The Transformation of Chinese Society in Postwar Singapore: Local Sentiment, Regional Network and Global Perspective) Xiamen, Xiamen daxue chubanshe, 2003, pp. 256–258.

past to the contemporary. Given the intrinsic disciplinary ties with foregoing happenings, it is inherent for all historians to have a respect for and an interest in the entire span of civilisational developments. However, in lieu of the personal limitation of time and energy and due to the academic trend of professional specialisation, most historians have to make a conscious choice to periodise and to pick a much narrower stretch of time to focus their research on. Wang is one of the few whose academic ability and portfolio stretch more widely from the ancient to the contemporary.

Wang's streak of "loving the ancient" (*haogu* 好古) derives mainly from his first leg of straddling over Chinese history which often boasts of a rich and continuous span of history and culture up-and-down the time scale of 5,000 years (*huaxia shangxia wuqiannian* 华夏上下五千年). It is his training and grounding in the history of China that have led him to reflect on and publish numerous writings relating to ancient Chinese history. This includes Confucianism and its politico-cultural system, imperial central governance from the First Emperor Qin Shihuang and how the various dynasties from the classical Shang–Zhou era down to the Manchu Qing had dealt with their neighbouring states.

It is partly due to the Confucian legacy and influence that have led Wang to develop a degree of hypersensitivity to terminology and the use of precise vocabulary to describe and analyse historical phenomena. Drawing upon Confucian classics, he believes that "in the Chinese tradition, there has always been much respect for the idea of *zhengming* 正名, or rectification of names. This is one of the important areas where we should practice *zhengming*".[23] It is this consciousness and proclivity that have given him the cutting edge to create the new

---

[23] Wang Gungwu, "Upgrading the Migrant: Neither *Huaqiao* nor *Huaren*", in Wang Gungwu *Don't Leave Home: Migration and the Chinese*, Singapore, Eastern Universities Press, 2003, pp. 153–154 (paper first presented at a conference in 1994, and published twice in 1996 and 1998). The other major influence is his heightened political sensitivity to the usage of confusing terminology that would be "dangerous to the people and countries concerned", especially in the context of Chinese migrants in Southeast Asia from the 1950s to 1970s.

sub-field of Chinese Diaspora Studies. By pondering over and sieving through the various specific terms, he has gone on to define terms and phrases to be used universally in that new realm. Sometimes he is unsuccessful in imposing his recommendations, but the academic community discussion that led to rejection and deviation has also enriched the field. His long and passionate struggle with terminology has included critical terms such as "Nanyang Chinese", "Huaqiao", "Overseas Chinese", "Chinese Overseas", "Ethnic Chinese", "Greater China" and "Chinese Diaspora".[24]

Parallel to his grounding in and influence by the ancient past, Wang crosses comfortably into the zone of the "contemporary". Unlike many conservative historians who would avoid the contemporary because they prefer having a longer distance of time to "let the dust of history settle" so as to secure greater objectivity, Wang is never hesitant about venturing into the much more recent past. He anchors the majority of his scholarly writings on this period. His previously cited 1967 inaugural professorial lecture had already signalled this inclination. He is intellectually committed to the utilitarian purpose of learning practical lessons to serve the present world. One of the specific uses of history in his mind is about knowing the past for the purpose of forging group identity, especially in lieu of the then looming climate of decolonisation and new nation-building.

Significantly, the bulk of his studies on the Chinese overseas communities focused on the effects of post-World War II decolonisation of Southeast Asia as well as on the impact of present-day Chinese migratory trends. The remarkable domestic policy and international relations changes in contemporary China after the communist takeover in 1949 and more so after Deng Xiaopeng's open-door and market reform of 1978 had fascinated him. Soon after his 1968 departure from Malaysia with its racially sensitive politics and his arrival in Australia

---

[24] For a detailed discussion of Wang's struggle with each of these critical terms and the importance this has on the epistemological production of knowledge in the field of Chinese Diaspora Studies, see Huang Jianli, "Conceptualizing Chinese Migration and Chinese Overseas: The Contribution of Wang Gungwu", pp. 1–21.

with much greater access to source materials and contact persons relating to communist China, he put forth the volume on *China and the World since 1949* for a publication series on "the making of the 20th century".[25] His 1996 return from Hong Kong to Singapore to restructure the Institute of East Asia Political Economy, and serve as the director of the new East Asian Institute (1997–2009) and later its chairman (2010–2018), had placed him in the pole position to lead the local and international scholarly community in order to interpret and contextualise the rapid rise of China today. Recent tell-tale contemporary publication titles helmed by him include *China: Two Decades of Reform and Change*, *Interpreting China's Development* and *China: Development and Governance*.[26]

Inter-Disciplinary Crossing: Beyond History, into the Social Sciences

Wang is also one of the few early historians who has ventured beyond his home-base discipline of history and its affiliated realm of humanities and is receptive to adopting social sciences approaches and theorisation. His history training has led him to be sensitive to the timing and circumstances of each situational happening. The natural historian gaze is on the particular and the proclivity is to avoid generalisation, especially with the word "theory" being almost pariah. Yet the post-World War II environment of emphasising science, technology and their scientific approaches, as well as the rapid rise of social sciences such as sociology and political science, have all created an environment which induces historians such as Wang to be

---

[25] Wang Gungwu, *China and the World since 1949: The Impact of Independence, Modernity and Revolution*, London, Macmillan Press, 1977; this 190-page book is partly written during his sojourn at the Oxford University.

[26] Wang Gungwu and John Wong (eds.), *China: Two Decades of Reform and Change*, Singapore, Singapore University Press and World Scientific, 1999; Wang Gungwu and John Wong (eds.), *Interpreting China's Development*, Singapore, Singapore University Press and World Scientific, 2007 and Wang Gungwu and Zheng Yongnian (eds.), *China: Development and Governance*, Singapore, World Scientific, 2013.

inter-disciplinary and open-minded about broader conceptualisation, if not theorisation. In the end, the new field of Chinese Diaspora Studies as pioneered by him has proven to be openly structured and able to attract scholarly participation from a wide range of disciplines, and never confined just to history.

Indeed, not satisfied with just charting the genealogy through chronological sequencing, one of Wang's early efforts is to bring his analysis of Chinese migration and settlement to a higher conceptual level by developing a formal typology of three categories of overseas Chinese and four patterns of Chinese migration (of which *Huaqiao* represented only one stage). It begins with his 1972 essay that argued that there were three major groups of Overseas Chinese as distinguished by their political interests and activities: Group A was "predominantly concerned with Chinese national politics and its international ramifications"; Group B was "principally concerned with community politics wherever it may be"; and Group C was "drawn into the politics of non-Chinese hierarchies, whether indigenous or colonial or nationalist".[27] At that stage, he was exploring only along the line of political orientation. By 1984, he had shifted to a newer classification by dividing Chinese migratory waves into four patterns, the first being the "*huashang* /trader", comprising merchants and artisans (inclusive of miners and other skilled workers). The second was the "*huagong*/coolie", constituted by the flood of peasants, landless labourers and urban poor who left China between the 1850s and the 1920s. Third was the "*huaqiao*/sojourner" who was "primarily determined by nationalism" and "enhanced by a close association with [the Chinese] revolution". Last was the "*huayi* /descent or re-migrant" who was confined to the post-1950s movement of people of Chinese descent from one foreign country to another.[28] Both typologies in the

---

[27] Wang Gungwu, "Political Chinese", pp. 130–132.

[28] Wang Gungwu, "Patterns of Chinese Migration in Historical Perspective", in Wang Gungwu, *China and the Chinese Overseas*, pp. 4–10, 21 (speech delivered in 1984, first published in 1989).

end have their fair share of limitations and proven not to be widely accepted by other scholars.[29]

Another major attempt at incorporating an inter-disciplinary angle is his 1985 essay on "The Study of Chinese Identities in Southeast Asia".[30] Here he even drew a diagrammatic quadrant matrix with four directional axes to outline his recommended sociological and political science approaches to understanding the normative identity of an Overseas Chinese. The nodal points of north-south-east-west are represented by the four identities: "Class" as forged by dominant pressures from economic norms, "Cultural" by cultural norms, "Ethnic" from physical norms and "National" by political norms. Each quadrant is then further sub-divided equally by a second set of northwest-south-east-northeast-southwest axes to represent his so-called "common multiple identities" of "Class-Cultural", "Cultural-Ethnic", "Ethnic-National" and "National-Class". How an Overseas Chinese reacts to and moves along with these four sets of varying normative pressure would then determine his positioning in the axes-and-sectorial diagram and his "multiple identity" at that moment in time.

In terms of identity politics, Wang's greater inter-disciplinary achievement was the opening up of a very important topic of "Chineseness". In 1991, he published a collection of essays he had written from 1957 to 1990 and titled it as *The Chineseness of China*.[31] In brief, the close nexus connecting a Chinese-looking person and the issue of him being often automatically associated as-a-matter-of-fact with Chinese speaking and writing abilities, as well as presumably someone with a knowledge of Chinese history and culture, derives

---

[29] For instance, see critiques by Leo Suryadinata, *Understanding the Ethnic Chinese in Southeast Asia*, Singapore, Institute of Southeast Asian Studies, 2007, pp. 65–68 and Adam Keown, "Conceptualizing Chinese Diasporas, 1842 to 1949", *The Journal of Asian Studies*, vol. 58, no. 2, May 1999, pp. 312–313.

[30] Wang Gungwu, "The Study of Chinese Identities in Southeast Asia", in Wang Gungwu, *China and the Chinese Overseas*, pp. 198–221 (paper presented in 1985, first published in 1988).

[31] Wang Gungwu, *The Chineseness of China: Selected Essays*, Hong Kong, Oxford University Press, 1991.

arguably from not just his ethnic physical features but also the lurking external background of "China Extraordinary". It is the extraordinarily large size of China's land and population, its rich and continuous history and cultural traditions, and its recent spectacular economic resurgence which have all contributed to the imagery overhang that not only defines China itself but also haunt every ethnic Chinese in all corners of the world. The reality, however, is that many ethnic Chinese outside of China cannot speak or write Chinese, nor do they know enough about Chinese history and culture, or even want to identify themselves as Chinese. Wang's surfacing of this identity notion of Chineseness has thus opened up a vibrant discussion on its embedded tensions. One of the breakthroughs emerging from the exercise is Ien Ang's 2001 classic work, *On Not Speaking Chinese: Living between Asia and the West*, in which she has interrogated Chineseness as "a prison-house" and tempering it with notions of fluidity and hybridity.[32]

Another of Wang's inter-disciplinary crossing is his contribution towards international relations studies through his chapter on "Early Ming Relations with Southeast Asia" in John K Fairbank's 1968 classic volume on *The Chinese World Order*.[33] While anchored on the Ming Dynasty, Wang went far beyond by conducting a *tour de force* exploration of China's foreign relations with its neighbours to the north, south, east and west, from the classical era down to some contemporary references. He highlighted the instances when the political reality with neighbouring states was clearly different from that of the Confucian world order, thus pushing the latter's language and idealised practices into the realm of myth, metaphor and convention. He characterised the ideational Chinese world view as undergirded by the notions of civilisational and moral superiority, of impartiality in not discriminating between various foreign rulers, as well as of inclusiveness in extending same treatment to all countries

---

[32] Ien Ang, *On Not Speaking Chinese.*
[33] Wang Gungwu, "Early Ming Relations with Southeast Asia: A Background Essay", in John K Fairbank, *The Chinese World Order: Traditional China's Foreign Relations*, Cambridge, MA, Harvard University Press, 1968.

regardless of their value to the Chinese empire's basic interests. The high point of this practice was the reign of Ming Yongle emperor with his eunuch and Sino-centric tributary diplomacy. At the conceptual level, Wang astutely pointed out that the paradox between equality and inequality/superiority in the traditional Chinese World Order was not really that dissimilar to the new post-19th century Western international system of "family of nations". Westphalian notion of nation-states with equal standing in the international system was practised in only a limited context until the 20th century, remaining today as neither self-evident nor permanently assured, often shading into degrees of inequality as determined by actual power and wealth. He thus argued that inequality was in fact the norm in international relations and the Chinese World Order sense of superiority was not exceptional.

A crossing over to the political science concern about balance of power and interest in outlining future scenarios also surfaces in that essay, with Wang asking what would happen if Communist China, then in the throes of Cultural Revolution, would one day re-emerge as a powerful giant nation-state. He has offered the following perceptive assessment as early as 1968: "There has been much speculation about what a Communist China will do when it becomes a power as strong as the strongest power in the world today. If its belief in Chinese superiority persists, it seems likely that the country will seek its future role by looking closely at its own history. The debate about this, centering on the degrees of continuity and of change, seems to be turning in favor of the view that the Chinese will return to some of their traditions. But here opinions divide sharply between the many who see any such return as pointing to future Chinese aggression and those who say that the tradition was one of superior and arrogant but peaceful indifference".[34] Indeed, today, after 40 years of remarkable Deng Xiaoping-initiated market reform and open door policy, the leading topic in political science discipline and its sub-field of international relations is on whether the ongoing rise of China would lead to a return

---

[34] Wang Gungwu, "Early Ming Relations with Southeast Asia", p. 62.

of hierarchical but reciprocal Chinese tributary-like relational order or whether there would be the emergence of a new competitive multi-polar balance of power.[35]

Intellectual Crossing: From the Academia to Public Activism

The last domain crossing of Wang Gungwu is his intellectual crossing from the academia to public activism. In the Western world with its history of a strong religious order and later secularisation, intellectuals in the academia are often depicted as being buried in their research and writing, cocooned in an "ivory tower" environment, and detached from the masses. There could be a handful who emerged to reach out to the popular masses and to shape the agenda of society, and they are termed as "public intellectuals". This distinction, however, did not operate in the traditional Chinese Confucian educational world. The university or academia strictly did not exist in China before the 20th century. The small self-educated, Mandarin-examination-driven educated class could only turn towards the very few bureaucratic positions or to assume the traditional gentry-leadership role back in their hometowns. Either way, they remained closely tied to the public domain. Hence, when the modern term of "intellectual" was imported and popularised in 20th-century China, it was translated as "*zhishi fenzi* 知识分子", a societal fragment of knowledge. This contextual Chinese historical positioning arguably has an influence on Wang and facilitated his early embrace of public activism.

Wang's plunge into activism began when he was an undergraduate with the University of Malaya (then located in Singapore) and elected as the first president of the newly formed left-wing University Socialist

---

[35] The literature on this international relations debate is too vast to cite. Two entry-level works which are also associated with Wang are Wang Gungwu and Zheng Yongnian (eds.), *China and the New International Order*, London, Routledge, 2008 and Zheng Yongnian (ed.), *China and International Relations: The Chinese View and the Contribution of Wang Gungwu*, London, Routledge, 2010.

Club in 1953.[36] Although Wang's engagement did not appear to be intense, the club as a whole played an important role in securing independence from Britain and in shaping the agenda of the post-colonial world for Malaya and Singapore. Waving the flags of decolonisation and nationalism, many other leaders of the club were to become deeply involved in the different emerging political parties. The club ran a campus magazine called Fajar (meaning "dawn" in Arabic) and members of its editorial board were put on trial for sedition by the British colonial authorities in May 1954. This trial was recognised as one key moment of local political awakening which signalled the impending end of British colonial rule.

After Wang returned from London with his PhD in history (1957) to be a junior faculty member of the University of Malaya, he opted to go over to the new campus in Kuala Lumpur and joined his university colleagues in building a new Malayan nation and in encouraging research on Malayan history. As mentioned earlier, he rose steadily through the ranks and became a full professor, giving an inaugural professorial speech with strong nationalist, nation-building undertone. In 1965, he was approached by his old friends from across the causeway who were now leaders of the ruling People's Action Party to chair a curriculum review of the Nanyang University in Singapore.[37] The "Wang Gungwu Report" released in August 1965 contained harsh recommendations to restructure the Nanyang University, going against the expectations of the Chinese-speaking community and creating a public furor and waves of student protest. The Singapore government

---

[36] Loh Kah Seng, *et al.*, *The University Socialist Club and the Contest for Malaya: Tangled Strands of Modernity* Singapore, NUS Press, 2013.

[37] Huang Jianli's chapter on "Language Fault Lines: The Wang Gungwu Report on Nanyang University" in Hong Lysa and Huang Jianli, *The Scripting of a National History: Singapore and Its Pasts*, Hong Kong, Jointly published by Hong Kong University Press and NUS Press, 2008, pp. 109–135. It is first published as Huang Jianli, "Nanyang University and the Language Divide in Singapore: Controversy over the 1965 Wang Gungwu Report", in Lee Guan Kin (ed.), "Nantah tuxiang: Lishi heliuzhong de shengshi" (Imagery of Nanyang University: Reflections on the River of History), Singapore, Global Publishing and NTU Centre of Chinese Language and Culture, 2007, pp. 165–220.

was forced to hold back its full implementation and the public image and standing of Wang took a major hit. The episode has reverberations even today but it is hard to ascertain exactly how much the event had dampened his inclination towards public activism.

In March 1968, he was briefly involved in the launching of Gerakan (People's Movement Party) which tried to alter the racial politics of Malaysia. However, his participation was transient and minimal because in that year he also left the University of Malaya to head the Far Eastern History Department of the Research School of Pacific Studies in the Australian National University. Notably, the 13 May 1969 racial riots of Malaysia took place soon after, changing dramatically the Malaysian political landscape.

Another instance of departure timing having an impact on his degree of activism was when he left Hong Kong University vice-chancellorship in 1996, on the eve of the sensitive People's Republic of China's takeover of British colonial Hong Kong to be its Special Administrative Region in July 1997. The decision and timing to leave after 10 years of holding the top university job, which also had a very high position in the political protocol within the British colonial order, must have been calculated to avoid the heated and highly politicised environment of the political takeover.

One final noteworthy dimension is that Wang's scholarly writings themselves are never apolitical, often crossing the thin red line between scholarship and politics. He has never hesitated to position himself as a scholar of Chinese ethnicity born and bred in Southeast Asia, and as one who is ideologically committed to the cause of campaigning against any insidious depiction of Chinese abroad as a unified threatening force for humanity in general and localised Southeast Asian nation-states in particular. The line between scholarship and politics in Wang's writings is often blurred. This has led Adam McKeown to call his writings as "politically conscious scholarship".[38] Gregor Benton and Liu Hong as editors of a volume of Wang's interviews and writings have

---

[38] Adam McKeown, "Ethnographies of Chinese Transnationalism", *Diaspora*, vol. 10, no. 3, Winter 2001, p. 342.

surmised that "his scholarship is characterized by a high-minded sense of social responsibility".[39] Philip Kuhn, in contributing a prologue to the festschrift volume for Wang's 70th birthday, has called him "a public-spirited intellectual", recognising that "Gungwu's concern to allay fears about China and the Chinese overseas is of long standing and forms a consistent part of his historical calling".[40]

Conclusion

In the review and reflection of Wang's academic career, it becomes obvious that the breadth and depth of his scholarship have been essentially underpinned by two major planks. First is the adoption of history as his disciplinary home base and his unwavering positioning as being first and foremost a historian. Second is his active engagement with multiple forms of domain crossing. This includes spatial crossing between inside and outside of China, temporal crossing from the ancient past to the contemporary, inter-disciplinary crossing from history to the social sciences, as well as intellectual crossing from the academia to public activism. It is his successful leveraging on these two critical supporting planks that has enabled him to venture and pioneer the totally new sub-field of Chinese Diaspora Studies and to leave behind an outstanding scholarly legacy for the new generation of researchers to match or surpass.

---

[39] Liu Hong and Gregor Benton, "Introduction", p. 4.
[40] Philip A Kuhn, "Wang Gungwu: The Historian in His Times", in Billy K L So, John Fitzgerald, Huang Jianli and James K Chin (eds.), *Power and Identity in the Chinese World Order: Festschrift in Honour of Professor Wang Gungwu*, Hong Kong, Hong Kong University Press, 2003, pp. 15, 25 and 27.

Chapter 2

The Southeast Asian-ness
of a China scholar

Anthony REID[1]

Wang Gungwu is certainly a card-carrying China scholar and a very distinguished one. He earned his PhD in Chinese History at the School of Oriental and African Studies, occupied the chair of East Asian History at Australian National University longer than any other professional appointment, and crowned his distinguished career as director and subsequently chairman of the East Asian Institute in Singapore. Most of his formidable list of books have 'China' in the title.

Nevertheless I will argue that he has had an even greater impact on Southeast Asian history. He never 'professed' this subject; he did not have to, since he was born Southeast Asian, and became the first 'Malayan' and one of the first Southeast Asians to make a real impact on the broader understanding of history. I met him in 1965 as my first boss — professor of History and head of Department at the University of Malaya, the first local to hold that or any history chair. Here I will address chiefly this Malaysian phase and the following Australian phase of his life, since they were the most influential on my own youthful career.

---

[1] Anthony REID is Emeritus Professor at the Australian National University. His last position was Director of the Asia Research Institute at the National University of Singapore from 2002 to 2007.

First Contact

As a young New Zealand graduate student at Cambridge looking for my first job in 1964–5, I was really anxious that it should be in the region. I was trying to be an Indonesianist, not yet a Southeast Asianist, but had spent far too little time in the country to be believable. I tried to become a volunteer of some kind in Indonesia, but that country's *Konfrontasi* of the new-born Malaysia was in full swing. Indonesia wanted nothing to do with even a normally harmless Kiwi since we had sent a part of our tiny armed forces to help defend Malaysia and thereby joined Sukarno's *Nekolim* — neo-colonialist imperialists. I applied for an advertised position at the University of Hong Kong, but I was more interested in being closer to Indonesia, in Malaysia. My associate supervisor C D (Jeremy), who was more interested in my thesis topic than Cambridge supervisor Victor Purcell, made enquiries on my behalf with his former colleagues in Singapore.

Ken Tregonning, the West Australian who had the chair at the University of Singapore, seemed from a distance to be doing well at establishing the first regional journal of quality (*JSEAH*, later *JSEAS*) and the first Centre for Southeast Asian Studies in the region, as well as acting as the first secretary-general of the International Association of Historians of Asia (IAHA).[2] Wang Gungwu would in fact succeed him in some of these regional leadership roles, hosting one of the first IAHA Conference in Kuala Lumpur in 1968. However, Tregonning replied in a clearly depressed letter to Cowan, later passed to me. Although Reid "sounds very interesting", he wrote, "no European can hope to be happy here as one of the few remaining expatriates". The local staff association, headed by Wong Lin Ken and Eunice Thio, was creating strong pressure on all expats to go. He advised trying the new University of Malaya in Kuala Lumpur where locals held most of the chairs and the resentment against expatriates was less. I remember Jeremy Cowan telling me that one's first head of department was crucial, and in Wang

---

[2] Ken Tregonning, *Home Port Singapore: An Australian Historian's Experience, 1953–1967*, Nathan, Queensland, Griffith University Centre for the Study of Australia-Asia Relations, 1989.

Gungwu I would find a good man and a fine scholar. So of course I wrote eagerly to this Professor Wang.

When I got a reply from the still-mysterious professor saying that he would be advertising a position, I rejected the offer from Hong Kong and set off from Cambridge with my wife in February 1965 on a long road trip heading perhaps to Malaysia, but if not to a default position in Auckland. We got as far as a campground at Adana, near ancient Tarsus on the south coast of Turkey, when a telegram from Gungwu somehow caught up with me, offering the job and telling me to start in April if possible. So our delightful dawdle through Asia turned into a more purposeful drive, towards Madras (later Chennai) to put our VW van onto the *SS Rajula* for Penang and the drive to Kuala Lumpur. Unfortunately for the department, we both arrived so weakened with what turned out to be hepatitis A that I was not able to teach for another couple of months.

Cowan could not have been more right about Professor Wang. Like his country, Malaysia, he was then in what I can only describe as a youthful, optimistic springtime. The early 1960s in general were turbulent but full of quasi-revolutionary hopes. Malaya was young and in the process of handing the jobs over to highly competent and optimistic locals. The formation of Malaysia, on the same date that Helen and I had formed our marital union in Cambridge, 31 August 1963, seemed still to be an exciting way of avoiding the dangers of either communism (in Singapore) or neo-colonialism (in Borneo) through forming a wonderfully diverse, multi-ethnic new rainbow country.

It also seemed to deal with a problem that Gungwu had identified in a series of perceptive articles of the 1960s.[3] At least two (or two and a half if Chinese nationalism were added) nationalisms and senses of national history competed in the young nation — that of 'Malaya' and that of *Tanah Melayu* (the land of the Malays). This divergence appeared in that springtime to be manageable through Malaysia with

---

[3] 'Malayan Nationalism' 1962, 'The Malaysian Split' 1966, 'Chinese Politics in Malaya' 1970, 'Malaysia: Contending Elites' 1970, all reprinted in Wang Gungwu, *Community and Nation: Essays on Southeast Asia and the Chinese*, Singapore: Heinemann, 1981.

good sense and generosity, though subsequent events seemed to make each reassertion of the hope fainter than the one before.

Wang Gungwu the Malaysian

At their early optimistic best, the country and the man seemed made for each other. We younger lecturers dreamed of how Gungwu (as I think everybody but the indispensable secretary Beng Thye called him) should before long be at least its foreign minister, if not more. As the country's most exciting public intellectual it was natural that he would be the one to give the new nation some intellectual substance, history and meaning. This he did by putting together the first encyclopaedic book on the subject — a collective work called simply *Malaysia: A Survey*.[4] This was one of the first books I acquired in Kuala Lumpur. He was a wonderfully generous boss, enthusiastic, universally curious, seemingly omniscient about the country I was naively but eagerly trying to understand.

He asked me to teach the course on Southeast Asia in the 16th and 17th centuries, a rapid learning experience that had everything to do with my becoming a Southeast Asianist and eventually defining that period as an 'age of commerce'. When I dedicated the first volume of *Southeast Asia in the Age of Commerce* (1988) to Gungwu, I recall trying to explain to him that I thought he had a great deal to do with my early conviction that Southeast Asia was not only endlessly exciting but fundamentally benign. An astute observer later suggested that this optimism was the most distinctive feature of my work.[5]

Gungwu was moved to the new university campus in 1959, soon after it was opened, and became dean of the faculty aged 32 and professor of history in succession to John Bastin at 33. When he became my first boss he was still a dynamic 35, and the first Malayan,

---

[4] Wang Gungwu, *Malaysia: A Survey*, Melbourne, Cheshire, 1964.
[5] Robert Cribb, 'The Past as Threat, the Past as Promise: The Historical Writing of Anthony Reid', in *Anthony Reid and the Study of the Southeast Asian Past*, Geoff Wade and Tana Li (eds.), Singapore, ISEAS, 2012, pp. 31–46.

later Malaysian, to achieve a number of milestones. His Southeast Asian-ness was never in doubt, as a leader of the new generation of western-educated Southeast Asia-born historians, first getting to know each other through IAHA. He was interested in every aspect of Malaysia's history. He encouraged Alistair Lamb and Brian Peacock in their pioneering archaeology in Kedah and Johor, getting his boots dirty in their excavations. He examined and wrote about the early history of Melaka with unrivalled expertise on the Chinese sources[6] and participated in the political debates of the moment. To my dismay he was ahead of me in mastering the Arabic-based *jawi* alphabet of Malay and I remember him practising writing his words in dull faculty meetings.

Since his student days in Singapore Gungwu had been a thoughtful 'Malayan' nationalist, excited by the retreat of colonialism and eager to speed that along in favour of a new multi-racial Malayan nation. Malaysia was a happy extension of that stance, providing a neutrally artificial name for the country. Though still young, still nationalist, he was in the 1960s naturally outflanked by more radical voices who seemed to want to reject whatever the colonials had built. The first of the issues of the University of Malaya Historical Society's journal after I got there well reflects the mood of these exciting beginnings. Zainal Abidin Wahid, feeling the weight of being the only Malay professional historian of the time, was the shrillest in deploring the "built-in weakness" of westerners who tried to write Malaysian history.[7] Rollins Bonney took a more Smail-ish position without quoting Smail, targeting the two most recent attempts to write Malaysian-centred history, by Tregonning and Jessy, as "in the context of Malaysian history, severe

---

[6] Wang Gungwu, The Opening of Relations between China and Malacca 1403–1305', in *Malaysian and Indonesian Studies*, Bastin and Roolvink (eds.), 1964 in Wang 1981, pp. 81–96. See also Wang Gungwu, 'The First Three Rulers of Malacca' from *JMBRAS*, 1968, in Wang 1981, pp. 97–107.

[7] Zainal Abidin bin Abdul *Wahid*, 'Some Aspects of Malay History', *Journal of the Historical Society, University of Malaya*, vol. 4, 1965/66, p. 6.

setbacks".[8] He made an early and eloquent call for marginalising the Europeans to the point of seeing the foundation of Penang and Singapore as events in Kedah and Johor history, not of the British empire. Asked to write the foreword for this issue, Gungwu was sufficiently concerned to warn against nationalist reinventing of the past with "echoes of Fascist and Nazi self-glorification".[9]

The older expat members of the department may already have felt some unease at the early stirrings of more exclusive nationalism, though found it all exciting. Gungwu himself was always generously inclusive, and ensured that the whole department regularly got together for dinners, welcomes and farewells, whether at his house or the Ma family's Muslim Chinese restaurant, which could deliver satisfactorily delicious Chinese meals without offending the liberal Muslims of the time (as they now seem). Although I could of course be biased, I would gamble my shirt on the Wang Gungwu era having been the happiest the University of Malaya History Department has known.

The End of the Springtime

Disenchantments were not long in coming, and of course earlier for Gungwu, whose identity was at stake, than for me. The abrupt departure of Singapore from Malaysia in August 1965 came as a rude shock, totally unexpected by most of us. It seemed to demonstrate dramatically that Lee Kuan Yew's 'Malaysian Malaysia' slogan after all defined the former 'Malayan' version of the country's identity too sharply to be acceptable. It was the first tough reminder that this multi-racial experiment just might not work; that even such an adeptly inclusive figure as Wang Gungwu might have to choose between the Singapore and the Malaysia paths. Each subsequent time Helen and I celebrated 'Malaysia Day' and our wedding anniversary on 31 August, we congratulated

[8] Rollins Bonney, 'Towards Malaysian History', *Journal of the Historical Society*, vol. 4, 1966, p. 20.
[9] Wang Gungwu, 'Foreword', *Journal of the Historical Society, University of Malaya*, vol. 4, 1965/66.

ourselves that however imperfectly, our marriage had done a great deal better than Singapore's with Malaysia.

The Indonesian coup attempt (Gestapu) followed within a month, and constituted for me and other wannabe Indonesianists a disenchantment like Singapore's expulsion for 'Malayans', though it took longer to make the greater horror of the mass killings clear. I remember very clearly hearing about the Untung coup of 31 September 1965 at one of Margaret's wonderful dinner parties, with the family all helping out. In those pre-TV days we clustered around the Wang radio to try to understand what was happening.

The Kuala Lumpur events of 13 May 1969 marked the definitive end of that 1960s Malaysian springtime. Singapore's departure had at least been bloodless, but the experience of Malaysians killing each other in the national capital was deeply traumatic, especially for the Chinese at the receiving end of most of the killing. Gungwu had already moved his family to Canberra and his Malaysian friends asked him how he knew that the dream of Malaysia was going to fall apart. Of course he did not, but was probably ahead of the trend in quietly perceiving how difficult life might become for non-Malays in Malaysia's universities. All we could do was to write about the anguish — he in Canberra and I in Kuala Lumpur.[10]

At the Australian National University (ANU)

The ANU wooed and eventually won Wang Gungwu in 1968 to become its second Professor of Far Eastern History in the Research School of Pacific Studies, in succession to Patrick Fitzgerald. Curiously, both Wang and Fitzgerald had been in a besieged Nanjing in 1948-9, the former as an 18-year-old student unlikely to have met the latter, a 48-year-old China hand, and well-known author though with no academic experience or degree.

---

[10] Wang Gungwu, 'Political Change in Malaysia', from *Pacific Community* 1970, in Wang 1981, pp. 224–31. See also Anthony Reid, 'The Kuala Lumpur Riots and the Malaysian Political System', *Australian Outlook,* vol. 23, no. 3, 1969, pp. 258–78.

I believe (though he does not) that ANU's brilliant choice to appoint Gungwu to a chair essentially in the China field had much to do with his role as a Southeast Asian. Fitzgerald's somewhat eccentric appointment, initially only as a visitor, had been on the initiative of ANU's first vice chancellor, Sir Douglas Copland, who had also been to Nanjing as Australia's envoy to China and known him there. It was a single foray at the time into Asia, defying the insistence of the Research School's academic architect, anthropologist Raymond Firth, that it should focus its attention on the ethnology of the small islands of the Pacific. This left Southeast Asia an embarrassing absence in the first decade of the existence of a Research School ostensibly set up to understand the countries of Australia's near north which had suddenly become vital to the country in the crucible of the 'Pacific War'.[11] Wang Gungwu became not only the second Professor of Far Eastern History (soon to be East Asian History) but effectively the first professorial level Southeast Asianist in the Research School. From where I stood as a junior scholar appointed to the School a year later and hoping to build up its Southeast Asian Studies, that was critical.

Through his exceptional lucidity and eloquence in English Gungwu quickly became the model academic Asian Australian. ANU had been not only very male but very Anglo in its early years and arguably its relatively low profile for Asians in Asian Studies still puts ANU a little behind many US campuses. He seemed to have single-handedly turned that around. As Director of the Research School (1975–80), President of Australian Academy of the Humanities (1980–83) and second President of the Asian Studies Association of Australia (1979–80), he played a prominent role in bringing an awareness of Asia into mainstream Australia. A key to this was I think his universal curiosity and sympathy. I remember him talking with enthusiasm about how his then role as director required him to go

---

[11] S G Foster and Margaret Varghese, *The Making of the Australian National University*, St Leonard, NSW, Allen & Unwin, 1996. See also Anthony Reid, 'Indonesian Studies at ANU: Why so Late?' for special issue in honour of Herb Feith, *Review of Indonesian and Malayan Affairs*, 43, part 1, 2009, pp. 51–74.

around the small Pacific Islands and attend the South Pacific Forum. He threw himself eagerly into such things.

Whereas the academic outsider Fitzgerald had struggled to attract mainstream China scholars and graduate students to join him in faraway Canberra, Gungwu attracted outstanding students and younger colleagues, not only from Australia but importantly from Malaysia and Singapore. Most of the Malayan students, including an important cohort of Nanyang University graduates (Yong Chin Fatt, Yen Chinhwang and Twang Peck Yang), studied not China but Chinese in Southeast Asia, more firmly a part of Southeast than of East Asian Studies. He was in effect my heavyweight mentor/protector in trying to build Southeast Asian history at ANU. He godfathered such key projects as *Perceptions of the Past in Southeast Asia* (Reid and Marr 1979) and *Southeast Asia in the 9th to 14th Centuries* (Marr and Milner 1986).[12]

Studying the Nanyang

During the time at ANU Gungwu became accepted as the leading authority on the Chinese in Southeast Asia and on the history of China-Southeast Asia Relations. I would argue that his most critical work has been in that field. As editor of a Southeast Asia Publications Series, I was eager to ensure that his perceptive work in this area appeared in book form as well as in the marvellous lectures and papers he was in great demand to give. He agreed, so long as I just did it and did not bother him, and so emerged the first of many published collections of his work in this format. [13]

Although Gungwu certainly strengthened his department's and the ANU's standing in China Studies proper, he immediately made ANU

---

[12] Anthony Reid and David Marr (eds.) 1979 *Perceptions of the Past in Southeast Asia*, Singapore, Heinemann for ASAA Southeast Asia Publications Series, with Preface by Wang Gungwu, 1979. See also David Marr and A C Milner, *Southeast Asia in the 9th to 14th Centuries*, Singapore, ISEAS, 1986.

[13] Wang Gungwu, *Community and Nation: Essays on Southeast Asia and the Chinese*, Anthony Reid (ed.), Singapore, Heinemann for ASAA, 1981.

a major force in the relatively undernourished field of the Chinese in Southeast Asia. He was able in 1980 to attract Jennifer Cushman to a post specifically in this field in 1980. Jennifer tragically died in1989, shortly after bringing out the book of the first major conference she and Gungwu organised.[14] When the International Society for the Study of Chinese Overseas, ISSCO, was established in 1992, Gungwu was again the indispensable figure as founding president, which he has remained.

As China began to open up, his was a persuasive voice for explaining the West and Southeast Asia to China, and China to them. He led a group of six Southeast Asianists from ANU to China in 1980 — my first visit to that country. His idea was twofold: to convince us that China had been entangled with Southeast Asia for a long time and had something important to say about it; and more importantly to pressure colleagues in China to accept the region on its own terms as 10 independent countries trying to integrate their minorities, not simply as a field of Chinese emigration seen through the lens of Chinese imperial sources and *huaqiao* interests. Our eyes were certainly opened and important contacts made. To judge from the enthusiastic reception his massively attended lectures received from younger Chinese academics and graduate students, the same was true on the other side. Following this visit, an important channel opened with Peking and Xiamen Universities, of which perhaps the most spectacular fruit was Tana Li. A graduate of Peking University in Vietnamese Studies, she did her PhD at ANU under David Marr and eventually returned to Canberra as his successor. After Gungwu's departure for Hong Kong in 1986 and Jennifer Cushman's death in 1989, she was able to ensure that Australia-China contacts continued, that our Southeast Asianists were aware of the richness of Chinese sources, while theirs could not ignore western scholarship on the region (some of which she in fact translated).

---

[14] Jennifer Cushman and Wang Gungwu, *Changing Identities of the Southeast Asian Chinese since World War II*, Hong Kong, Hong Kong University Press, 1989.

Conclusion: A Model for Our Times

I have recently become aware that scholarship on Southeast Asia is entering a new era, with China-educated scholars entering as never before the global discussion in English on Asian histories. The scholarship on China and Southeast Asia is enriched by their numbers and their learning, but they also bring an unprecedented danger of a kind of Sino-centrism in writing about Southeast Asian connections with China. The Chinese sources on Southeast Asia, like European ones, are both more abundant and easier to fit into a modern narrative sense of state history than the Southeast Asian written sources. Those brought up on such sources risk interpreting the so-called 'tribute system' and the dismissive approach in the imperial records of traders who operated outside this system as 'pirates', in wholly misleading ways. My generation learned how to combat Euro-centrism by reading between the lines of the western sources, and bringing a good deal of local sensitivity to interpreting more opaque Southeast Asian sources. A new generation may have a similar challenge in regard to China.

There is no better guide to how to do this right than Wang Gungwu. Having lived his life in Southeast Asia and Australia, he sees China, its history, its sources, sympathetically but from the margins; not quite from outside, but certainly not from inside. He uses Chinese sources but is intensely aware that they cannot safely be used in isolation; that there are other sources from the region and the West that have quite different priorities and perspectives. He has shown how to recognise and celebrate Chinese threads in the rich tapestry of Southeast Asia, not as part of anyone's nationalist project, but as the essence of the hybrid, cosmopolitan crossroads the region represents.

Chapter 3

History Meets Policy in the Age of Donald Trump and Xi Jinping

Paul EVANS*

Introduction

At the conference honouring Wang Gungwu on the occasion of his 80th birthday, I compared his writings on China to those of John Fairbank, the subject of my 1988 biography. The essay assessed how each of them saw part of their historian's vocation as linking China's past to contemporary affairs, what Fairbank called probing history's important but "indeterminate relevance".[1]

In this brief chapter, I will examine some of the elements of Wang's ideas as they relate to current international relations, that "indeterminate relevance" for what all of us see as a turbulent juncture in global affairs. There are many connective threads but I will look briefly at three: Chinese conceptions of world order; the Thucydides trap as a

* Paul EVANS is Professor of Asian and trans-Pacific international relations in the School of Public Policy and Global Affairs, University of British Columbia.
[1] See "Historians and Chinese World Order: Fairbank, Wang and the Matter of 'Indeterminate Relevance'", in Zheng Yongnian (ed.), *China and International Relations: The Chinese View and the Contribution of Wang Gungwu*, London, Routledge, 2010; and Paul Evans *John Fairbank and the American Understanding of Modern China*, New York and Oxford, Basil Blackwell, 1988.

way of framing and avoiding a possible US-China collision; and new elements of Beijing relations with overseas Chinese communities.

China and World Order

Fifty years ago Wang attracted international attention with an essay on Ming relations with Southeast Asia in an oft-cited volume edited and introduced by John Fairbank. The book was a pioneering effort to lay out elements of the normative underpinnings and practices of the imperial tribute system and made some broad connections to the lingering resonance for Mao-era foreign policy.[2]

Fast forward to 2018 when the concept of "world order" is doing box office business as a central dimension of international discourse, in part because many of its key elements seem to be unravelling and in part because China's role in determining its future seems dramatically greater and more contested than even a decade ago. What China thinks matters because China matters on a global stage that is being severely shaken in the era of Donald Trump's America First and Xi Jinping's China Dream.

Wang's writings run orthogonal to those who see China as the creator of a new order or, alternatively, the sustainer of an existing American-centred system. His main idea about Chinese thinking centres on change: orders rise and fall. The current international order is not *the* international order but rather the product of the values and interests of the victors in the second world war. China accepts and will support elements of a world order that are in its own interest but not the system itself. The rules, norms and institutions underpinning the much touted "rules-based order" are neither universal nor permanent and China is neither a revisionist nor a status quo power. Categories in Western international relations theorising and diplomacy fit uneasily with Chinese history.

---

[2] Wang Gungwu, "Early Ming Relations with Southeast Asia: a Background Essay", in John K Fairbank (ed.), *The Chinese World Order: Traditional China's Foreign Relations*, Cambridge, MA, Harvard University Press, 1968.

Avoiding the Thucydides Trap

Graham Allison's *Destined for War: Can America and China Escape Thucydides's Trap* elegantly outlines the argument that power transitions are particularly dangerous with a high likelihood of a military confrontation between an established and a rising power. The book is not a prediction that war is inevitable but a warning that unless extraordinary measures of diplomacy and accommodation are taken the chances of it happening are high.

A legion of Western writers and officials have argued that China must adjust its ambitions and find a way to live within the "rules-based order" currently dominated by the United States. Some including Henry Kissinger and Graham Allison have talked about co-evolution and mutual accommodation as difficult but both necessary and possible.

Wang's argument takes a different cut. Accommodation might be possible because China's past makes it a different kind of actor from other imperial powers. China's aspirations are not those of the United States. China's phase of expansion ended long ago and it has not demonstrated the will for regional or global dominance in the form of spreading its political or economic model to other countries. As he noted in an extended interview in 2010:

> "[I]f the Chinese were thought to have conceived a world order that they could dominate, then no such world order existed. The concept of a world order is a Western one. The Chinese did have an idea of order that was hierarchical, one in which they saw themselves as the most civilized and the most developed. But theirs was not a concept of world order that led them to justify any kind of military intervention or the expansion of Chinese territory".[3]

Many are sensitive to the possibility that Xi Jinping's recent posturing and ambition suggest a potential change in direction.

---

[3] *Wang Gungwu; Junzi, Scholar-Gentleman,* in conversation with Asad-Ul Iqbal Latif Singapore, Institute of Southeast Asian Studies, 2010, p. 99.

In looking at that future, the wisdom of Wang is that the greatest danger that China poses is not a re-enactment of Chinese ambitions and practices from the past — the revival of Middle Kingdomism and a hierarchical tributary system much feared in China's immediate neighbourhood — but rather its potential emulation of the imperial behaviour of Japan in the first half of the 20th century or the United States. If it comes to mimic or share American conceptions of domination, that clash is almost inevitable.

The prospect of accommodation or co-evolution depends precisely on the maintenance of difference rather than convergence in the spheres of what Thucydides identified as honour, fear and interest. Ironically, China's adoption of the American way would be a recipe for disaster rather than peace.

Overseas Chinese and the Great Chinese Rejuvenation

Accompanying China's rise are expanding fears of what that rise means for Beijing's expectations of and connections with overseas Chinese communities. Wang's writings and entrepreneurial efforts have been seminal in the development of academic study of overseas Chinese. At a moment when Chinese overseas are growing rapidly in number and influence in many parts of the world and when Beijing is making great efforts to connect to them as an asset in its domestic and global agendas, new kinds of questions are arising for policymakers and academic analysts.

What are the implications of the blurring of the distinction between *huaren* and *huaqiao* in Xi's statements on the rejuvenation of the Chinese nation? What are the operational implications of the merger of the Office of Overseas Chinese Affairs into the United Front Work Department of the Chinese Communist Party? What are the extraterritorial implications for Chinese outside of China of increased surveillance systems inside China and emergence of new forms of monitoring and reporting under the Social Credit System?

Some of the underlying alarm is related to geo-politics and economic frictions. In recent months it has expanded to include foreign influence activities. In Australia, there has been major media and governmental attention on perceived interference in its domestic political and academic institutions, including the domination of the Chinese language media. This has triggered new legislation and growing strains in bilateral relations. In the United States, a Congressional commission has investigated sharp power influence and proposed new laws. The director of the FBI testified to a Senate committee about new intelligence risks posed by "non-traditional information collectors" that are part of a "whole of society" threat of foreign manipulation from China. In Singapore, government officials have spoken of new risks posed by recent immigrants from China trying to reshape public attitudes.

This kind of backlash signals new vulnerabilities for Chinese outside China and a major policy challenge for Beijing trying to maximise overseas assets in a way that meets its developmental objectives while avoiding backlash and recrimination in host countries. As China becomes more deeply integrated into the world the threads that connect — diplomats, clan associations, business and scientific networks, professors, students and migrants — risk being seen as enemies or potential risks.

Deeper understanding of the dynamics of identity and assimilation and new mechanisms for transparency and codes of conduct are even more essential now than when Wang pioneered the field a generation ago.

Going Forward

Not long before his death in 1991 John Fairbank stated that he hoped to be remembered above all not as an historian or a China scholar but rather as an educator. Wang has expressed a similar cosmopolitan sentiment, reminding us that knowing the past is just one part of living well in the present and that history presents a recurring set of evolving questions rather than permanent answers defined by any single civilisation or state.

Chapter 4

Globalisation and the Chineseness of the Chinese State*

ZHENG Yongnian[1]

State transformation in contemporary China is the result of the country's irreversible integration into the world market and global capitalism. Despite difficulties, the Chinese leadership has made enormous efforts to adjust the state structure to accommodate globalisation and facilitate the process of China's integration into the global system. It is too early to judge whether all these attempts have made the Chinese state stronger than before, but it is certain that the Chinese leadership

---

* ZHENG Yongnian is Professor of the East Asian Institute, National University of Singapore. This chapter was written during the period of 2002-2003. Inspired by Wang Gungwu's discussion on the Chinese-ness of China over the country's long history, the author wanted to examine the theme in the contemporary context. During the writing, Professor Zheng had several discussions with Wang and some of his deep insights about the (un)changing nature of the Chinese state have been incorporated. Professor Zheng has revised it for inclusion in this volume in honour of Wang Gungwu. Other cases such as Xi Jinping's "China Dream movement" were not added as they will not value add in a significant way. More importantly, the theme of this chapter is highly relevant today when the West, particularly the United States, is giving up on the idea that the Chinese state can be changed despite the reform and open door policy initiated by the late Deng Xiaoping.
[1] Zheng Yongnian, *Globalization and State Transformation in China*, Cambridge and New York, Cambridge University Press, 2004.

wants to make the state more modern. This chapter discusses the impact of globalisation on the nature of the Chinese state.

To explore the nature of the Chinese state is to assess the Chineseness of the Chinese state. To a great degree, to say that the Chinese state has become more modern means that the Chinese state has become more "westernised". As discussed elsewhere, the Chinese leadership has rebuilt the state by selectively importing Western products, or more correctly, Western ideas of state building. Whether it is the market economy, federal-style taxation system, central banking system, or the rule of law, the building of all these systems is not a natural development of the state system. Instead, they are the conscious efforts of China's leaders. In the process, while the Chinese state becomes more westernised, it also gradually loses its Chineseness.

Will China become another Western democratic state with rapid globalisation? Some Western scholars and policymakers tend to believe so. Such an optimistic perspective stems from their belief that capitalist economic development would induce democratisation. This argument has been very popular since Seymour Lipset conceptualised the linkage between economic development and democracy in 1959.[2] The reasoning is like this. Based on the experience of political development in East Asia, promoting economic growth while monopolising political power is an almost impossible balancing act in the long term, especially in a world increasingly linked by communications and trade. As people's income rise and their horizons broaden, they are more likely to demand for the right to participate in governance and to enjoy full protection under the rule of law. So, in the first news conference of his second term, US President Clinton said that "the impulses of the society and the nature of the economic change will work together, along with the availability of information from the outside world, to increase the spirit

---

[2] Seymour M Lipset, "Some Social Requisites of Democracy: Economic Development and Political Legitimacy", *American Political Science Review*, vol. 53, no. 1, 1959, pp. 69–105. For a comprehensive review of this argument, see Dietrich Rueschemeyer, Evelyne H Stephens and John D Stephens, *Capitalist Development and Democracy*, Chicago: The Chicago University Press, 1992.

of liberty over time" and that China could not hold back democracy, just as eventually the Berlin Wall fell.[3]

The reality, however, is more complicated. The modernisation or Westernisation of China's political-economic order also resulted in enormous unexpected consequences and thus resistance to globalisation. In order to deal with all these consequences, the leadership has pursued the Chineseness of the state. To do so, the leadership has its own rationale because the newly established systems (or Western state products) not only take time to take root and begin to be effective in dealing with the problems in China, but also cannot provide a sound base for the political legitimacy for the current regime. Regime survival sometimes becomes more important than regime modernisation. To survive, the leadership has to appeal to the Chineseness of the state. The Chineseness of the state has been pursued in different ways. First, the leadership has imported Western state products very selectively and gradually. Total and wholesale Westernisation did not occur. Second, institutional innovation has taken place. To import a Western state product is not the same as importing a foreign machine. In order for the Western state product to function in China, these products have to be modified with domestic contents added. Third, in some cases, the leadership has directly appealed to traditional Chinese products to counterbalance the efforts of Western state products. This is very true in the case of the leadership' proposal that the rule of law has to be accompanied by the rule by virtue.

Overall, China has globalised in quite a balanced way and achieved an equilibrium between "Westernisation" and "Chineseness". The nature of the Chinese state exists in such an equilibrium which is not a spontaneous consequence of China's development; instead, it is a goal consciously pursued by the Chinese leadership. This chapter discusses this changing nature of the Chinese state from a historical perspective. It will first discuss how this mentality was formed in China and then compare three cases — the New Life Movement under Chiang

---

[3] Lee Siew Hua, "China Will Be 'More Democratic over Time'," *The Straits Times*, Singapore, 30 January 1997, p. 1.

Kai-shek, the Learning From Lei Feng Movement under Mao Zedong and the Rule by Virtue under Jiang Zemin — to see how the Chinese political elite has tried to maintain such an equilibrium. This comparison shall enable us to see the (un)changing nature of the Chinese state.

(Un)changing Nature of the Chinese State

The Chinese state is a multifaceted political entity. Most studies on the Chinese state have focused on its organisational and institutional side.[4] In discussing the Chineseness of the Chinese state, one often refers to the cultural or civilisational side of the Chinese state. While it is easier for scholars to detect organisational and institutional changes, great controversy has existed among scholars on whether the nature of the Chineseness is changeable.

Those influenced by cultural essentialism have argued for the enduring nature of the Chineseness. The so-called "ultrastable cultural identity" among China scholars is such an example. Sun Longji wrote, "This tendency toward stagnation is also evident in the personality of every Chinese individual. A Chinese is programmed by his culture to be 'Chinese. In other words, in-bred cultural predispositions make the Chinese what they are and prevent them from being full-blown individuals. Dynamic human growth is an alien concept to the Chinese."[5] Quite similarly, Jin Guantao argued, "China has not yet freed itself from the control of history. Its only mode of existence is to relive the past. There is no accepted mechanism within the culture for the Chinese to confront the present without falling back on the inspiration and strength of tradition".[6] This is also true among scholars in the West. Tim Oakes pointed out, "China's history is trapped by a cultural

---

[4] For example, David Shambaugh, *The Modern Chinese State*, New York, Cambridge University Press, 2000; Stuart R Schram (ed.), *The Scope of State Power in China*, Hong Kong, The Chinese University Press, 1985 and Stuart R Schram (ed.), *Foundations and Limits of State Power in China*, Hong Kong, The Chinese University Press, 1987.

[5] Cited in Geremie Barme and John Minford, *Seeds of Fire: Voices of Chinese Conscience*, New York, Hill & Wang, 1988, p. 136.

[6] Cited in Geremie Barme and John Minford, *Seeds of Fire*, p. 133.

geography, an ultrastable spatial identity of 'Chineseness'".[7] In this context, Lucian Pye argued that China is a civilisation pretending to be a nation-state".[8]

Other scholars, though less influenced by cultural essentialism, have tried to identify some enduring features of the Chinese state. For example, Benjamin Schwartz pointed out that "one of the most striking characteristics of Chinese civilisation is what might be called the centrality and weight of the political order within that civilisation".[9] While Schwartz referred to the centrality of the political order, David Shambaugh stressed on some of the enduring functions of such a political order or the state. According to him, for more than a century, the Chinese state has had three enduring missions regardless of their fundamentally different cast. These missions include modernisation of the economy, transformation of society and defence of the nation against foreign aggression. Shambaugh argued,

> As one [the state] evolved to the next, some elements of the past survived each transition and were woven into new institutional frameworks. Each new departure was never total, although all were sharp and each sought to 'overthrow' and replace the former. In reality, though, each new Chinese state maintained certain features of the old. Moreover, in each phase, different foreign elements were imported and grafted on to the evolving indigenous root, creating an ever more complex hybrid.[10]

Though Shambaugh noted that the Chinese state has added something new to itself over its long evolution, he nevertheless under-emphasised that the Chinese state has to transform itself to not only

---

[7] Tim Oakes, "China's Provincial Identities: Reviving Regionalism and Reinventing 'Chineseness'" *The Journal of Asian Studies*, vol. 59, no. 3, August 2000, p. 668.

[8] Lucian Pye, "China: Erratic State, Frustrated Society", *Foreign Affairs*, vol. 69, no. 4, Fall 1990, p. 1.

[9] Benjamin I Schwartz, "The Primacy of the Political Order in East Asian Societies: Some Preliminary Generalizations", in Stuart R Schram (ed.), *Foundations and Limits of State Power*, p. 1.

[10] David Shambaugh, "Introduction: The Evolving and Eclectic Modern Chinese State", in Shambaugh (ed.), *The Modern Chinese State*, pp. 1–2.

accommodate changing socio-economic circumstances, but also lead socio-economic development. In other words, in pursuing its missions, the state has also transformed itself. To understand the changing nature of Chineseness is to understand how the state has transformed itself.

Indeed, many other scholars have searched the dynamics of the changing "Chineseness". As Wang Gungwu has pointed out, China today is radically different from China in 1900 and almost every aspect of Chineseness has undergone considerable change during the past 3,000 years. In order to understand these changes, Wang suggested that "our understanding of Chineseness must recognize the following: it is living and changeable; it is also the product of a shared historical experience whose record has continually influenced its growth; it has become increasingly a self-conscious matter for China; and it should be related to what appears to be, or have been, Chinese in the eyes of non-Chinese".[11] Thus, the question is not whether "Chineseness" changes or not, but how much it has developed and changed.

The Chinese state can refer to a complex organism and include different components such as ideas, values and institutions. In this context, "Chineseness" means something quintessentially Chinese which is the remarkable sense of continuity that seems to have made the civilisation increasingly distinctive over the centuries.[12]

Though the state needs to be better understood as a whole, its different components do not change simultaneously. The organisational side of the state can be made easier than its cultural side, which in some cases, does not follow changes on the organisational side at all. Wang even argued that "Chineseness was surely not dependent on the empire".[13] Indeed, throughout modern history, Chinese revolutionaries from Sun Yat-san to Chiang Kai-shek to Mao Zedong, established very different regimes, which were all typically Chinese. The reason is their

---

[11] Wang Gungwu, *The Chineseness of China: Selected Essays*, Hong Kong, Oxford University Press, 1991, p. 2.

[12] Wang Gungwu, *The Chineseness of China*, p. 2.

[13] Wang Gungwu, *The Chineseness of China*, p. 6.

Chineseness which lied underneath very different organisational and ideological forms.

While Wang pointed to why Chineseness could survive different forms of states, other scholars have explored how this very Chineseness has changed. For example, in a recent article, Oakes discussed how "Chineseness" has been reinvented in the light of China's provincial identities. Noting that there exist various enduring features of provincial identity, Oakes stressed that Chineseness is a result of changing relations between the centre and the provinces, causing Chineseness to change as well.[14]

So, this chapter will explore the Chineseness of the Chinese state from different layers with the answering of these questions: (i) what are the basic components of Chineseness; (ii) how have they changed in a new socio-economic environment; and iii) what are the dynamics of this change.

Defining Chineseness

There is no precise definition of Chineseness. Nevertheless, there is a consensus among scholars that the Chinese state is a Confucian state. In such a state, Confucianism, as a body of ideas and institutions, supports and perpetuates an empire-state. Some Confucian measures included, among other things, state sponsorship of Confucian learning and selection of public officials, the use of Confucian criteria to determine all matters of public morality, and broad categories of duties and relationships. The consensus is that Confucianism provides powerful support for an authoritarian system.[15]

For most scholars, what makes the Chinese state peculiar is its emphasis on morality as the basis of politics, just as the emphasis on the rule of law makes Western states peculiar. Hayek once described the role of legislation in the functioning of Western states and regarded it as "among all inventions of man the one fraught with the gravest

---

[14] Tim Oakes, "China's Provincial Identities", pp. 667–692.

[15] Wang Gungwu, *Nationalism and Confucianism*, Singapore, UniPress, 1996, pp. 5–6.

consequences, more far-reaching in its effects even than fire and gunpowder".[16] Morality to the Chinese state is hence just like legislation to the states in the West.

According to Confucianism, morality was the central factor of politics and political order was contingent upon the moral qualities of the ruler: the sage-ruler achieved good government through self-cultivation. Moreover, morality was the expression of a "natural" order, immutable and prior to politics. The political order based upon it was the only proper order. The people were not the subject of politics but the materials of the transforming power of the sage; they were to be educated, fed and protected by political leads informed by morality.

Confucianism actively tried to restrict the power of the state by the burden it placed on the ruler: moral cultivation was most crucial in the ruler, whose example determined the political condition. It declared that the powers of government had to be limited. The ruler's primary obligation was to perform the imperial rites regularly and meticulously. He was also obliged to adhere to the traditions embodied in the examples of sage-kings. Harmony was primarily ensured by the regulatory power of social norms (*li*). Strict performance of the rites heightened the likelihood that the ruler would conform with *li*. Rule by benevolence was another obligation imposed on the ruler.

Furthermore, Confucianism granted society a great deal of independence from the state. As Shils pointed out, "Confucius never recommended that the government take over or regulate the work of merchants, peasants, or craftsmen. They were to be left on their own, and they — especially the peasants — were to be treated with disinterest. ... Confucius praises the ruler 'who achieved order without taking any action'".[17] Even rebellion could be justified when the ruler

---

[16] F A Hayek, *Law, Legislation and Liberty*, vol. 1, London, Routledge and Kegan Paul, 1973, p. 72.

[17] Edward Shils, "Reflections on Civil Society and Civility in the Chinese Intellectual Tradition", in Tu Wei-Ming (ed.), *Confucian Traditions in East Asian Modernity: Moral Education and Economic Culture in Japan and the Four Mini-Dragons*, Cambridge, MA, Harvard University Press, 1996, p. 46.

failed in the performance of his duties and the preservation of harmony.

Unlike Confucianism, the legalists rejected morality as an operative principle of politics and instead took the pursuit of self-interest by each and all as its empirical starting point. Men invariably put their private interests before all else. This inevitably brought them into conflict with one another over limited resources. The only solution under such circumstances was the minute regulation of duty and privilege through the *li*.

As defenders of state power, the legalists resisted all moral restrictions on the ruler's power and regarded society as the tool for its maximisation. They also rejected particular interests, though the emphasis on private pursuits inevitably encroached on the prerogatives of the state. Without believing in morality other than state interests and its condition-power, their stratagem for eliminating competition and conflict was the total organisation of society. In contrast to Confucian reliance on social norms, politics in the legalist scheme was relegated to the administration of power emanating from a single source — the state.[18]

In reality, the Confucian state never failed to make use of other traditions, especially legalism, to rule the country. Theoretically, the two main traditions, Confucianism and legalism, contradict each another but in the political realm, they are complementary. The Chinese Confucian state waned and waxed but it survived for thousands of years, longer than any form of state that ever existed in this world. So, many China scholars regarded it as an ultrastable political structure.

The Confucian state and Western state products

What brought down this Confucian imperial state during the course of the 19th century was Western power, a new power based on superior science and technology, political and economic organisations and a

---

[18] Arif Dirlik, "The Ideological Foundations of the New Lift Movement: A Study in Counterrevolution", *Journal of Asian Study*, vol. 34, no. 4, August 1975, p. 969. See also H G Greel, *Chinese Thought: From Confucius to Mao Tse-tung*, New York, 1960, pp. 125–31.

revolutionary vision of indefinite progress. Against this power, mere Chineseness, however confident, was no match. It was the coming of this Western power that triggered century-long political changes in the Chinese state.

Liu Shu-hsien, a Confucian scholar, believes that the development of Chinese thought since the middle of the Qing dynasty has gone through three stages. In the first stage, the Chinese were shocked by the superiority of Western science and technology. They tried to absorb such Western achievements into their own culture while still believing in the basic soundness of the foundation of their own traditional culture. Representative of this first wave was Zhang Zhitong (1837–1909) who advocated "Chinese learning for *ti* (substance, essence) and Western learning for *yong* (function, utility). In the second stage, the Chinese were thoroughly disappointed with their own tradition and could not find anything valuable about it. Tradition only served as the stumbling block to any move towards future progress. Hope lied only in a quick and totalistic Westernisation process. Representative of the second wave is Hu Shih (1891–1962) who advocated wholesale Westernisation or whole-hearted modernisation. In the third stage, the Chinese came to see the flaws in the Western system and the value of their own tradition. The Western culture, as well as the modernisation process, had its problems. They soon realised that though many traditional habits of the heart had to be eradicated, some cultural insights deeply rooted in the tradition should be reconstructed in such a way that they might make significant contributions in the move towards the future. A synthesis based on the realistic understanding of the problems of humanity and its environment had to be sought. Representative of the third wave may be said to be Mou Tsung-san who advocated the revitalisation and reconstruction of traditional Chinese philosophical insights.[19]

---

[19] Liu Shu-hsien, "Confucian Ideals and the Real World: A Critical Review of Contemporary Neo-Confucian Thought", in Tu Wei-ming (ed.), *Confucian Traditions in East Asian Modernity: Moral Education and Economic Culture in Japan and the Four Mini-Dragons*, Cambridge, MA, Harvard University Press, 1996, p. 100.

The political front is quite similar to the intellectual front. Facing Western powers, the Chinese political elite had to do something about the old form of the state in order to cope with and survive amid changing external and internal circumstances. In doing so, they also faced enormous constraints. According to Bunger, the Chinese rulers faced three choices: (i) to reform the institutions, which had strengthened in the course of history; (ii) to copy the Western model; or (iii) to develop her own new institutions, drawing, where appropriate, on foreign examples.[20] Apparently, the Chinese political elite did not realise they had these three options. Instead, as Liu described, they learned of these options from their political practice over a long historical period and the learning was often by trial and error.

The first option no longer existed since the old order was unable to counter Western powers. The realisation led the Chinese political elite to begin to make efforts to rebuild the state by learning from the West and importing Western state products. Nevertheless, in their struggle to modernise China's political institutions in the late 19th century, they found that they had to give priority to military modernisation since the international system then was still very much imperialistic. Among European states and the United States, a nation's power was based almost invariably on its ability to wage war successfully. The intrusion of Western powers in East Asia shattered the traditional Chinese idea of a world order centred around the Middle Kingdom. Western powers brought the idea of nation state to China without recognising China as a sovereign state. This international system had a significant impact on China's choice of state-building alternatives. It seemed to the Chinese elite that only a modernised military force could prevent further intrusion of Western powers. They realised that if China was to gain respect abroad and to protect itself, it had to first strengthen its armed forces. Military modernisation was thus given the highest priority.

---

[20] Karl Bunger, "The Chinese State between Yesterday and Tomorrow", in Stuart R Schram (ed.), *The Scope of State Power in China*, p. xvii.

Despite its efforts at military modernisation, China was defeated in the Sino-Japanese war (1894–95). The Chinese elite then realised that without a modern state, military modernisation alone would not save China and rebuilding a modern state through government reforms was the only way for China to be strong. Intellectuals like Wang Tao, Yan Fu, Kang Youwei and Liang Qichao all suggested that a modern Chinese state had to be built based on the power of the people.[21]

In examining the evolution of the late imperial state from the mid-16th century to the 1911 Revolution, Miller showed how the weakening of the imperial state led to reforms and served as the bridge to republicanism — a more modern state for China.[22] The late imperial state was the product of, among other things, a moralistic ideology (neo-Confucianism) propagated through a variety of state organs. The educational system was highly elitist and the tool for propagating and inculcating the official cant lied in the educated literati who staffed the state. With neo-Confucian orthodoxy as the ethical-moral basis of rule, there was a natural ritualistic basis of state authority. There was also no routinised process of elite turnover or regime change.

Nevertheless, this Confucian state increasingly became weak on different fronts of state power. Fiscally, the late imperial state had a weak capacity to extract resources and revenue from the populace. The imperial court did not possess the means to redistribute resources to needy sectors or invest in strategic priority projects. A value-added tax on commerce would have gone far to fill state coffers and stimulate growth in key industries. The social stratification of society, which placed merchants at the bottom of the social ladder, was a further impediment. Finally, the limits on state power at the local level and the persistent centrifugal forces in Chinese history made it difficult for the sovereign to extend total rule over its subjects in such a far-flung

---

[21] Zheng Yongnian, *Discovering Chinese Nationalism in China*, Cambridge, Cambridge University Press, 1999, pp. 24–25.

[22] H Lyman Miller, "The Late Imperial Chinese State", in David Shambaugh (ed.), *The Modern Chinese State*, pp. 15–41.

empire. China developed a highly centralised and specialised bureaucracy but encountered real difficulties extending its writ over society.

The weakening of the late imperial state first gave rise to the "self-strengthening movement" of the 1870s and then the attempted reforms of 1898. All these reform efforts, despite ultimately failing, set the Chinese state on the paths of modern industrialisation, military modernisation, scientific inquiry and Western educational reform. These reform movements were inspired by studying a combination of Japanese Meiji reforms, European industrial and military strategies, and American science and education. After enormous efforts, the Qing court attempted to establish a constitutional monarchy to strengthen state power while people's power or popular sovereignty and political participation could be expressed to some degree.

Nevertheless, only after the importation of various schools of Western ideas such as nationalism, liberalism and socialism did the radicalisation of the Chinese intellectual-political elite occur. Westernisation became a prevalent paradigm for China's state building. As Gernet correctly pointed out, "The [Chinese] imitation of Western institutions was inspired simply by the desire to copy those things which led to the success of the West".[23] In this context, Japan was regarded by the Chinese, at the end of the 19th and the beginning of the 20th centuries, as the most exemplary model. To the Chinese elite, the success of Japan was because of its emulation of Western institutions.

Indeed, the 1911 Revolution was inspired by the Western idea of a republican state. After 1911, China had attempted to import Western political institutions. In fact, as Bunger pointed out, imitating and importing Western models of the state became a major theme of China's state building during the greater part of the 20th century.[24] The various constitutions of a Western type bore witness to this. However, all these efforts were without any success and did not help bring about

---

[23] Jacques Gernet, "Introduction", in Stuart R Schram (ed.), *The Scope of State Power in China*, p. xxxii.

[24] Karl Bunger, "The Chinese State", p. xxii.

a modern and strong China. Instead, the importation of Western state products led to China's rapid disintegration. The reason is also quite simple. According to Bunger, "Their obvious failure is based in large part on the initial failure to take account of China's real situation, and in the lack of understanding of the difference between the historical preconditions in Europe and in China. The political institutions and theories which have been taken over from Europe owe their origin there to the peculiarities of the course of European history, which in China are in part completely absent and in part only approximately valid".[25]

The failure of Westernisation projects led to the third option of devising China's own new institutions while learning from the outside world. It has been a long and difficult process, but in the end, it became the most promising for the Chinese leadership. Following the radical "May Fourth Movement" was very serious criticism of modern Western ideas in the 1920s, including an attack on Confucianism at the root of Chineseness. Those who attacked the baneful influence of Confucianism and called for total Westernisation believed that only by importing Western ideas and state products could Chineseness be revitalised.

In the political realm, the building of a more modern state during the Republic era (1911–1949) was by trial and error. Sun Yat-sen envisioned "Three People's Principles" (nationalism, people's rights and people's welfare) as a blueprint for a modern democratic state, a modern society and a modern economy. This proved to be unrealistic. Even early political radicals like Liang Qichao did not believe that Sun's vision would materialise in the Chinese context. Liang argued that the Chinese people were not ready for such modernity. He instead contended that an extended "enlightened autocracy" was required for an indeterminate period of tutelage. Indeed, the republic's first president, Yuan Shikai, ruled as an autocrat. Yuan even attempted to restore the monarchy and crown himself emperor in 1916. However, Yuan's efforts failed. By the early 1920s, the Republic state began to disintegrate as a constitutional and parliamentary entity, and as a bureaucratic force. China entered a period of chaos and warlordism, during which

---

[25] Karl Bunger, "The Chinese State", p. xxiii.

centralised rule and national unity collapsed in the face of warlords, and various military strongmen vied for control of the national government.[26]

This anarchic period came to an end when Chiang Kai-shek emerged as the leader of the Republic. Chiang launched the "Northern Expedition" from Guangdong in 1927 and his efforts succeeded in unifying much of the country under a single government established in Nanjing in 1928. Thereafter, prior to the Japanese invasion, the Nanjing government under Chiang was able to build a seemingly more modern state.[27] In this process, Chiang did not hesitate to borrow "foreign parts". He did not give up on Sun Yat-sen's ideology and imported a Leninist state structure. He was also willing to borrow from China's past to make the state work. For example, he initiated the New Life Movement to make Confucian values a part of the new state. All these efforts seemed quite promising until the Japanese invasion. The anti-Japanese War inadvertently stopped Chiang's efforts at state building.[28] The consolidation of the Chinese Communist Party (CCP) during the Anti-Japanese War not only further nullified the Nanjing government but also ultimately drove the Kuomintang government out of the political scene in the Mainland.

The CCP promised to be the vanguard of a Chinese millennium and the revolution it led succeeded in establishing the People's Republic in 1949. Chiang Kai-shek attempted to redefine the Chineseness of the state by combining Western and Chinese values. Similarly, the Communist Party under Mao Zedong wanted to redefine it by combining Marxist-Leninism and the Thought of Mao Zedong. For Mao, Confucianism could play no part in the dominant ideology. From the mid-1950s to the end of the Cultural Revolution period in 1976, there

---

[26] Edward McCord, *The Power of the Gun: The Emergence of Modern Chinese Warlordism*, Berkeley, CA, University of California Press, 1993.

[27] Julia Strauss, *Strong Institutions in Weak Polities: State Building in Republic China, 1927–1940*, Oxford, Clarendon Press, 1998.

[28] Ramon H Myers, "The Chinese State During the Republic Era", in David Shambaugh (ed.), *The Modern Chinese State*, pp. 42–72.

was an all-out attack on all vestiges of Confucianism, including the teachings of Confucius, Mencius and their followers throughout Chinese history. Enormous political efforts made after 1957 were to eliminate all "feudal" ideas. The Cultural Revolution again aimed to bury Confucianism and the methods used by Mao and his radical followers reminded us of Qin Shihuangdi's decision to bury Confucians more than 2,000 years ago. In some cases, other traditions were drawn upon to denigrate the central tenets of the official Confucianism that had provided the pillars of the Chinese traditional state.[29]

Nevertheless, as Wang has pointed out, China cannot free itself from traditional Chineseness overnight. Mao Zedong rejected modernisation along Western lines in 1949 but did not totally accept socialism along the path of the Soviet Union. In the 1960s, Mao turned to China's own resources for a modern state. Once a Soviet styled state structure was planted, Mao showed his dissatisfaction with its highly bureaucratic characteristics. The Great Leap Forward and the Great Proletarian Cultural Revolution were all efforts by Mao to restore the Chineseness of the state.[30] In doing so, traditional Confucian values were revitalised under disguise. The political campaign of "Learning from Comrade Lei Feng" in the 1960s was an example of such efforts.

Post-Mao reform has witnessed a slow and gradual restoration of Confucianism and other traditional values. Though the state was reluctant to give up the Marxist-Leninist doctrine and the Thought of Mao Zedong, it became increasingly accommodative of Confucianism. Various factors contributed to the revival of Confucianism and other traditional values.

In China, development means national prosperity domestically and national unity externally. In order to pursue domestic prosperity, the leadership was willing to appeal to Confucianism. The dynamic economic success in East Asia, especially in Japan and the "Four Dragons", impressed China's reformist leaders. It seemed to them that what had contributed to East Asia's economic success were Confucian values as

---

[29] Wang Gungwu, *Nationalism and Confucianism*, pp. 7–8.
[30] Wang Gungwu, *The Chineseness of China*, p. 7.

the Confucian tradition was prevalent among Chinese in Taiwan, Hong Kong and Singapore, as well as non-Chinese in Korea and Japan. If the presence of Confucian qualities expressed through kinship structures, educational ideals and practices and entrepreneurial initiatives were factors for their success, there is no reason to reject them in China where Confucianism originated.

Although the Chinese government did not officially claim Confucianism as a value system to support domestic development, the revival of Confucianism was seen at local levels without any formal declaration. As Wang has observed, "Down in the provinces and townships where reviving traditional practices is less inhibited, there is considerable evidence that local officials give credence to the importance of certain Confucian concepts as spurs to entrepreneurship. The Confucian classics have been reprinted with modern translations and annotations. Lectures, seminars, symposiums on a whole range of philosophical and historical tests have been organized regularly. Under a strongly utilitarian banner, Confucian values are being sifted for the help they can give to modern needs".[31]

Similarly, national unity and national unification required that the leadership appeal to Confucianism. After so many years of separate development in different parts of China, namely, Taiwan, Hong Kong and Macao, there was nothing in common except for their cultural origins. Confucianism was the backbone of the great achievement of Chinese civilisation and therefore the very essence of the national spirit. It would be difficult to imagine the Chinese nation without the contributions of Confucian values. In other words, Confucianism can be easily used to achieve the leadership's political goal of national unification.[32]

There are also concerns for the political legitimacy of the CCP regime among Chinese intellectuals and government officials. In the 1980s, liberal intellectuals regarded much of the Chinese tradition as "feudal residues" which they attacked as barriers for China to become

---

[31] Wang Gungwu, *Nationalism and Confucianism*, p. 19.
[32] Wang Gungwu, *Nationalism and Confucianism*.

a modern state. The Enlightenment Project was called to import Western ideas and state products. However, since the early 1990s, such an intellectual environment has changed drastically. There have been intellectual concerns about moral support for the new socialist market economy. Revolutionary ideals guided earlier generations of cadres and ordinary Chinese as well. When the old revolutionary ideology no longer appeals to most Chinese, what can be done to save China from becoming an increasingly money-grubbing society? Chinese intellectuals appealed to their Confucian tradition for a new source of political legitimacy.[33]

The leadership seemingly did not meet with any great difficulty in making such a transition from anti-Confucianism to pro-Confucianism. It is willing to import Western state products in order to build a strong state but is not ready to accept Western value systems. Somehow, Chinese leaders have come to realise that a Western value system can completely undermine the modern state they are trying to build. Anti-Westernisation has been a consistent theme throughout the reform period, especially in the 1980s, when waves of so-called anti-spiritual pollution campaigns and anti-bourgeois liberalisation campaigns were initiated against liberals.[34] While the leadership seemed to defend its mandate to rule through these anti-Westernisation movements in the 1980s, it began to move on the offensive to define a Chinese way to modernity as well as guide its cadres and people. It is no longer hesitant to turn to Confucianism for help. This is the background of the "rule by virtue" movement by Jiang Zemin.

Evidently, there is a change in the nature of the Chinese state. From the traditional imperial state to the Republic state to the Communist state, the transitions changed not only the organisational structure of the state, but also its Chineseness. In other words, the nature of the Chineseness was redefined in the new context. The following section compares the three campaigns, namely, the New Life Movement, the

---

[33] Zheng Yongnian, *Discovering Chinese Nationalism*, p. 70–76.
[34] Merle Goldman, *Sowing the Seeds of Democracy in China: Political Reform in the Deng Xiaoping Era*, Cambridge, MA, Harvard University Press, 1994.

Learning From Lei Feng Movement and the "Rule by Virtue" campaign, to highlight how the equilibrium between importing Western state products and maintaining the Chineseness of the state has been achieved.

The Three Movements Compared
Chiang Kai-shek and the New Life Movement

On 19 February 1934, Chiang Kai-shek inaugurated the New Life Movement in Nanchang, Jiangxi, which was "designed to cope with the spiritlessness of the country".[35] Why did Chiang initiate such a political movement? In essence, by initiating such a movement, Chiang wanted to build a new state which was capable of coping with the enormous political difficulties he encountered as well as a state he could manage. The Confucian spirit was highlighted by the Movement because of not only Chiang and other Kuomintang leaders' belief in Confucianism, but also the utilitarian functions of Confucianism.

Chiang and other Kuomintang leaders believed that the material and spiritual degeneration of the people should be responsible for China's continued crisis. In his inaugural speech, Chiang attributed China's inability to achieve equality with other nations to the inferiority of the "knowledge and morality" of her citizens compared to those of other countries. The Movement was expected to purge every Chinese of these characteristics that weakened the nation and hindered its development. For the Kuomintang leadership, the campaign was to mobilise the population to improve public and private hygienic and behavioural standards, and lead to the moral regeneration of the Chinese people and thus enhance public awareness of and concern for China's problems. Therefore, the movement would not only strengthen the polity at a time of crisis, but also lay the groundwork for a national renaissance.

---

[35] Samuel C Chu, "The New Life Movement, 1934–1937" in John E Lane (ed.), *Researches in the Social Sciences on China*, The East Asian Institute of Columbia University, 1957, p. 1.

According to Chiang, the way of life reflected the people's level of civilisation as well as its moral, spiritual and intellectual make-up. To modernise the way of life became crucial to any nation aspiring to be civilised. The lives of modern Westerners were governed by public morality, including "orderliness", "cleanliness", "simplicity", "frugality", "promptness" and "precision". So, to modernise the way of life was to establish such Western public morality among the Chinese. The way of life should also be based on ethical principles that formed the basis of Chinese morality and civilisation in the past: *li-yi-lian-chi*, or propriety, righteousness, integrity and sense of shame. In this sense, to modernise the way of life was not to Westernise it, but to revive "native morality".[36]

While the leadership insisted from the very beginning that the primary goal of the movement was to modernise China, it also emphasised that the new Chinese civilisation was to be erected upon a native moral foundation. For Chiang, these two were complementary. The modernisation of the way of life coincided with the revival of traditional morality that had fallen into disuse. Traditional morality could be revived to provide the guiding principles of the way of life. Only by doing so could China reach the level of modern civilisation without abandoning her native roots.[37]

There were also many practical driving forces behind the Movement. First, there was political threat from within the Kuomintang. As mentioned earlier, in 1926, the Kuomintang initiated the Northern Expedition, which by 1928, united the nation under Kuomintang auspices. Initial success of the Expedition was due less to its military prowess than to popular sentiment in favour of national unity. Until the mid-1930s, effective Kuomintang control did not extend much beyond the central and lower regions of the Yangtze valley. Local warlords and regional commanders withdrew their allegiance to the national government under Chiang Kai-shek. Throughout the early 1930s, open conflict broke out sporadically between the national

---

[36] Arif Dirlik, "The Ideological Foundations of the New Life Movement", p. 956.

[37] Arif Dirlik, "The Ideological Foundations of the New Life Movement", p. 960.

government and powerful warlords. China was united only in having a central government to represent the nation; in reality, the nation was torn by regional factionalism.[38] Apparently, it was imperative for Chiang to forge political loyalty to the national government and especially to himself within the Kuomintang.

Second, there were challenges from society. Since the 1920s, student and labour movements in the cities, as well as peasant movements in the countryside were on the rise, representing new social forces on the political scene. These forces in turn reflected deeper, irreversible changes in Chinese society. The rise of market economy lent a new significance to urban centres and their immediate environment. The cultural radicalism of the intelligentsia, crystallised around the Versailles Treaty issue in 1919, turned into organised political action in the 1920s. The peasantry, while not that politically aroused at that time, was nevertheless increasingly released from its traditional moorings. Different imported ideologies including communism found their strong support in different social groups. For the Kuomintang leadership, "[p]olitical success depended on the extent to which these new forces could be incorporated into a new political structure".[39] In this sense, the New Life Movement can be seen as a response to the intellectual and social mobilisation that had dominated Chinese politics since the 1920s. According to Dirlik, the Movement "represented the Kuomintang effort to overcome public alienation from the government, to mobilize the public not only to support the state but also to help in its reform".[40] Chiang hoped that the Movement would simultaneously eliminate social radicalism and convert the masses into instruments of his will.

Third and most importantly, there was the threat from the CCP as an organisation and an ideology. During the Northern Expedition, CCP leaders like Mao Zedong worked with the Kuomintang in the belief that a national revolution to unite the country was a prerequisite

---

[38] Samuel C Chu, "The New Life Movement", p. 1.

[39] Arif Dirlik, "The Ideological Foundations of the New Life Movement", p. 947.

[40] Arif Dirlik, "The Ideological Foundations of the New Life Movement", p. 947.

to a proletarian revolution. When initial success was achieved by 1927, a break between the conservative and moderate elements of the Kuomintang on the one hand, and the radical elements including the Communists on the other, became inevitable. Chiang, supported by the right-wingers, succeeded in driving the Communists out of their positions in central China. The Communists under Mao Zedong and Zhu De entrenched themselves in Jiangxi and set up a Soviet regime independent of the control of the national government. Confucianism again became useful as Chiang used it to replace all "imported doctrines" including Communism.[41]

The New Life Movement embedded all these agendas. To forge political loyalty within the Kuomintang and among the people, Chiang realised that it was important to create a collective sense of political identity. Such an identity represented a social and political consciousness. It seemed to Chiang that the key to such a social and political consciousness was the cultivation of group orientation, namely, collectivism. Chiang and other leaders believed that the Chinese were traditionally selfish and thought only of themselves or of their families, with little awareness of or concern for the larger society and the nation. The cultivation of group life became imperative for national survival and strength since it could stimulate the awareness of the nation and build the spirit of responsibility and sacrifice.

To achieve this, the New Life Movement leadership believed that the people's collective consciousness could be awakened by politicisation and mobilisation. Political mobilisation was expected to increase people's awareness of the group and subject their own will to that of the collectivity, that is, from the family to the state. The emphasis of political mobilisation was on self-restraint, self-sacrifice, obedience and loyalty. State interest was extended ad infinitum, while private interest was rejected as "selfishness".

Traditionally, the Chinese viewed politics in two different ways, as in Confucianism and Legalism. Confucianism conceived politics as essentially a moral question and obviated the need for organisation.

---

[41] Samuel C Chu, "The New Life Movement", p. 12.

It focused on the moral improvement of the individuals as the means to good society. By contrast, legalism envisioned ideal society as a bureaucratic machine with the sole purpose of serving the cause of the state. According to Dirlik, the interplay of these two conflicting conceptions of politics shaped the New Life Movement.[42]

The New Life Movement placed an overwhelming emphasis on the centrality of individual morality. The transformation of the behaviour and attitudes of individuals was regarded as the primary task; institutional change was secondary because institutions were worth no more than the individuals operating them. Nevertheless, the New Life Movement was not a total restoration of Confucianism. As Dirlik pointed out, the New Life ideology broke with Confucianism in its understanding of both politics and morality and consequently, of the relationship between the two. It rejected the idea of social-political order as an immutable, natural order; instead, it stressed the role of the state and state bureaucracies and other organisational agents in making such a social-political order. It also regarded morality as the tool of the state, existing only to serve the ends of the state. This contrasted with the original Confucian views of the state. In Confucian political theory, the state derived its legitimacy from the ruler's morality, demonstrated through his ability to establish conditions of harmony that would enable the people to realise their potential for virtue and pursue their natural and social obligations. This criterion was lacking in the New Life ideology.[43]

The Movement aimed to educate the public as Chiang indicated in his various speeches. Equally important, it also aimed to educate those in power. Chiang desired a thorough bureaucratisation of society, with each individual having a specific function to perform in order to achieve the goals of the organisation. The values the movement tried to instil in the people included functional morality, hierarchical conception of society, uniformity assured by specific rules, regularity and

---

[42] Samuel C Chu, "The New Life Movement", p. 968.
[43] Samuel C Chu, "The New Life Movement", p. 971.

order, and the necessity of obedience to the dictates of the collectivity personified in superiors and so on.[44]

According to Dirlik, the New Life Movement "was intended not to challenge but to enhance the existing structure of authority. Its goal was not to extend political participation to the people but to mobilize them in support of state goals, to convert them into voluntary functionaries of a bureaucratic machinery that encompassed the whole nation".[45] The Kuomintang leadership did not attempt to restore China's traditional values but use these values to build a new vision of the state. The Movement seemed to have revived the Chineseness of the Chinese state but in reality, as Dirlik argued, "it was not a traditional but a modern response to a modern problem".[46]

Mao Zedong and the "Learning from Lei Feng" movement

On 15 August 1962, Lei Feng died in an accident. In January 1963, the National Defence Ministry named the squad that Lei Feng was associated with before his death as the "Lei Feng Squad". Meanwhile, Lei Feng was posthumously honoured by the Chinese Youth League as An Excellent Instructor of the National Young Pioneers. The People's Liberation Army's General Political Department, the Central Committee of the Chinese Youth League, the National Trade Union and the National Women's Association issued the notice to all their members to learn from Lei Feng. On 5 March 1963 Mao Zedong wrote the famous calligraphy, "Learning from Comrade Lei Feng". Days thereafter, other major leaders such as Liu Shaoqi, Zhou Enlai, Zhu De, Deng Xiaoping and Chen Yun also wrote similar calligraphies. This kick-started the national movement to "Learning from Lei Feng".

After its initial wave in 1963, the "Learning from Lei Feng" movement experienced several major peaks. According to a statistical study,

---

[44] Samuel C Chu, "The New Life Movement", p. 972.
[45] Samuel C Chu, "The New Life Movement", p. 953.
[46] Samuel C Chu, "The New Life Movement", p. 945.

there had been six peak periods: (i) before 1973; (ii) 1973–76; (iii) 1977–82; (iv) 1983–89; (v) 1990–93; and (vi) after 1993.[47] All these movements had very different themes, depending on the socio-economic and political circumstances at that time. This discussion focuses on only the initial wave of the movement.

According to official narrative, Lei Feng was born in 1939 to a poor peasant family in Hunan province.[48] His early childhood was one of extreme poverty and tragedy. His father died when he was only five years old, the victim of a brutal beating by the Japanese. His elder brother died the following year of tuberculosis contracted in the sweatshop where he was compelled to labour. Soon after, Lei Feng's younger brother succumbed to typhoid fever. Lei Feng's mother, who was a servant in a landlord household, gave in to humiliation and despair after being raped by the son of the landlord. She hanged herself. Lei Feng was thus made an orphan at an early age. He managed to survive until 1949 when his hometown was finally liberated by the PLA.

From then on, good fortune had befallen on the young Lei Feng. He entered a local primary school in 1950. After completing junior primary school, he attended a senior primary school where he worked diligently and became a member of the Young Pioneers in 1954. A year thereafter, when a new school was built closer to his home, he entered this new school and helped to organise a new branch of Young Pioneers. When he was in the sixth grade, the local agricultural producers' cooperative began a literacy campaign and Lei Feng encouraged his friends to join him in establishing a night school for the local peasants.

After graduating from senior primary school in 1956, Lei Feng was assigned as a messenger in the local authority offices. Due to his hard work and the spirit of volunteerism, he was promoted to work for the

---

[47] Wu Hai-gang, "Lei Feng de meiti xuanchuan yu shidai biange") (Changes over Time in the Media Propaganda of Lei Feng), *Ershiyi shiji* (The 21st Century), Hong Kong, no. 4, 2001, pp. 137–142.

[48] This narrative is based on Chen Guangsheng, *Lei Feng xiaozhuan* (Brief Biography of Lei Feng), Beijing: Zhongguo qingnian chubanshe, 1963; and Chen Guangsheng and Cui Jiabo, *Lei Feng de gushi* (The Story of Lei Feng), Hong Kong, Sanlian shudian, 1973.

party committee. During this time, he was chosen as a model worker and accepted into the Youth League. After a brief period in which he helped to build a dam, he volunteered to work at a farm and later as a tractor driver in 1958. After the Great Leap Forward was launched later that year, he volunteered to go north to work in the Anshan Iron and Steel Company. During his short stint at the company, he had been voted an advanced worker three times, a pacesetter 18 times, a red standard bearer five times and became a model member of the Communist Youth League.

When the PLA was searching for local recruits, Lei Feng was said to have begged his way into the army after being refused several times because of his height and lightweight. When he was eventually admitted into the PLA, his physical stature was described as a "handicap" but which he was able to overcome through sheer strength of will and diligence. In the military, after a brief stint with his unit's amateur culture troupe, Lei Feng was eventually assigned to drive a truck. Once he almost single-handedly saved a processing factory which had gone into flames. Thereafter, he joined a team even though he was ill at that time to fight a flood which almost led to the collapse of the dam at a local river.

Lei Feng was also known to have done many good deeds, albeit mostly very small ones. He gave his coat to a poor old peasant even though it meant he would have nothing to put on while working outside in the cold. He gave his lunch to a comrade saying he was not hungry just because he thought his comrade needed the food more than him. He bought a ticket for a stranger he met at a train station who lost her ticket and did not have enough money left for her journey home. While riding on the train, he cleaned the floors and washed the windows just to give a helping hand to the train attendants. During a heavy rainstorm at a construction site, without available tarpaulins, Lei Feng used his own bedding and his own clothing to cover up some bags of cement that otherwise would have been ruined by the rain. While the other men in his barracks slept, Lei Feng secretly stayed up at night to wash their laundry and mend their socks just because he knew they were all tired. He not only contributed his salary for various philanthropic projects but also encouraged his comrades to do so. Due to all his good deeds, he was given the honour of membership in the CCP on 8 November 1960.

On the morning of 15 August 1962, Lei Feng was returning to his barracks in his truck with a comrade. Lei Feng got out of the truck to direct his fellow soldier who was at the wheel. The road was slippery and while backing into a narrow space, the truck hit a pole which came crashing down on Lei Feng's head, killing him almost instantly.

Why did Mao Zedong initiate such a nationwide movement to learn from Lei Feng? Mao wanted the "Learning from Lei Feng" movement as Chiang Kai-shek wanted the New Life Movement. The two movements aimed at fashioning a citizenry responsive to national needs, willing to endure hardship for the good of society and ready to exert the maximum effort for the achievement of national progress. Like Chiang, Mao also wanted to forge a new identity among the people and party cadres towards the party, especially towards Mao himself. While Chiang borrowed traditional values to solve modern problems, Mao utilised his concept of class struggle to achieve his goals. Arguably, Lei Feng's experience could be considered as, in the Confucian spirit, a form of class struggle.

China under Mao was regarded as a virtuocratic society where people were selected for schooling and occupational opportunities primarily on the basis of their moral virtue.[49] Anyone, regardless of intellect, social status and education or skills, with morally and politically upright behaviour could reap societal rewards of his/her actions. A virtuocratic system was very beneficial for the party leadership. It could help to transform society from the old to the new by rewarding behaviour that was in keeping with socialist objectives and further economic goals through mass mobilisation of the workforce. What Susan Shirk called virtuocracy played the role of "moral incentive" which Lindblom used to explore the Communist systems such as China and the Soviet

---

[49] Susan Shirk, *Competitive Comrades: Career Incentives and Student Strategies in China*, Berkeley, CA, University of California Press, 1982.

Union.[50] Virtuocracy is helpful to understanding the Learning from Lei Feng movement under Mao Zedong. The virtues Lei Feng had were what Mao wanted for China's state-building and consolidating his power as well. While in pre-modern China the student who aspired to work in the government service focused on the Confucian classics as the source of orthodox traditions, Lei Feng forged his virtues by reading Mao's teachings. While the Confucian student gave loyalty to his emperor and showed filial piety to his parents, Lei Feng combined these two into the single-minded devotion he gave to the party, the people and above all, Mao Zedong. So Reed argued, "although he [Lei Feng] was a hero designed to promote socialist construction, he displays certain virtues and characteristics that link him with Chinese models of the past".[51]

What virtues did Lei Feng possess? The most important quality Lei Feng had was, of course, his loyalty to Mao Zedong and his party. On 5 March 1963, *People's Daily* re-issued a paper written by Lo Ruiqing, the vice premier of the State Council and general chief of staff of the PLA. Lo wrote,

> There are many fine points in Comrade Lei Feng which are worthy of study, but I feel that one of the fine points which deserves our study, the most basic and salient point which enabled Lei Feng to become a great fighter, is the fact that he repeatedly studies the works of Chairman Mao, faithfully observed every instruction of Chairman Mao in carrying out his work, and devoted himself to being a good fighter of Chairman Mao. Lei Feng believed that Mao Zedong's ideas are "food, weapons and a compass".[52]

Lei Feng owed all he had achieved to Chairman Mao and the party. His gratitude to Mao and his party knew no bounds. He transferred

---

[50] Charles E Lindblom, *Politics and Markets: The World's Political-Economic Systems*, New York, Basic Books, 1977.

[51] Gay Garland Reed, *The Lei Feng Phenomenon in the PRC*, PhD Thesis, University of Virginia, 1991, p. 67.

[52] Lo Ruiqing, "Xuexi Lei Feng" (Learning from Lei Feng), *People's Daily*, 5 March 1963. The paper was published originally in *Zhongguo qingnian* (The China Youth), 2 March 1963.

filial allegiance and appreciation from the family to the party. This made Lei Feng stand out. Lei Feng was a person of only average, or even below average, physical and cultural endowments. However, he so desperately wanted to make his contribution, out of gratitude to the party, devotion to Chairman Mao and love for his country and his people, that he always worked harder and longer than others just to make up for the difference.

"I originally was an orphan", he was quoted as having said. "Born into a bitter life I was later raised in sweetness. The party and the people have given everything to me. I want to give everything back to the party and the people". The fact that Lei Feng was an orphan was significant because he was a person without familial ties which could interfere with his dedication to Chairman Mao, to the party and to the people. In his diary, Lei Feng claimed, "I feel in my bones that it is the happiest thing to live in a socialist society, in a big revolutionary family, in the great era of Mao Zedong". Among the many songs associated with Lei Feng is one called, "To Sing a Song to the Party":

> To sing a song to the party
> I take the party as my mother
> My mother only gave me my body
> The party's radiance shines in my heart
> In the old society
> The whip was beaten on my body
> My mother could only cry
> But the Communist party called us to revolution
> And we wrest the whip from the enemy
> And beat the enemy

The second most important virtue of Lei Feng was his profound hatred for class enemies. In his diary, Lei Feng quoted a well-known passage which expressed the appropriate class stand and revealed no ambivalence about what to hate and what to love:

> Towards our comrades we should be as warm as spring
> Towards work as hot as summer

Towards individualism like the autumn wind seeping away the fallen leaves
Towards our enemies as ruthless as winter.[53]

Lei Feng's Confucian style of filial allegiance to and appreciation of Chairman Mao, his party and his people, and his class consciousness, exactly met Mao Zedong's political needs in the early 1960s.

During the 1958–1961 period, China experienced the greatest famine in human history.[54] The famine radically changed China's political development. Maoist radical idealism was deemed to be responsible for this famine. Consequently, pragmatism became prevalent in the party leadership and Liu Shaoqi, Deng Xiaoping and other leaders came to the forefront of the political scene. In 1961–62, China instituted new economic policies to counteract the devastation wrought by the three disastrous years of the Great Leap Forward. The new policies shifted the responsibility for production from party committees at different levels to the hands of industrial, commercial and agricultural experts who were given considerable autonomy and latitude in meeting their state quotas.

As the economic adjustment was quite effective and economic incentives were introduced into the system, China's economy quickly recovered. Nevertheless, such positive economic adjustments also brought about changes to the distribution of political power within the party. With pragmatic leaders dominating the area of economic development, Maoist radicalism seemed to have been "sidelined". Economic incentives increased morale and output but diluted the collectivist ideals of the party. More importantly, the rise of a new class of managers and technocrats challenged not only Maoism but also the party's hegemony. Various criticisms were directed at the Great Leap Forward and Mao's individual dictatorship among social groups.

Once Mao felt threatened by such new developments, he took decisive action to regain his power and domination of the party

---

[53] Gay Garland Reed, *The Lei Feng Phenomenon*, p. 98.
[54] Yang Dali, *Calamity and Reform in China*, Stanford, CA, Stanford University Press, 1996.

leadership. Class struggle again became the most effective tool for Mao to achieve his goals. Mao claimed that the party leadership and indeed the Chinese bureaucratic system had been deeply affected by Khrushchev's pernicious virus. To save the party (read as to save himself), a series of class-struggle movements became imperative.

On 25 December 1962, the Central Committee of the Communist Youth League emerged from their "Fifth National Conference on Work for Young Pioneers" in Beijing with a resolution to strengthen the communist ideological education of the children. This was followed by a series of political campaigns, including the campaign to learn from the PLA, the movement to cultivate revolutionary successors, the Socialist Education Movement and the Campaign to Learn From Lei Feng and other role models.

Notably, all these movements were interrelated. When Mao was alienated from the Chinese bureaucracy, he turned to the military supported by Lin Biao. Mao believed that the party apparatus no longer served his revolutionary cause and he wanted to use a member of the PLA as a model for universal emulation to produce revolutionary successors.[55] Spence pointed out that Mao's call to the entire country to learn from the PLA put the army in the position previously enjoyed by the party.[56] Together with Lin Biao, Mao rapidly expanded military influence in the party and government organs. From 1963, the political department had been set up in each ministry, which was staffed by military cadres. By doing so, the military established its own power network in China's political system, which effectively served to implement Maoist continuous revolution.[57]

The socialist educational movement was virtually a class education campaign aimed at raising class consciousness among those who had not experienced the oppression and exploitation of the pre-revolutionary period. The "Learning from Lei Feng" movement integrated well

---

[55] Gay Garland Reed, *The Lei Feng Phenomenon*, p. 128.

[56] Jonathan Spence, *The Search for Modern China*, New York, W W Norton & Co, 1990, p. 597.

[57] Wu Hai-gang, "Lei Feng de meiti xuanchuan yu shidai biange", p. 138.

with the socialist educational movement. To forge class consciousness, the issue of "red and expert" was again raised. According to Mao, a revolutionary successor had to be both "red and expert". On the surface, this appeared to be a combination of virtuocratic and meritocratic criteria. In effect, the "expert" part of the equation was couched in virtuocratic rhetoric.[58] For Maoists, the only justification for becoming "expert" was the advancement of the proletarian cause and service to the motherland. As one commentator argued in *China Youth*,

> It will be extremely good if you decide to become a red specialist of the working class and render active service to the socialist and communist cause with your scientific accomplishments. It will be very bad if you use your scientific and technical accomplishments as personal capital to pursue personal fame and benefit and serve whoever satisfies your private ends.[59]

Lei Feng fitted well with this Maoist ideal of class consciousness. More importantly, Lei Feng also served the growing personality cult of Mao. As Mao himself was ageing, he wanted to put forth a youthful image for the country to follow. Reed correctly pointed out that this image was not a new leader but a youth who followed the leader without question, and not a young man with new ideas on how to serve the party and the people but a young man who followed, without question and without any qualms, the ideals already set forth.[60] Mao wanted such a youthful face to carry on his revolutionary mission. The creation and promotion of a model of such devotion, purity and virtue could only reflect positively on Mao and the party. Mao needed Lei Feng's Confucian style of loyalty but did not want the Confucian style of questioning the legitimacy of his power. Lei Feng's filial appreciation of Mao and his class consciousness made him an ideal figure for Mao when he encountered serious challenges from within and outside the party.

---

[58] Gay Garland Reed, *The Lei Feng Phenomenon*, p. 133.
[59] Cited in Gay Garland Reed, *The Lei Feng Phenomenon*, p. 133.
[60] Gay Garland Reed, *The Lei Feng Phenomenon*, p. 103.

Jiang Zemin and the "Rule by Virtue" movement

The movement of "Rule by Virtue" proposed by Jiang Zemin can be regarded as a continuation of the tradition of the New Life Movement and the Learning from Lei Feng movement. Like his predecessors Chiang Kai-shek and Mao Zedong, after Jiang came to power, he also aimed to consolidate his power within the party by initiating the movement of rule by virtue. The leadership believed that such a movement could bring some positive results such as bringing rampant corruption under control, soliciting consensus among party leaders, forging loyalty to the party (especially to the Jiang-centred leadership) among party cadres and people as well, and strengthening the base of political legitimacy.[61]

What does rule by virtue mean? Jiang did not explain it clearly. However, his loyal theoretical thinkers had provided some useful definitions. According to a group of scholars in the Shanghai Academy of Social Sciences, though this concept originated from ancient China, it needs to be redefined in China's new context. They argued that while rule by virtue normally refers to the role of morality in governing the country, today, it "means not only morality, but also ideal (*lixiang*) and believing (*xinnian*)".[62] More concretely, rule by virtue implies:

(1) building a socialist moral thought system compatible with socialist legal system and Marxism-Leninism, Mao Zedong Thought and Deng Xiaoping theory as its bases;
(2) serving the people as its core, collectivism as its principle and "love the country, people, work, science and socialism" as its basic requirements;

---

[61] For a discussion, see The Editorial and Writing Group, *Yifa zhiguo he yide zhiguo jiben fanglue xuexi duben* (The Reader of Basic Strategies of the Rule of Law and Rule by Virtue), Beijing, Zhonggong dangshi chubanshe, 2001.

[62] Zhang Qian and Ji Haiqing, "Fade jianzhi, jianshe you Zhongguo tese shehuizhuyi fazhi guojia" (Rule of Law cum Rule by Virtue: Building a Socialist State of Rule of Law with Chinese Characteristics), *Shanghai shehui kexueyuan jikan* (Quarterly Journal of the Shanghai Academy of Social Sciences), no. 2, 2001, p. 189. This paper is a summary of a conference on Jiang's concept of rule by virtue, held in the Academy.

(3) employing professional ethics, public morality and family virtue as a basic starting point;

(4) emphasising moral standards in the selection and promotion of party cadres and government officials;

(5) requiring leading party cadres to be a role model for the people; and

(6) recognising the importance of the rule of law[63]

As Jiang Zemin claimed that the CCP represents the most advanced Chinese culture, it would be irrational for him to directly borrow this ancient concept; instead, he needed to assign some new meanings to the concept. His loyal scholars argued that rule by virtue could not be understood only in the context of China's cultural development as it has also to be explained in terms of socio-economic progress. By proposing the rule by virtue, Jiang did not mean to go back to such an ancient virtue or to repeat China's traditional values but to modernise these values under modern socio-economic circumstances.

Certainly, rule by virtue requires a defence in modern terms. Its traditional contents no longer fit modern needs as it has to be based on modernity, rationality and advancement. What is the modern context of rule by virtue? According to these scholars, its modernity lies in the context of China's modern practice of rule of law. Rule by virtue "is required because of the need for spiritual development and the need for rule of law per se".[64]

Thus, what is important is the relations between rule of law and rule by virtue. For those who support the concept, rule of law and rule by virtue are not in conflict, but complementary. First, both aimed at nurturing the good and discarding the evil, purifying the social atmosphere, lifting the quality of citizens and facilitating social progress. Second, a sense of morality is necessary for lawmakers who formulate

---

[63] Zhang Qian and Ji Haiqing, "Fade jianzhi, jianshe you Zhongguo tese shehuizhuyi fazhi guojia"; and The Editorial and Writing Group, *Yifa zhiguo*, p. 16.

[64] Zhang Qian and Ji Haiqing, "Fade jianzhi, jianshe you Zhongguo tese shehuizhuyi fazhi guojia", pp. 189–90.

the law and law implementers who enforce the law. Third, without the support of rule by virtue, the system of rule of law will not work effectively. Since the implementation of reform and open door policy, China has made many laws and regulations without enforcing them. One major problem is that many law enforcers are themselves not morally qualified. There is also a large gap between people's moral quality and their demands for law. To a great degree, the problem associated with law enforcement is the underdevelopment of a moral basis. Socio-economic development may have facilitated legal development, but people's moral progress is still lagging far behind. Certainly, when great legal development has been achieved, it becomes politically significant to realise moral progress.[65]

What makes rule by virtue possible? Or how can such a system materialise? Jiang Zemin and his followers differ from the New Life Movement and the "Learning from Lei Feng" movement in this regard. Both Chiang Kai-shek and Mao Zedong were more ambitious and idealistic than Jiang. Chiang and Mao wanted to use the movement to educate not only party cadres and government officials, but also social members. Jiang did not have this capability to command such nation-wide movements. All he could do was to limit the movement within the party and government. According to Jiang's supporters, "rule by virtue means first to rule the party (government officials) rather than the people; furthermore, in order to rule the party, it is necessary to rule party cadres, especially high-rank cadres first".[66]

How can rule by virtue play an important role in educating party cadres and government officials? According to these proponents, in order to do so, the leadership has to (i) emphasise the moral dimension of administration and social justice; (ii) cultivate (*jiaohua*) party cadres and government officials, the most important function of rule by

---

[65] Zhang Qian and Ji Haiqing, "Fade jianzhi, jianshe you Zhongguo tese shehuizhuyi fazhi guojia", 190.

[66] Zhang Qian and Ji Haiqing, "Fade jianzhi, jianshe you Zhongguo tese shehuizhuyi fazhi guojia", p. 189.

virtue; (iii) demonstrate as moral rulers; and (iv) balance between law and morality during legislation and administration of justice.

There is also an institutional side of rule by virtue. Without certain institutions, virtue will not be able to play its proper role in government. As Jiang's supporters alleged, the realisation of virtue in government can be assured by building a set of institutions including (i) establishing a system of moral evaluation and moral supervision; (ii) building ethic codes in different areas of administration and political, economic and religious activities; and (iii) developing individual professional ethnic codes.[67]

Even though Jiang Zemin showed his genuine enthusiasm and even great passion for rule by virtue, and the party's propaganda made enormous efforts to spread the idea, the movement received a very cold reception. The movement only provided political conservatives with an opportunity to lay claim to the moral superiority of the party and justify its existing authoritarian rule. Naturally, the propaganda movement was extremely unpopular among liberal-minded intellectuals and serious criticisms followed even with tight political control of the media. It not only reminded them of the quasi-fascist nature of the New Life Movement and how Mao's personal dictatorship was justified by the "Learning from Lei Feng" movement, and how the movement had pushed Mao's personal cult during the Cultural Revolution.[68]

Even among Jiang supporters, there was no consensus on the rule by virtue. They seemed to have reached an agreement that rule of law is China's basic strategy for political development, but they disagreed with one another if rule by virtue could be assigned the same importance. Was rule by virtue another basic strategy for the country's political construction? Many would say no. Instead, they would like to see

---

[67] Zhang Qian and Ji Haiqing, "Fade jianzhi, jianshe you Zhongguo tese shehuizhuyi fazhi guojia", p. 191.

[68] For a serious criticism, see Wei Yi, "Zhongguo xin dezhi lunxi: gaige qian Zhongguo daode hua zhengzhi di lishi fanxi" (An Analysis of New Theory of Rule by Virtue in China: A Historical Reflection of Chinese Moralized Politics in Pre-Reform China), *Zhanlue yu guanli*, no. 2, 2001, pp. 25-38.

rule by virtue becoming a basic strategy for party building and argued that rule by virtue should be used to rule party cadres and government officials instead of the people. Some cast serious doubt on whether it was realistic to do so. Since rule by virtue needs implementation from above, without knowing what modern virtue was, it was dangerous to implement it. How to modernise virtue for it to be compatible with the market economy was another pertinent issue. It has taken a long time for China to develop a market economy; developing a modern virtue could take much longer. Therefore, it is too idealistic to talk about rule by virtue and placing too much emphasis on rule by virtue will certainly undermine the progress of the rule of law.[69]

Chineseness and Democracy

I have briefly described the three movements in the context of China's state-building in the modern era. What conclusions can be drawn from this discussion about Chineseness and democracy? Since China was forced to open its doors to the West, modern Chinese politics has been organised around various Western concepts such as "democracy", "popular sovereignty", Marxism, Leninism and so on. For better or worse, they have had an impact on the political elites' mindset of how Chinese development needs to be directed. The democratic images of Sun Yat-sen's "republic", Taiwan's presidential election and mainland China's rural elections did not originate from China's tradition. Obviously, democracy is spreading gradually and slowly in China but whether it will take root depends on various factors. These factors can be organised around the following three lines, namely, nationalism versus democracy, liberalisation versus democratisation and capitalism versus democracy.

Nationalism versus democracy

Nationalism played an essential role in the development of Western democracy. Modern Western nation states were created by the interplay

---

[69] Zhang Qian and Ji Haiqing, "Fade jianzhi, jianshe you Zhongguo tese shehuizhuyi fazhi guojia", pp. 189–92.

of two types of sovereignty: national sovereignty and popular sovereignty. Nationalism first implies that the nation itself is called upon to defend its freedom. However, more importantly, nationalism means the triumph of individual liberty. Without the rise of popular sovereignty, it is difficult to understand the evolution of Western modern nation states.[70]

However, when Western nationalism spread to China, national sovereignty became separated from popular sovereignty. The former became dominant and the latter was replaced by state sovereignty as China encountered a different international environment. When China began to modernise itself, it was in an age of imperialism and the Chinese elite had no choice but to modernise. Nevertheless, the highest priority had to be given to national survival, rather than individual freedom or democracy. Democracy was desirable, but it had to subordinate itself to national survival.

This was the theme of Chinese nationalism proposed by Sun Yat-sen, the founder of the Republic of China. For Sun, nationalism's chief concern was to ensure the survival of the Chinese nation because it had suffered from foreign aggression. According to him, the meaning of Chinese nationalism was multifold. First, nationalism was equivalent to the doctrine of the state as China had been developing a single state out of a single race ever since the Qin and Han dynasties. Second, nationalism was key to the development and survival of the Chinese nation; and third, nationalism called for equality of all human races and was the way to restore freedom and equality to China.[71] These ideas were reflected in Sun's design of the three stages of Chinese political development — military government, guided democracy and constitutional democracy.

Li Zehou, a well-respected Chinese scholar, argued that the priority for national survival was in conflict with democracy in modern China.

---

[70] Hans Morgenthau, "The Paradoxes of Nationalism", *Yale Review*, vol. xlvi, no. 4, 1957, pp. 481–96.

[71] Chou Yu-sun, "Nationalism and Patriotism in China", *Issues and Studies*, vol. 32, no. 11, 1996, pp. 67–87.

National survival required an authoritarian regime, even a dictatorship. For Chinese elites, nationalism means national freedom, rather than individual freedom, collectivism rather than individualism. Facing a hostile international environment, a strong regime only means statism.[72] Li raised his argumenti n the mid 1980s, but his argument was criticised by the Chinese government. This does not mean, however, that China has resolved the contradiction between a strong state and democracy.

After Deng Xiaoping took over power, China began to seek a favourable international environment in order to give highest priority to domestic development. China was successful in improving its relations with major powers and with its neighbouring countries as well. It also achieved a high rate of economic growth in the 1980s. Ironically, however, rapid economic development did not make the Chinese state stronger than before. Indeed, state power has been on the decline ever since.

The decline of central power was a natural result of the Chinese style of reform — decentralisation. Throughout its modern history, China's modernisation encountered a dilemma. China's system was highly centralised where blanket implementation of top-down policies at the provincial levels might not suit local conditions. Yet the national government was not able to modernise a country that had great diversities. The only strategy for modernisation was decentralisation. However, decentralisation produced growing pressure at other levels of the polity for participation in the political process and participation further limited central autonomy in decision making. As elite involvement at the local level expanded, it was increasingly accompanied by expectations that not only local men should manage local affairs, but also elite views should be considered by officials in formulating national policy. Local political participation made it difficult for the national government to effectively organise its resources and implement its policies.[73]

---

[72] Li Zehuo, *Zhongguo jindai sixiangshi lun* (History of Modern Chinese Thoughts), Beijing, Renmin chubanshe, 1987.

[73] For a discussion of this trend, see, Paul A Cohen, "Post-Mao Reforms in Historical Perspective", *Journal of Asian Studies*, vol. 47, no. 3, 1988, pp. 519–41.

The experience of post-Mao China is a classic example. Decentralisation promoted economic growth, the impact of which went beyond the economic arena. Central revenue has shrunk continuously since the implementation of reform. A new fiscal system was established to centralise fiscal power but local resistance was strong. Without strong fiscal capacity, the national government was not able to coordinate development among regions. Income disparities widened consistently and led to complaints among local residents and government officials in poor areas. Regional disparities generated a great momentum for ethnic nationalism. Many Chinese intellectuals, especially the new leftists, fear that China will follow the footstep of Yugoslavia which led to national disintegration with decentralisation.

Even before the 1989 Tiananmen Incident, many Chinese intellectuals began to talk about neo-authoritarianism. The collapse of European communism made many Chinese top leaders believe that if China adopts political liberalisation, the CCP may not be able to avoid a similar misfortune. The collapse of the Soviet Union also had a great psychological impact on Chinese attitude towards revolutions or radical reform movements. People began to overwhelmingly appreciate social stability and economic development rather than political democratisation. With this change in attitude, people become more indifferent to the regime's authoritarian measures against civil society. Under such circumstances, democratisation becomes more difficult.

Another important factor is the rise of various anti-China theories such as the "China threat" and "containing China" in the West. Many Chinese now believe that China's international environment could deteriorate and domestic development could be endangered. This perception led to the rise of popular nationalism against the West, especially the United States. For the leadership, this new nationalism is justification for the regime's authoritarian rule. Democratisation is regarded as a destabilising force. As long as the Chinese dream of a strong state is not realised and nationalistic ideal is not materialised, democratisation is unlikely.

Liberalisation versus democratisation

Many scholars in the West believe that economic development will necessarily lead to liberalisation which, in turn, will lead to political democratisation, as shown in South Korea and Taiwan. In the long run, this may become a reality. However, the causal linkage between liberalisation and democratisation is rather weak in the context of Chinese political development.

The necessity of liberalisation is obvious. The state must lift its control and let individuals have the freedom to promote economic development. If the national government wants local government officials to make laws or regulations appropriate to local conditions, it must not impose any top-down restrictive and unified laws. If economic performance becomes a foundation of CCP's political legitimacy, liberalisation will follow. Put it in another way, individual and local autonomy is a precondition for rapid economic development. Economic reforms would require the national government to withdraw from economic affairs and decentralise economic decision-making power to individuals and local units. Without individual and local economic initiative, rapid development will be impossible.

Economic liberalisation also leads to political liberalisation to some degree. Many Chinese reformist leaders, especially Deng Xiaoping, realised that a Marxist-Leninist state is incompatible with a market economy and political reforms are needed to make the system more accommodating to economic growth. China's political system has departed from old totalitarianism, as discussed in this chapter. Economic and political liberalisation, however, will not necessarily call for a Western style of democracy. Political democracy does not necessarily facilitate economic growth and other aspects of social progress. In fact, in a recent study of 141 countries, Adam Przeworski and his colleagues confirmed that there is no causal linkage between the nature of political regimes and economic growth.[74]

---

[74] Adam Przeworski, et al., *Democracy and Development: Political Institutions and Well-Being in the World, 1950–1990*, New York, Cambridge University Press, 2000, p. 270.

Historically, economic growth took place under different forms of government, not necessarily democratic government. This is especially the case of East Asia. Development requires a strong and efficient government committed to development and able to mobilise savings and other resources. Democratisation took place in Taiwan and South Korea recently but social chaos also followed. What Chinese leaders have seen from their transition to democracy is that a drastic political transformation to a full democracy will bring China more chaos. Therefore, "development first, democracy later" has become a major guiding principle among Chinese leaders for the country's modernisation.

Deng Xiaoping consistently argued that China would not follow a Western style of democracy, such as checks and balances, separation of power and so on. Deng thus regarded all efforts that could lead to political democratisation as "bourgeois liberalisation". From the late 1970s when he took over power to the early 1990s, Deng established a firm legacy by adhering to this approach. The Jiang-centred third generation of leadership had certainly lived under the shadow of Deng. Like Deng, for many years, Jiang made great efforts to consolidate his power in the party and strengthen party control rather than introduce any genuine political reform. Once political liberalisation poses a political threat to the CCP's rule, the leadership comes down hard to reassert control. As long as the party-state stays above Chinese society, political liberalisation will be very limited, not to mention democratisation.

Capitalism versus democracy

It is widely believed in the West that capitalism and democracy are twins, that capitalism and economic wealth are conducive to a democratic government, and that democracy as a form of government is likely only in market or capitalist economies. This theme is reflected in works by contemporary scholars such as Lindblom, Huntington,

Lipset and Moore.[75] All these authors saw the historical and logical connections between capitalism and democracy.

On this basis, China's rapid capitalistic economic growth would lead to political democratisation. However, the inter-connectedness between capitalism and democracy as perceived in the West is not easy to replicate in China. The development of democracy in China cannot be understood as a natural result of economic development alone. Instead, democratic development must be considered in the context of the inter-connectedness between the state and development. The state in a developing country like China is not only an agent of political order, but also responsible for facilitating socioeconomic development. In other words, unlike states in the West, state authorities in China have to generate capitalism and economic development. Consequently, the state faces a dilemma between economic development and democracy. The state must attempt to establish legitimacy and order on the one hand and promote socioeconomic development from above on the other. However, the state authorities often find that these two sets of goals are in conflict. Whereas democracy requires that the state accommodate many competing demands, effective performance of developmental functions pushes the state to stand above society in order to act as a rational agent of change. This tension seems to be irreconcilable in China's case, at least in the short run. The state often enforces its "rational" order on society, which tries to free itself from the state.

Furthermore, democracy requires a nonpolitical and societal sphere. Development, however, demands that the state penetrates society. In other words, both economic growth and the creation of civil society are political tasks. The state is thus in command of socioeconomic change. State domination of society makes it difficult for democracy to develop.

---

[75] Charles E Lindblom, *Politics and Markets*; Samuel Huntington, "Will More Countries Become Democratic?" *Political Science Quarterly*, vol. 99, Summer 1984, pp. 193–218; Seymour M Lipset, *Political Man: The Social Base of Politics*, New York, Doubleday & Company, Inc, 1963; Barrington Moore, *The Social Origins of Dictatorship and Democracy*, Boston, Beacon Press, 1966.

Democracy is thus more likely to occur as a gift from the political elite to society and less likely to be the result of a political system created of its own volition by significant social forces as had occurred in the West.

As shown in this chapter, capitalism has spread all over China and gained momentum, especially since Deng Xiaoping's southern tour in 1992. The CCP has also formally legalised a capitalistic economy. For a long time, promoting economic development became a, if not *the*, major standard for judging government officials' political achievements. Indeed, the rise of the local developmental state has been the major cause of China's rapid economic growth in the past decade. Local officials become key political and economic actors and are highly entrepreneurial in promoting their local interests.

While local developmental states promoted rapid economic growth, it is also in conflict with democratic development in China. With the withdrawal of the national government from local affairs, the local governments stepped in to fill this vacuum and became highly interventionistic. Decentralisation will not necessarily lead to the rise of civil society. As decentralisation is concerned with interest distribution, local governments, as interest maximisers, took over the power that the state wanted to dispense to individuals, which is not democractic. As local officials monopolise both political and economic power, decentralisation has produced many small local "dictatorships". These dictators make their own "laws" and regulations in order to gain social control and elicit social compliance within their territories. At the same time, they limit the reach of state power, which is finding it increasingly difficult to have its policies reach the grass-roots. Even though in the long run, local dictatorship might play a positive role in checking state power as shown in the development of Western European modern democracies, it is apparently undemocratic because it deprives individuals of political and economic rights.

The Chinese political elites have played an important role in rebuilding the Chinese state by importing Western state products. However, they also want to borrow from tradition to consolidate their power, survive rapid socioeconomic changes and make the new state work.

They do so because of not only their self-interest, but also civilisational constraints. The Chinese state is not just a man-built state, but is more importantly, a civilisational state. Bunger once said that "the state is a historical concept. Its emergence and development does not follow the fixed laws of natural sciences. It is man-made, and has many forms".[76] In this sense, we can be sure that whatever form the Chinese state takes, it will always be a Chinese civilisational state.

---

[76] Karl Bunger, "The Chinese State", p. xv.

Chapter 5

"Chineseness" in History Textbooks: The Narrative on Early China

QIAN Jiwei and Ryan HO*

"Our understanding of Chineseness must recognize the following: it is living and changeable, it is the product of a shared historical experience, it has become an increasingly self-conscious matter for China, and it should be related to what appears to be, or to have been, Chinese in the eyes of non-Chinese".

Wang Gungwu (1991)[1]

"In the recent decades, we have had enough of the oppression from the imperialists. As a result, this has triggered our nationalist consciousness. Under this consciousness, we all hope to produce a general textbook for Chinese history, so as to have a better understanding of our ethnic composition, and also to have a good discussion on which territories are ours".

Gu Jiegang and Tan Qixiang (1934)[2]

---

* QIAN Jiwei is Senior Research Fellow at the East Asian Institute, National University of Singapore. Ryan HO is Research Assistant with the same institute. This chapter is developed and translated from Qian Jiwei, "Lishi Jiaokeshu zhongde Zhongguo: Yi Zaoqi Zhongguo Xushi Weili" (The Study of Chineseness in History Textbooks: the case of Early China), *Tsinghua Sociology Review*, vol 11, 2019, pp. 107–118.
[1] Wang Gungwu, *The Chineseness of China*, Hong Kong, Oxford University Press, 1991, p. 2.
[2] Gu Jiegang and Tan Qixiang, "Foreword", *The Chinese Historical Geography*, vol 1, Issue 1, 1934.

The concept of "Chineseness" is complex. As a result, there has been much scholarly debate on the concept of "Chineseness". Professor Allen Chun of Academia Sinica argues that "Chineseness" has become so politicised that one can question whether its propagation has anything to do with culture.[3] The growing dominance of China in the media and in trade has not only altered the balance of power with societies on its periphery, but also given "Chineseness" a new politicising spin. Professor Chun also states that "what it means to be Chinese has been constructed in completely different ways in different societies".[4] The geopolitical aspect would mean that "Chineseness" in mainland China would be vastly different from those defined in Taiwan, Hong Kong, Singapore and other Chinese-speaking communities. These developments have been part of an ongoing and subtle shift in the meanings and application of "Chineseness" throughout the world.

The narrative of Chinese history has always been an important part of the definition of "Chineseness". Professor Wang Gungwu's greatest contribution to the scholarly debate on the concept of "Chineseness" in the study of Chinese history is the recognition that the concept of "Chineseness" is the product of a shared historical experience which has continually influenced its growth, making it living and changeable.[5] According to Professor Wang, the self-awareness of being Chinese emerged with the writings of Confucius and his contemporaries during the sixth to fifth centuries BC; in the later history of China, however, there has been less general agreement on how much this "Chineseness" has developed and changed.[6]

Other scholars like Ge Zhaoguang have used a perspective from East and Inner Asia to discuss the narrative of Chinese history since the

---

[3] Kevin Sprague, *Forgetting Chineseness*, 8 March 2017, <https://www.international.ucla.edu/apc/article/172547> (accessed 25 July 2019).

[4] Kevin Sprague, *Forgetting Chineseness*.

[5] Wang Gungwu, *The Chineseness of China*, p. 2.

[6] Wang Gungwu, *The Chineseness of China*, p. 2.

Song Dynasty to explain the development of "Chineseness".[7] Prasenjit Duara has approached the study of Chinese history from local and regional angles to explain the concept of Chineseness.[8] In Philip Kuhn's discussion of the formation of China in the contemporary period, the uniqueness of the concept of "Chineseness" was emphasised.[9] These academic debates among historians revolve around the concept of "Chineseness", which has much to do with changes in the socioeconomic conditions. Chinese history when viewed from the "inside" differs markedly from an "outside" view. For example, Chinese, American and Japanese scholars have different understanding of what "Chineseness" is.[10] Scholars of different generations also have different opinions of the concept of "Chineseness" in history due to the difference in social and economic contexts that they live in. An example is that of scholars of the second Sino-Japanese War and the reform and opening up period of the late 1970s. The complexity of "Chineseness" is also due to the vast territory of China and the many ethnic groups/nationalities living within its boundaries. For example, Jiang Yongli has pointed out that the definition of "China" during the Ming period is different from the territorial definition of the China we know today. For the Ming ruling elite, "China" refers to the geographic area of China proper. The Miao minority regions in Hunan, Guangxi and Guizhou were not considered to be part of China in that period.[11] Most importantly, the academic debate between social scientists and historians, as well as the dialogue between archaeologists and scientists, has increased our knowledge of the ancient past and the beginning of civi-

---

[7] Ge Zhaoguang, *What is China? Territory, Ethnicity, Culture, and History*, Harvard, Harvard University Press, 2018, [Translated by Michael Gibbs Hill].

[8] Prasenjit Duara, *Rescuing History from the Nation: Questioning Narratives of Modern China*, Chicago, University of Chicago Press, 1995.

[9] Philipp Kuhn, *Origins of the Modern Chinese State*. Stanford University Press, 2002.

[10] Wang Gungwu, *The Chineseness of China*, p. 2.

[11] Jiang Yongli, "Thinking About the 'Ming China' Anew: The Ethnocultural Space In A Diverse Empire-With Special Reference to the 'Miao Territory'", *Journal of Chinese History*, vol. 2, no. 1, 2018, pp. 27–78.

lisations. For example, in recent years, some social scientists have researched on how factors such as human cooperation, resource extraction, warfare and income inequality significantly impacted the trajectory of a country's history.[12]

History textbooks are very important to the narrative of a country's history. For China, history textbooks discuss the state formation of China in terms of the country, civilisation, geography and nationalities. The college and university textbooks reflected the changing understanding of the academia towards the concept of "Chineseness" and the historical narratives show the influence of the political environment of the time.

This chapter utilises a collection of college and secondary school levels history textbooks to explore the changes in the understanding of ancient China from the intellectual community and changes in the socioeconomic context that caused the changes in the concept of "Chineseness". The narratives of history textbooks have not changed much, especially from the period of Han China and after, due to the availability of official records since Han Dynasty. If there were any changes to the historical narratives of Han China and the later periods in history textbooks, it is due to the selective use of materials by the authors.[13] To analyse the selective use of historical materials by different

---

[12] For the impact of income inequality, see Carles Boix, *Political Order and Inequality*. For the impact from the modes of resource extraction, see Ian Morris, *Foragers, Farmers, and Fossil Fuels: How Human Values evolve*. For a general discussion about the topic, see Tuong Vu, "Studying the State through State Formation", *World Politics*, vol. 62, no. 1. See also Dal Bó, Ernesto, Pablo Hernández, and Sebastián Mazzuca, "The Paradox of Civilization: Pre-Institutional Sources of Security and Prosperity", no. w21829, National Bureau of Economic Research, 2015. An interesting piece about the impact of geography on China can be found in David Keightley "What Did Make the Chinese 'Chinese'?" *Education About Asia*, vol. 9, no. 2, 2004, pp. 17–23.

[13] According to Yao (2016), the main aim of the selection of historical materials is to use history to provide lessons for the present and guidance for the future, for judging the responsibility of a historical figure and for detailing the process of historical changes. See Yao Dali, *Sima Qian he Tade Shiji*, Fudan University Press, 2016. Professor Wang Gungwu believes that Chinese historians have been more practical in the implementation of historical knowledge. He believes that history was used to govern the country. See <http://www.thepaper.cn/newsDetail_forward_1530109> (accessed 3 July 2019).

authors would therefore complicate our discussion. To have a detailed discussion of the changes in historical narratives, this chapter only focuses on changes in the narrative of "Early China" (before Han Dynasty) in history textbooks.

"Early China" refers to the period between the earliest beginnings of Chinese civilisation to about 220 AD.[14] From the 1930s, college and university history textbooks began to have many different interpretations of this period. Three reasons accounted for this. Firstly, the the authors of the history textbook of this period are incomplete. For the period of "Early China", the authors of the history textbook have relied on the same sources. For example, there are limited historical materials about the Yellow Emperor (*Huangdi*). In the 1920s, *China's History*, written by Gu Jiegang and Wang Zhongqi, and *Zhongguo Tongshi* (General History of China), written by Bai Shouyi, considered the Yellow Emperor to be a myth. Gu Jiegang and Wang Zhongqi assumed that the late-Zhou era scholars fabricated the myth of the Yellow Emperor. Like Gu Jiegang and Wang Zhongqi, Bai Shouyi believes that the Yellow Emperor is a myth; he argues that the myth proves the existence of the Yellow Emperor's tribe and infers the location of the tribe to be in northern Shaanxi.

Secondly, Chinese official history has generally provided the narrative for mainstream Chinese history. However, it may not be the case for the history of "Early China". The concept of China as a nation/civilisation in "Early China" was still fluid due to the ongoing political, economic and societal developments. In *Guoshi dagang (A General History of China)*, Qian Mu argued that the process of China's historical development cannot be compared to the Western one. Qian Mu believed that the process of the West's historical development was impacted by foreign factors, while China's was domestic-driven. In the West, there was a competition for existence among the different kingdoms, which affected their historical development, unlike China,

[14] The same definition of Early China can be found at the *Society for the Study of Early China* website, <https://www.cambridge.org/core/membership/ssec/about> (accessed 14 July 2019).

which saw itself as the centre of the *Tianxia*.[15] Hirase Takao's *A History of China* argues that subsequent generations have incorporated the Han-era *Tianxia* view in the narrative of the *Spring and Autumn* and *Warring States* period. However, the concept of a "territory-based country" was more important during this period. This exposes the different trajectories which Chinese history could have developed. A recent work by Zhao Dingxin has also emphasised the importance of the *Spring and Autumn* as well as the *Warring States* period in the development of Chinese history.[16] In other words, the historical narratives of the Xia, Shang and Zhou dynasties reflect many possibilities of an alternative historical development.

Thirdly, since the 20th century, archaeological discoveries have changed the narrative on China's civilisation.[17] The oracle bones unearthed from the *Yinxu* or ruins of *Yin* (located near modern Anyang city) have confirmed 23 out of the 30-king lineage of the *Shang* Dynasty which was recorded in Sima Qian's *Shiji* (The Records of the Grand Historian). The bronze inscriptions from Shaanxi have also confirmed 11 out of the 12-king lineage from the *Zhou* dynasty documented in *Shiji*. As a result of these archaeological findings, *Shiji's* credibility as a historical source has increased. Some history textbooks have also narrated the development of ancient China using the discovery of the *Yinxu* in the 1920s. The discovery of both the *erlitou* site and the Zhengzhou Shang Dynasty ruins in the 1950s has also greatly changed the view of the academia towards the Shang era which is reflected in the narratives of history textbooks.

This chapter also uses a social science-based research method called meta-analysis to uncover how history textbooks from the 1900s to

---

[15] According to Zhao (2006), *Tianxia* has three meanings. The first is the equivalent of 'the universe' in Western languages; the second refers to the 'general will of the people' and the third refers to a universal system for the world. For more discussion on the ancient *Tianxia* system, refer to Zhao Tingyang, "Rethinking Empire from a Chinese Concept 'All-under-heaven' (Tian-xia, 天下)", *Social Identities,* vol. 12, no. 1, January 2006, pp. 30–36.

[16] Zhao Dingxin, *The Confucian-Legalist State: A New Theory of Chinese History,* Oxford, Oxford University Press, 2015.

[17] See a general discussion from Liu Li and Chen Xingan. *The Archaeology of China: From the Late Paleolithic to the Early Bronze Age,* Cambridge University Press, 2012.

2010s deal with the idea of "Chineseness" in early China. Specifically, this chapter analyses how history textbooks in this period narrates three dichotomies: "Centre and Periphery", "Reunification and Separation" and "Myths and Recorded History" before proceeding to discuss factors that influence the narrative of the textbooks towards these three themes. These three themes shed light on the concept of "Chineseness". "Centre and Periphery" details the place of origin of China's civilisation. "Reunification and Separation" describes the different organisational forms of China's society and politics, which are also linked to the uniqueness of China. "Myths and Recorded History" analyses the authenticity of information of the historical period.

This chapter posits that there are three factors affecting the narratives of early China in Chinese history textbooks. Firstly, the historical context leading to the writing of the textbook are associated with the generation of the narrative in the textbook. Secondly, the authors' academic background also affects the narrative. Thirdly, when the textbook becomes academic material, the mass knowledge of the academic community has a large impact on the historical narrative.

Historical Textbooks Discussed

The publishing of the seven history textbooks (see Table 1) under discussion in this chapter in mainland China, Hong Kong, Taiwan, Japan and the United States was between the 1900s and the 2010s. The list includes two secondary school textbooks, three university textbooks and two books for the public, which are somewhere between the secondary school and university level. Hirase Takao's original version of *A History of China* is in Japanese, but this chapter uses the Chinese-translated version published by Guangxi Normal University press. The publisher of Yao Ta-Chung's *History of China* is Taiwan's San Min Book, but this chapter uses its translation in simplified Chinese published by Huaxia printing press.

In the discussion that follows, this chapter will use the authors' names to refer to the different history textbooks. There are a few reasons why

Table 1: The List of Textbooks

	Author	Date of Publication	Place of Publication	Title of Book	Type of Book
1	Xia Zengyou	1904–1906	Mainland China	*The Newest Secondary School Chinese History Textbook*	Secondary school level
2	Gu Jiegang and Wang Zhongqi[18]	1923	Mainland China	*China's History*	Secondary School level
3	Qian Mu	1940	Mainland China/Hong Kong	*Guoshi Dagang*	University level
4	Yao Ta-Chung	1981	Taiwan	*History of China*	University level
5	Bai Shouyi	1991	Mainland China	*Zhongguo Tongshi*	General Public
6	Hirase Takao	2005	Japan	*A History of China*	General Public
7	Li Feng	2013	United States	*Early China: A Social and Cultural History*	University level

Source: Qian Jiwei, "Lishi Jiaokeshu zhongde Zhongguo" (The Study of Chineseness in History Textbooks), *Tsinghua Sociology Review*, vol. 11, 2019, pp. 107–118.

these books are chosen. Firstly, we have chosen some of the most well-known history textbooks which have been reprinted several times. Some of them were printed in different eras in China such as the Republican period and the post-1949 period. This includes history textbooks written by Xia Zengyou, Qian Mu and Bai Shouyi. These textbooks were supposed to have great influence in the formulation of historical narratives. Secondly, the history textbooks are from different geographical areas, such as mainland China, Hong Kong, Taiwan, Japan and the United States. Thirdly, we have chosen history textbooks written by authors with a certain level of expertise towards the subject. This includes textbooks authored by Gu Jiegang, Qian Mu and Hirase Takao.

---

[18] Reprinted in Gu Jiegang Quan Ji, *History papers*, vol. 12, Zhonghua Shuju, 2010.

Research Methodology

This chapter uses a social science research methodology of meta-analysis.[19] It will code the three dichotomies in a given textbook as 0 or 1. For example, in discussing the "Centre and Periphery", authors of some textbooks believed that China's centre of civilisation was the Yellow River (defined as 1 in this case), while some advocate multiple centres of civilisation (defined as 0). In some traditional interpretations, the peripheral areas were also centres of civilisation. After discussing the positions taken by the textbooks, this chapter will discuss the factors affecting them.

Centre and Periphery

The centre of China's civilisation is an important part of China's historical narrative. This centre refers to both the geographical sense and the cultural sense. The bronze sculpture of the Western Zhou Dynasty refers to China as the area around Luoyang where the central plains are. Figuring out the geographical centre will bring about the location of the cultural centre. For example, the geographical concept of "shadowless at *Luozhou*" (*Luozhong Wuying*) means that as *Luozhou* (modern day Luoyang) is the "centre of the *Tianxia*", it is shadowless during noon. According to official records, the core areas of Chinese civilisation after the Qin and Han dynasties are very clear and not subject to much debate. However, the centre and periphery of early Chinese civilisation still has room for different interpretations. Some think that there were various locations that marked the beginnings of Chinese civilisations. In 1981, Su Bingqi's *Six Big Archaeological Cultural Sites* raised the idea that the archaeological cultural site in the central plains, which was considered as the major origin of the Chinese civilisation ("cradle of civilisation"), was only one of the six sites during the Neolithic age.[20] Chang Kwang-chih argued that

---

[19] E J Rinquist, "Assessing Evidence of Environmental Inequalities: A Meta-Analysis", *Journal of Policy Analysis and Management*, vol. 24, 2005.

[20] Su Bingqi, *A New Look into the Beginnings of Chinese Civilization* [Zhongguo wenming qiyuan xintan], Taipei, Sanlian Book Company, 1999.

Chinese civilisations were interlinked. Chinese civilisations along the Yellow River, Yangtze River, Liaoning and Shandong during the Neolithic Age were all interlinked.[21] Some scholars also believe that the centre of Chinese civilisation should be found near the Yangtze River delta and not the Yellow River.[22] Yan Wenming raised the theory of the "Central Plains culture at the forefront". This theory believed that despite the development of Chinese civilisation during the Neolithic age in many areas, the culture along the Central Plains area was always more superior. Thus, the earliest kingdom was formed around the Central Plains area.[23]

Similar to debates in the academia, there have been many narratives about the centre and periphery in secondary school and university textbooks. The authors of many textbooks seem to believe that there is no historical source to back the story of the Yellow Emperor, but when it comes to explaining the relationship between the Yellow Emperor and China's origins as a civilisation and country, the authors held different stances. Gu Jiegang and Wang Zhongqi only mentioned the myth of the Yellow Emperor without stating his impact on the development of the Chinese civilisation. Xia Zengyou pointed out that the Yellow Emperor unified the *tianxia*. Qian Mu argued from archaeological evidence that civilisations existed in not just the Yellow River area, but also the lower reaches of the Yangtze River and the Yunnan-Sichuan during the Neolithic age. However, the earliest discovery of Chinese civilisation should be at the Shanxi-Shaanxi area. Despite the argument that the Yellow Emperor was just a myth, there was evidence that the tribe resided in the Henan-Shanxi area. Yao Ta-Chung believed that the Yellow River was the core of early Chinese civilisation. The northeast region, northwest region and Yangtze River civilisations during the

---

[21] Chang Kwang-chih, *Bronze Sculptures*, Qingtong Huizhu, Shanghai, Shanghai Wenyi Publishing Press, 2000.

[22] Olga Gorodetskaya (Guo Jingyun), *Xia Shang Zhou: From Myth to Historical Truth* [Xia Shang Zhou: cong shenhua dao shishi], Shanghai, Shanghai Guji Publishing, 2013.

[23] Chen Xingcan, "Archaeological Discoveries in the People's Republic of China and Their Contribution to the Understanding of Chinese History", *Bulletin of the History of Archaeology*, vol. 19, Issue 2, 2009.

Neolithic age had been deeply influenced by the civilisation in the central plains. Bai Shouyi believed that at that time there were four tribes in China, and the Yellow Emperor tribe was just one of them but was the most advanced in its economics and culture.

Li Feng discussed how to utilise the archaeological theories developed in the 1980s (for example Su Bingqi and Chang Kwang-chih's theory) to understand China's civilisation during the Neolithic age.[24] However, Li also points out a big problem with these theories. The theory of multiple civilisational areas fails to explain why Chinese civilisation originated from the central plains area but not from any other areas. Li's book mentioned that Yan Wenming's explanation of the "superior culture of the Central Plains" has huge persuasive power, but lacks adequate archaeological evidence.

Unification and Separation

Unification and separation is a very common dichotomy in the narrative of Chinese history. It is also a topic worth discussing. Whether a dynasty was fully unified or not was highly relevant to the discussion of the historical narrative of this dynasty.[25] For example, Yang Lien-Sheng classified unified dynasties as "major dynasties" and called separated/ fragmented dynasties as "minor dynasties".[26] Unlike other periods in Chinese history, academics could not come to a clear conclusion as to whether there was political unity in early China. The Shang Dynasty was the first recorded dynasty in history, but it coexisted with four other vassal states.[27] The Zhou Dynasty was the first kingdom to push

---

[24] Li Feng, *Early China: A Social and Cultural History*, Cambridge, Cambridge University Press, 2013.

[25] Ichisada Miyazaki, *History of China* (Zhongguo Shi), Zhejiang: Zhejiang People's Publishing Press, 2015.

[26] Yang Lien-sheng, "Towards a Study of Dynastic Configurations in Chinese History", *Harvard Journal of Asiatic Studies*, Issue 17, 3/4, 1954.

[27] David Keightley "The Shang: China's First Historical Dynasty", in *The Cambridge History of Ancient China: From the Origins of Civilization to 221 BC*, Cambridge: Cambridge University Press, 1999.

the frontiers to current day northern China.[28] Before the *Spring and Autumn* period, kingdoms that were city-states were the norm. The land between the city-states was outside the control of the kingdom.[29]

Like the academic world, secondary and university textbooks have different interpretations regarding the political unity of early China. Based on archaeological evidence, Yao Ta-Chung believed that the territorial domain which the Xia, Shang and Zhou dynasties could actually control had been expanded gradually. From the *Spring and Autumn* period, China had evolved from city-state to a sovereign-based one. Qian Mu pointed out that during the Xia, Shang and Zhou period there had always been a relationship between the central power and the four vassals. Gu Jiegang and Wang Zhongqi held the same opinion. On the other hand, Takao Hirase believed that China had a concept of "cultural areas" before the Qin-Han period. Other than being dynasties that ruled a unified China, the Xia, Shang and Zhou's "cultural areas" and "territory-based kingdoms" had interactions with other polities in the peripheral areas. The *Sanxingdui* civilisation in Sichuan is one example. Li Feng also believed that the Shang Dynasty was a city-state as most of the political and religious activities were carried out in the city. However, it was a bit different in the Zhou Dynasty. During this period, there was a network of cities that became the foundation of the political power of the Zhou. The idea of a "territory-based state" emerged during this period and it was a precursor to the later imperial states.

Myths and Recorded History

The difference between "myths" and "recorded history" is where the credibility of the narrative of Chinese history is drawn. Due to insufficient historical materials, early China is important to the understanding

---

[28] Li Feng, *Landscape and Power in Early China: The Crisis and Fall of the Western Zhou 1045–771 BC*, Cambridge, Cambridge University Press, 2006.

[29] Zhao Dingxin, *The Confucian-Legalist State: A New Theory of Chinese History*, Oxford, Oxford University Press, 2015.

of the "myths" and "recorded history". In the modern era, there have been many discussions about the myths and recorded history in early China. Particularly since the 1930s, Gu Jiegang has represented a school of thought called the "Doubting Antiquity School (*Gu Shibian*)" that believes the ancient history of China to be a myth. Gu argues that China's ancient history is "layered, accumulated and fabricated". He was also doubtful of the political unity of early China. However, archaeological findings in the past half century, including those at *Erlitou*, Zhengzhou Shang city and Yinqueshan Han Tombs Bamboo Slips, have confirmed that the historical records of the Xia and Shang civilisations are reliable. All these archaeological findings have undermined persuasive power to the group led by Gu Jiegang.

In the textbooks that they authored, Gu Jiegang and Wang Zhongqi doubted the historical writings of early China. For example, on the myths of Emperor Yao and Shun, Gu and Wang write that, 'We have been used to the fact that there really is a wise Yao and Shun. However, it is in fact only a myth created by late-Zhou era scholars. The lies they create make later people believe that it was true'. Xia Zengyou believes that the myth of the 'Three Sovereigns and Five Emperors' originated

Table 2: Summary of Textbooks in Their Opinion Towards the Three Binary Themes

Theme	1	0
Core and Periphery	Yellow River civilisation was the core of Chinese civilisation (Xia Zengyou)	There are many centres in Chinese civilisation (Li Feng)
Unification and Separation	Xia, Shang and Zhou were unified states (Qian Mu and Yao Ta-Chung)	Xia, Shang and Zhou eras were all city-state models (Takao Hirase)
Myths and Recorded History	The historical myths before the Pre-Western Zhou era had a high level of credibility (Qian Mu and Li Feng)	The historical myths before Western Zhou have no historical credibility and were mostly myths and layers of interpretation from later history (Gu Jiegang and Wang Zhongqi)

Source: Qian Jiwei, "Lishi Jiaokeshu zhongde Zhongguo" (The Study of Chineseness in History Textbooks), *Tsinghua Sociology Review*, vol 11, 2019, pp. 107–118.

from the Zhou Dynasty. Yao Ta-Chung agreed with Gu's interpretation that the myth was built upon by generations of people relying on the late-Zhou era scholars' fictional portrayal of Emperors Yao and Shun. However, through the myths, China's different stages of civilisation development became evident. For example, the myth of the Yellow Emperor proved that a political organisation existed in Chinese tribes. Qian Mu does not agree with Gu's interpretation. Instead, Qian suggested that ancient Chinese history was rational and close to the truth, unlike other nationalities which have ancient histories based on myths. Li Feng also points out that the group represented by Gu which views ancient history as a myth has focused too much on textual analysis and neglects the study of archaeology.

Analysis and Discussion

Based on the three themes aforementioned, this chapter concludes that there are three main factors affecting the narrative of "Early China". Firstly, the historical context at the time of writing the book affects the historical narrative. The second quotation at the beginning of this chapter is from Gu Jiegang and Tan Qixiang's declaration in the inaugural issue of *Yugong* where Chinese history writing was related to nationalist consciousness under the pressure of imperialism. Qian Mu's *Guoshi Dagang* was written in the 1930s, before the war with Japan and the Chinese Civil War (1946–1949) which brought disaster and suffering to the country. He emphasised the traits of Chinese civilisation, promoted the consciousness of Chinese culture and the framework of dynastic rise and decline in Chinese history. Gu Jiegang and Wang Zhongqi's *China's History* was written after the new culture movement (i.e. May fourth movement). They used a scientific method to view Chinese historical materials, belonging to what Qian Mu called "reform group" historians (*Gexinpai shixue*). Gu and Wang believed that the story of the 'Three Sovereigns and Five Emperors' was a myth and books on them were obviously affected by the historical background of their time (e.g. new culture movement).

Besides those political, social and economic contextual determinants, for history textbooks, another determinant in historical contexts affecting the narrative of the book is the teaching guidelines of the officials in power. The narrative of "Early China" therefore suited what the officials wanted to be taught in the classroom. For example, during the period of the *Beiyang* government, the elementary and secondary school history teaching guidelines on the "Early China" history narrative spelled out that "the mythical period of the Chinese nation was during the Yu, Xia, Shang, and Zhou period". The temporary teaching guidelines issued by the 1929 Nanjing nationalist government for elementary and secondary school history textbooks stated that the role of history was to chart the development of China's politics and economy, and to highlight the imperialist oppression on China so as to arouse the nationalist spirit of the students. For the part on "Early China" history, the theme was, "The building of the Chinese nation". Thus, the teaching guidelines of the administration in power shaped the narrative of the history textbooks produced during this period. For example, Gu Jiegang and Wang Zhongqi's stance is quite bold in the sense that they believe that the story of the 'Three Sovereigns and Five Emperors' is a myth. This was in opposition to the teaching guidelines, which was why during the late 1920s the education ministry of the Nanjing nationalist government had banned these books nationwide.[30]

Secondly, the author's academic background also affects the historical narrative. Gu Jiegang and Wang Zhongqi's *China's History* was very clearly influenced by the school of thought which dismissed ancient history as myths. Xia Zengyou passed the imperial civil service examination and Chen Yinke, a prominent historian of the republican period, labelled Xia as having special insights in the analysis of history.

---

[30] See a discussion in Hon T K, "Ethnic and Cultural Pluralism: Gu Jiegang's Vision of a New China in His Studies of Ancient History", *Modern China*, vol. 22, no. 3, 1996, pp. 315–339. See also<http://news.ifeng.com/history/zhongguojindaishi/200909/0925_7180_1364650.shtml>and <http://www.thepaper.cn/newsDetail_forward_1322479>(accessed 17 February 2018).

Published before the end of the *Qing* Dynasty, Xia's *The Newest Secondary School Chinese History Textbook* relied on old historical sources.

Qian Mu's academic background had a greater impact on his book, *Guoshi Dagang*. Yen Ken-wang wrote in his diary that Qian Mu had knowledge and analytical skills which were out of the ordinary. Yu Ying-shih went even further to claim that *Guoshi Dagang* had been extraordinary.

Thirdly, the accumulated knowledge of the knowledge community also affects the historical narrative of textbooks. Thomas Kuhn linked the scientific community to the "paradigm" of scientific research.[31] The knowledge community's link with the paradigm in the study of history is hence evident. Bai Shouyi, Hirase Takao and Li Feng published their works after the 1990s, implying that these books tapped their research on the archaeological discoveries in the 20th century. Li Feng's work especially discussed the different theories based on their explanatory power to the archaeological sites. Bai Shouyi's book, *Zhongguo Tongshi*, centred on almost all of recent China's archaeological discoveries, while Hirase Takao's work was a combination of almost all of the research on China's ancient dynastic history and city-state history conducted by Japanese sinologists since the Edo period. Qian Mu's book is believed to have reaped the fruits of success in the knowledge community's research in ancient history since the May Fourth period.

Conclusion

In general, the concept of "Chineseness" is very fluid and complex, as pointed out by Professor Wang Gungwu,[32] resulting in much scholarly debate over it. The concept of "Chineseness" varies in different contexts and societies. "Chineseness" viewed in mainland China contrasts with

---

[31] Thomas Kuhn, *The Structure of Scientific Revolutions*, Stanford, Stanford University Press, 1970.
[32] Wang Gungwu, *The Chineseness of China*, p. 2

the version of "Chineseness" understood in Taiwan, Hong Kong, Singapore and other Chinese-speaking communities.

What factors have affected the narrative of early China in history textbooks? This chapter uses different textbooks with different interpretations of early China to uncover the reason. Early China differs from later periods in Chinese history as historical sources on it are scarce. In addition, during the period of Early China, the idea of 'China' as a civilisation and a country was still in development and fluid, so detailing the different textbooks with different interpretations will shed light on the factors behind the different narratives. Variations of political, economic and social development contexts as well as the authors' own experiences contributed to the differences in historical narratives. Changes in the knowledge community such as the discovery of archaeological sites have a huge part to play in the changing historical narrative too. This chapter has chosen to use history textbooks in mainland China, Taiwan, Hong Kong, United States and Japan to discuss the reasons behind the different narratives of Early China. It also discussed three relevant binary themes, namely, 'Core and Periphery', 'Unification and Separation' and 'Myths and Recorded History', which are related to the narrative of early China.

Findings show that the time in which the textbooks were written, the social background, academic background, historical circumstances and the stock of knowledge accumulated by the knowledge community, will influence the writing of China's historical narrative. However, due to limited resources, the authors only select representative textbooks on the three themes in the narrative on "Early China". Future research on this issue could involve a wider range of textbooks and utilise relevant themes in the writing of the historical narrative of "Early China" and in the focus on "Chineseness".

Chapter 6

The Logic of Political Reform in China: 1978–2018

ZHENG Yongnian[1]

Introduction

To a great degree, the 40 years of China's reform and opening up have altered the trajectory of the world's modern history. These 40 years (1978–present) also witnessed major historical changes in China, be they material or non-material. The sudden changes in the economy, society, politics, culture, lifestyle and technology have dumbfounded onlookers and before one can comprehend or notice a change, another occurs. At the ideological level, all modern "isms" or "ideologies" can find room to develop and receive considerable support in China as reflected by the different strange looking architectures emerging in the cities. However, many of the changes could also just be illusions. There are "utopias", but there is also goodwill.

Notwithstanding the changes, China will always be China, which is indeed becoming more "Chinese". All kinds of transformations and reforms are possible in a liberal environment, but in China, they have

[1] ZHENG Yongnian is Professor in the East Asian Institute, National University of Singapore. The chapter was originally in Chinese. The author is grateful to Ryan Ho, research assistant at the East Asian Institute, for his translation. It was revised and rewritten based on the translated text.

to be first applied and tested, like what the late Deng Xiaoping emphasised during China's initial period of reform and opening up that "practice is the sole criterion for testing the truth". The pursuit of the "truth" can be executed, but it has to be applied and tested to become the "truth" that China needs. The many transformations that the country is undergoing may give it a multifaceted façade, but in no way will they be able to cover the real China, let alone replace it.

Historically speaking, transformations and reforms are not the only themes of the last 40 years. The pressure on the transformation from the objective environment, or the subjective willingness of the reformers these last 40 years cannot be compared to the turmoil that the country faced in the late Qing and the Republic Era. In that period, China was defeated by not only the faraway West, but also its former student and neighbour Japan. People of that era lamented that it was a change that China had never experienced before in the 3,000 over years. China went from a traditional agricultural economy to a modern industrial economy, from an imperial system to a republican one and from learning Confucian studies to modern sciences. However, not all changes were successful as evidenced by China's continued war, revolutionary struggles and "continuous revolution" in the following half century. The late 1970s and early 1980s witnessed another transformation of modern China, with history still wielding its influence and shaping China to what it is today.

What is change? How much change is needed? How to change? How to remain unchanged in the process of change? How to achieve the necessary change while remaining unchanged? These are the questions that many have attempted to answer. Although there are many answers to these questions, politics remains as the factor that decides the answers. While participation in politics could be mass based, or politics is open to the influence of the masses, politics needs to have a leading agent. Without a leading agent, changes are doomed to fail. The various transformations of early modern China were not destined to fail from the start, but the flop in the transformation from an imperial to republican system could have a large part to play for the eventual let-down in many aspects. Without the leading agent, transformation and changes could go out of hand. The transformation and reform since the 1980s has a leading agent in control — the Chinese Communist Party (CCP) — and with this leading agent, China has set out in its reform process, picking up the theme of transformation and reform left behind by its early modern history. While the CCP remains the most important political organisation in China, this organisation has been unduly understudied in the field of China studies.[2]

China today has entered a new era, or it can be said to be at a turning point. Therefore, the importance of political transformation is very obvious. The phrase 'entering a new era' would assume the passing of an "old era", bringing into question where and what is the "new" in the "new era". To understand the transformation would require an understanding of the "grand discourse" ("isms" and ideologies such as "market economy" and "democracy") and more importantly, the "little facts on the ground" (the events that happened in reality). Simply by looking at the "grand discourse" would not enable one to have a clear understanding and objective analysis of the changes as subjectivity will set in. In understanding the logic of China's political reform, the "little facts on the ground" are even more important than the "grand discourse" as they are essential if the "grand discourse" is to become reality.

Within the academic circle, the consensus is that the idea of a "grand discourse" in political reform cannot fully explain the logic behind China's political changes in the last 40 years. Scholars in the

---

[2] In the field of China studies, a large body of the literature has been in the subjects such as local democracy, nongovernmental organisations and social protests which fit general themes of research in the West. There are a few works on the CCP, including David Shambaugh, *China's Communist Party: Atrophy and Adaptation*, Washington, DC and Berkeley, CA, Woodrow Wilson Centre Press and University of California Press, 2008; Zheng Yongnian, *The Chinese Communist Party as Organizational Emperor: Culture, Reproduction and Transformation*, London and New York, Routledge, 2010; Lance L P Gore, *The Chinese Communist Party and China's Capitalist Revolution: The Political Impact of Market*, New York and London, Routledge, 2011; Kjeld Erik Brodsgaard and Zheng Yongnian (eds.), *The Chinese Communist Party in Reform*, London and New York, Routledge, 2006 and Zheng Yongnian and Lance L P Gore (eds.), *The Chinese Communist Party in Action*, London and New York, Routledge, forthcoming.

West generally believe that China did not experience any meaningful political reform because they have measured political reform in China against the scale of Western democracy. This is echoed by many scholars inside China who hope to see China follow the West in its road to democracy. They measure China's political reform against its progress in democratisation at every stage of its political development.

In the past 40 years, the reforms of the political system were in reality the reform of the leading agent, the CCP. To deny that political reform occurred in China will make it hard to explain transformation and changes in other areas.[3] The CCP has not simply adapted to the new environment and new challenges as a result of its reform, but also more importantly, initiated and led other areas of reforms. Obviously, the existence of a unified power centre has differentiated contemporary reforms from those in the late Qing and Republic eras.

At different levels and in a different era, different leaderships and different circumstances lead to a different understanding of political reforms, which leads to a different direction of reform. Three distinct eras can be differentiated, namely, the 1980s, the 1990s–2012 and the "new era" from 2012. Every era adopted a different political thinking, each with its own unique logic. Although the 1980s and the 1990s had different political developments, they both belonged to a reform paradigm set up by the late Deng Xiaoping and thus can be termed as the "old era". The concept of a "new era" was coined at the 19th party congress in 2017. Substantial developments occurred within the timeframe of the 18th to 19th party congress. It was the changes during these five years that basically laid the ground of the "new era". In this sense, the "new era" has its beginnings from the 18th party congress in 2012.

Political Reforms in the 1980s

The political thinking of the 1980s was those of the late Deng Xiaoping and his colleagues such as Chen Yun and Peng Zhen. Although Deng

---

[3] Central to the argument that China did not experience political reform is that China did not experience democratisation in the Western sense. See Susan Shirk, *The Political Logic of Economic Reform in China,* Berkeley, CA, University of California Press, 1993.

Xiaoping identified himself as the "second generation leaders" along with Peng Zhen and Chen Yun, it is difficult to differentiate the "first generation" leaders like Mao Zedong from the "second". The two groups of leaders had the same revolutionary experiences and experienced the same political life in the party. With their common political experiences, they could achieve a common consensus vital for the collective effort to reform.

The domestic problem faced by this group of post-Mao leaders was economic development. The quest for "rich nation strong army" was the driver behind the CCP's revolutionary programme. It was also a dream for political elites throughout the history of modern China. The common consensus for leaders in the political spotlight in the 1980s was that they needed to change the situation that China was in, a poor socialist country.

The Soviet-American rivalry still raged on in the 1980s, but in general there was still relative peace. The Anglo-Americans started the reforms led by "neo-liberal economists" in which economic reform remained the crux. A new wave of globalisation began with the West leading the process. The Chinese leadership viewed the international situation as "an opportunity to develop", with Deng Xiaoping observing that peace and development were the two critical issues of the world.

However, there was still no concrete plan or answer for economic reform at that time. Deng Xiaoping remarked that the efforts to reform were like "touching the stones to cross the river", implying that there was no clear plan and steps were taken one at a time. At the ideological level, China spent 14 years transitioning from a planned economy to a socialist market economy (from 1978 to 1992). China followed closely the reform experiences of former Soviet satellites like Hungary and other Asian countries like Japan and the "Four Dragons". Although the change in the economic ideology was very slow, at the practical level, the direction was very clear. The move towards a market economy can be seen from the rural reforms, the decentralisation of the economy and the economic reforms in the urban areas.[4] The number of national

---

[4] Barry Naughton, *Growing Out of the Pan: Chinese Economic Reform, 1978–1993*, Cambridge and New York, Cambridge University Press, 1995 and *The Chinese Economy: Transition and Growth*, Cambridge, MA, MIT Press, 2008.

ministries and commissions had also reduced from 100 in 1981 to 41 in 1988, signalling a move towards marketisation of the economy.[5]

As economic reforms went underway, the central leadership was also seeking to initiate political reforms. From the early 1980s to the late 1980s, Deng had also expressed his views about political reform, which were also shared by others in the central leadership. On the whole, these reforms were not affected by the heated discussions of "political democratisation" at the societal level but was made to solve the problems faced in Chinese politics. Therefore, reforms were not made to realise the dream of "political democratisation" but were instead made to solve the practical issues on the ground.

The reforms encompassed a few points. The first was the rule by law. On one hand, the rule by law was directed at society and the other was directed at political activities within the party. The "continuous revolution" during the Mao era had destroyed some aspects of the rule by law, leaving party infighting unchecked and resulting in the death of many cadres due to political struggles.[6]

Second was the reform of the cadre classification and recruitment system. The "Four Modernisations" standard of the cadres was to ensure that they could aid China's economic development.[7]

Third was the reform of the party and leadership system. The relationship between the leadership and the system was addressed after it was destroyed during the Cultural Revolution. There was also a selection process among the junior cadres to resolve the succession issue. The retirement issue of the old cadres was also addressed, for example

---

[5] Zheng Yongnian, *Globalization and State Transformation in China*, Cambridge and New York, Cambridge University Press, 2004, chapter 5.

[6] Zheng Yongnian, *Contemporary China: A History since 1978*, Oxford, Wiley-Blackwell, 2014, Chapter 1.

[7] Lee Hong Yong, *From Revolutionary Cadres to Party Technocrats in Socialist China*, Berkeley, CA, University of California Press, 1991; and "Political and Administrative Reforms of 1982–1986: The Changing Party Leadership and State Bureaucracy", in Michael Kau Ying-Mao and Susan H Marsh, eds., *China in the Era of Deng Xiaoping: A Decade of Reform*, Armonk, NY, M E Sharpe, 1993, pp. 41–48.

with the setting up of a central advisory commission as a temporary solution to abolish the lifelong tenure of cadres.

From the middle to the end of the 1980s, political reforms gathered considerable strength. This was because of not just the societal pressure to democratise, but also the attraction of democracy for young leaders such as Hu Yaobang, Zhao Ziyang and many others.[8] As a result, political reforms accelerated and the leadership decided that political reforms would follow the direction of the separation of the party from the government (*dangzheng fenkai*). Those who held this line of thought attributed the high concentration of power in the leader's hands that led to a tragedy like the Cultural Revolution and to the failure to separate the party from the government. Additionally, political reforms were about protecting the successes of economic reforms and carrying on the momentum for further reforms. At the societal level, the then Soviet leader Mikhail Gorbachev's "Perestroika" had made a huge impact on Chinese society, leading the intellectual circles to come to a common consensus that China must follow Western democracy.

Notably, political reforms of the early 1980s and the mid-end 1980s differed. The early reforms were made to address the facts on the ground, but the later reforms slid towards democratisation. The early reforms were largely successful, with political life normalised, the cadre recruitment system successfully implemented and the retirement system of old cadres established. However, the separation of the party and the government did not succeed, leading to many fatal issues and to the party and the state becoming two separate entities; for a long time, government organisations were undergoing reform, but areas related to the party did not, leading to a major problem. The reforms weakened the CCP's leadership even though it was an unwritten rule that the party's leadership could not be challenged. This set the stage for a crisis like the Tiananmen Movement when the party had to democratise to change itself in the late 1980s.

---

[8] Carol Lee Hamrin, *China and the Challenge of the Future: Changing Political Patterns*, Boulder and London, Westview Press, 1990.

The theme of "separation of party and the government" lasted from the mid 1980s to the Tiananmen Movement of 1989. In reality, the separation of party and state led to the breakdown of party and the state. In the official narrative of the Tiananmen Movement, the crisis for the ruling party occurred when relations between the party and state broke down due to a serious disagreement in the highest leadership of the party. After the Tiananmen Movement, Deng Xiaoping reorganised the party's central leadership. Despite Deng Xiaoping's emphasis on collective leadership, the experiences of the 1980s and the political reality of the time called for a new political thinking. This political thinking drove political changes of the 1990s.

Political Reforms in the 1990s

The political reforms of the 1990s can be considered to have lasted from the 1989 Tiananmen Movement to the 18th party congress in 2012. If 1978 is to be regarded as the start of the reforms, then the 23 years from 1978 to 2012 can be considered as the "Deng Xiaoping Era". This "Deng Xiaoping Era" can be divided into two small eras, with the "first era" from the 1980s to 1989 and the "second era" from 1989 to 2012. The leadership period of Jiang Zemin and Zhu Rongji can be said to be the peak of this "second era". Although the leadership of Hu Jintao and Wen Jiabao spanned this "second era", they did not develop a new direction for reform and only sought to solve the problems brought about by the political reforms during Jiang Zemin's era. A new direction for political reforms only formed after the 18th party congress in 2012.

The crisis of the late 1980s changed the direction of the political reforms. Between 1989 and the 14th party congress of 1992, a new political reform direction was in the making. Due to the West's total embargo on China, China's economic development stalled and worsened; however, the CCP leadership remained conservative and was reluctant to initiate new reforms. The dissolution of Soviet and Eastern European Communist states hastened the search for a new direction of reforms for Deng Xiaoping. The new reform direction was to separate the reform of economics and politics, with an emphasis on economics. In the Soviet Union, Gorbachev's Perestroika democratisation efforts were not all smooth sailing as his economic reforms were hindered by different interest groups in the Soviet Union. Western democracy resulted in not only the dissolution of the Soviet Union, but also the collapse of communist regimes in the Eastern European satellite states. This had a big impact on the CCP leadership.

China learned two lessons from this. The first was that economic and political reforms could not go hand in hand, and that political reforms could not be depended upon to push economic reforms. The second was that the goal of instituting political reforms was not to lead to a Western style democracy, but to strengthen the power and capability of the ruling party. Based on observations of the end of the Cold War in the early 1990s, Deng Xiaoping believed that Soviet Communism collapsed because the leadership could not bring about economic prosperity to keep the people contented and not simply because of the attractiveness of Western-style democracy. The lack of legitimacy of the communist party in the Soviet Union also led to its downfall in 1991.

The 14th party congress in 1992 was indicative of many of Deng Xiaoping's new reform directions from his "Southern Tour". The highly debated "Market Economy" concept was officially promulgated as "Socialist Market Economy".[9] This new concept provided a new ideology for economic reforms. In the mid 1990s, China sought to enter the World Trade Organisation. To facilitate its entry into the global economic system and global society, China revised a series of internal laws and policies to meet the "international standards" of a market economy. The internal reforms and opening up to the world gave China's economic reforms a huge boost. China achieved near double-digit economic growth by 2012, a mere 20 years after the 14th party congress.

---

[9] John Wong and Zheng Yongnian (eds.), *The Nanxun Legacy and China's Development in the Post-Deng Era,* London and Singapore, World Scientific/Singapore University Press, 2001.

In the domain of politics, the reform was more focused on the "little truths" — solving practical issues on the ground. These reforms focused on a few political areas. First, in 1992, the advisory committee was disbanded and at a formal institutional level, the problem of the retirement of old cadres was solved. Second, a term limit of no more than two terms was instituted for the president, vice president, premier and other important posts. Third, an unwritten age limit was set up for members of the Standing Committee of the Political Bureau to retire when they reached the age of 67. Fourth, the practice of collective leadership and democracy within the party was established. Although Deng Xiaoping established a "party core" concept after the 1989 Tiananmen Movement, he also concurrently stressed the need for collective leadership and democracy within the party.[10]

The most important reform in the domain of politics was the establishment of the "3 in 1" system in which the posts of general secretary of the party, chairman of the Central Military Commission and state presidency is held by an individual concurrently. In the 1980s, the aforementioned posts were held by different individuals, and both state president and vice-state president were only symbolic titles. This led to many problems in the exercise of power and to the Tiananmen Movement. The political reform which placed the title of general secretary of the party, chairperson of the central military commission and state president in one person's hands was a clear rejection of the "separation of the party and the government", a theme of the 1980s. China thus went on a path of reform that once again merges the party with the government, a fact which was explicitly acknowledged only after the 19th party congress in 2017.

During the era of Jiang Zemin and Zhu Rongji, there was a reform that could be classified under "the pursuit of the grand discourse". The "rule of law" reform was put forward at the 15th party congress in 1997. Before that, the official language was "rule by law". "Rule of law"

---

[10] John Wong and Zheng Yongnian (eds.), *China's Post-Jiang Leadership Succession: Problems and Perspectives*, London and Singapore, Singapore University Press and World Scientific, 2002 and Zheng, *Contemporary China*, chapter 2.

and "rule by law" had very different meanings, despite having the same Chinese characters. The former meant that law was a tool for the ruling party and its government, and the latter meant that the party and the government also had to abide by the law.[11] Yet for a long while, the "rule of law" remained largely as a concept and without any concrete plan for its implementation. It was only until the Fourth Plenary Session of the 18th CPC Central Committee that the CCP started to use the concept of "rule of law" as a core idea for reform. There was also a "three represents" concept mooted during Jiang Zemin's era, which sought to solve the political identity crisis of the newly emerging class. Although the "three represents" allowed the newly emerging class to join the CCP, strengthening the social foundations of the party, it also brought about long-term ramifications.

During the Hu Jintao-Wen Jiabao era from 2002 to 2012, many new political initiatives had been launched, but many problems surfaced as well, thus signalling the need for change. At the societal level, the previous prioritisation of economic growth brought about societal and environmental problems. This posed pertinent questions on the kind of growth that China should pursue and led to the advocation of "Scientific Development" by the Hu-Wen leadership.

The organisational structure reform inherited the thinking of the 1980s. The separation of party and government was not brought up, as the party and government started to integrate. However, from 1992 to 2012, only the reform of the organisational structure of the government and not the party was initiated, making the party-government organisations very uncoordinated. For example, the constitution stipulated a two-term limit for the state presidency and vice-state presidency, but there was no such limitation to the term limit for the general secretary of the party and chairman of the central military commission. This inconsistency can lead to huge problems internally. In 2002, when the chairman of the central military commission reached two terms, he

---

[11] Zheng Yongnian, "The Rule by Law vs. the Rule of Law", in Wang Gungwu and Zheng Yongnian (eds.), *Reform, Legitimacy and Dilemmas: China's Politics and Society*, London and Singapore, World Scientific, 2000, pp. 135–163.

continued to serve for another two years as there was no term limit for this position. Thus, from 2002 to 2004, the three top leadership posts in China were not in the hands of the same person.

In these 10 years, the most important initiative was democratisation within the party or intra-party democracy. The reform direction of "democratisation within the party to lead democratisation for the people" was brought up at the 17th party congress in 2007. At this point, the party decided to use the voting system to select cadres as the best way to try out the democratic system. However, the lack of experience and the fact that many unwritten or hidden rules remained, some political figures started to assert control of the voting process to its detriment. This is the main reason for the scrapping of the voting system at the 19th party congress.

At the practical level, the search for democracy within the party also posed contradictions and critical problems. To demonstrate its commitment to democracy within the party, the idea of "party core" had been dropped after 2002. This went against Deng Xiaoping's directive that the party needed a core to function as the party core represented political responsibility. Many reasons could have led to the abandonment of the idea of party core, but one important reason was the CCP's determination of collective leadership and democracy within the party.

The search for democracy within the party also led to the sharing of responsibilities and workload within the party's leadership, with one person in charge of one domain. Although this practice can be superficially considered as more "democratic", it led to many negative ramifications in reality, with the formation of cliques in the party. The party's general secretary was reduced to a mere "figurehead". The purged personnel after the 18th party progress, Zhou Yongkang, Ling Jihua, Xu Caihou and Guo Boxiong were the heads of the different cliques in the party. These party cliques established their own power network and recruited members that were loyal to them. Their power and influence stretched from the central to local governments, including many ministries and commissions. Empirically speaking, these cliques within the CCP could have developed into a multi-party system like the West, a development the CCP will do everything to avoid. The Boris Yeltsin era in Russia was stained with different major cliques within the party and post-independence Ukraine was also plagued with the same problem.

On the search for democracy, there had always been outside pressure since the opening up and reform period. Western liberalism has this sense of mission to expand itself to different parts of the world. In the 1980s, when China was in the first decade of its reform, liberalism sought to thrive in China. Deng Xiaoping believed that the Tiananmen Movement was the product of the interaction between external forces and China's internal environment. In the 1990s, after the dissolution of the Soviet Union and the collapse of communism in Eastern Europe, Western liberalism thrived in Russia and Eastern European countries. Due to China's internal reform and opening up, China did not face great pressure on the issue of democracy. However, entering the 21st century, China faced increasing pressure during the Hu-Wen era to democratise as democracy has already taken root in Eastern Europe and Western liberal democracy once again turns its attention to China.

Since the opening up of China, the Chinese leadership has vehemently opposed the introduction of Western-style democracy in China despite the fact that they have not given up on the search for a localised form of democracy. This search for a localised democracy has to some extent relieved the pressure from the West to democratise China. After the West successfully integrated China into the Western-led economic system, it was hard for them to accept the fact that China remains authoritarian. A continuously "un-democratic China" is often the source of the "China threat" view in the West. This view has gained traction in recent years when Western-style democracy begins to face problems.

On the whole, from 1992 to 2012, Deng Xiaoping's legacy has continued and strengthened in the domain of Chinese politics. The search for democracy within the CCP has brought about increasing problems. By the 18th party congress in 2012, problems of critical issues were on the verge of breaking out or had erupted, a distress which was evident at the 18th party congress. All these signalled that a new direction and thinking for reform in China had to be sought.

Political Reforms in the "New Era"

Although the concept of a "new era" was officially raised at the 19th party congress, the 18th party congress was the starting point. The concept of a "new era" was coined on the basis of the reform practices during the five years from the 18th to the 19th party congress.

After the 18th party congress, the central leadership began to implement "effective centralisation" in view of the increasing corruption within the ruling party, especially the rise of cliques within the party. Effective centralisation was implemented not solely for fighting corruption on a massive scale, it was part of the need to further reforms. It was needed to surmount the resistance from vested interest groups when reforms after the 18th party congress emphasised on the "comprehensiveness" and "deepening" of reform, requiring the so-called "top-level design". As the reform deepened, the resistance from vested interest groups became greater.[12]

Evidently, what the ruling party needed most is political reform. After the 18th party congress, the Chinese economy entered the phase of a "new normal". High growth was neither possible, nor essential. Political reform, on the other hand, had become a pressing issue as indicated by the various political problems faced prior to the 18th party congress, basically plunging the ruling party into an inner-party governance crisis. A reform of the inner-party governance system thus became the focus, an area which was neglected since the 1980s with the adherence of the "separation of party and government" principle. After the 18th party congress, the "Four Comprehensives" was coined, referring primarily to comprehensively building a moderately prosperous society, comprehensively deepening of reform, comprehensively implementing the rule of law and comprehensively strengthening Party discipline. Apparently, the most crucial among the "Four Comprehensives" was comprehensively strengthening of Party discipline. In China, the Communist

---

[12] Robert S Ross and Jo Inge Bekkevold (eds.), *China in the Era of Xi Jinping: Domestic and Foreign Policy Challenges*, Washington, DC, Georgetown University Press, 2016.

Party is the perennial ruling party. Its well-being will impact on all other areas and lead eventually to a full-blown crisis.

The inner-party reforms that followed have their grounds. To begin with, the top-level leadership experienced a power reshuffle. This was done by establishing four leading groups (revamped into "committees" after 19th party congress). Even though leading groups before the 18th party congress were in existence, there was a difference between the old and the new. The old leading groups were informal and their members and activities were not made public whereas the new leading groups were the exact opposite. The newly established leading groups (other than military-related) have Xi Jinping as their group leader and Li Keqiang as the deputy leader, while the other members of the Political Bureau Standing Committee are assigned to different leading groups. The old leading groups were each headed by a member of the Political Bureau Standing Committee. The new arrangement improves coordination of power at the top-level as well as efficiency of the operations, and the power reshuffle also prevented the recurrence of "clique politics" that existed previously.[13]

Power centralisation at the top-level was facilitated by the massive anti-corruption campaign and the top-level design of policies. Although anti-corruption has been in progress since the reform and opening up of the 1980s, fighting corruption at the top-level has not been easy. The investigations of many high-ranking politicians (including former Political Bureau Standing Committee members and incumbent Political Bureau) after the 18th party congress is no doubt an outcome of power centralisation.

Throughout this political process, the top-level leadership also reaffirmed the concept of the "party core".[14] As discussed earlier, the CCP has not been deploying the concept of "party core" since the 16th party congress in 2002 to allow more elements like "intra-party democracy",

---

[13] Zheng Yongnian and Weng Cuifen, "The Development of China's Formal Political Structures", in Ross and Bekkevold (eds.), *China In the Era of Xi Jinping*, pp. 32–65.

[14] Chris Buckley, "Xi Jinping Is China's 'Core' Leader: Here's What It Means", *The New York Times*, 30 October 2016.

which led to the reduction of power at the top level. However, the reduction of power at the top level had brought about problems of political responsibility. By bringing back the concept of "party core", it not only represents power centralisation, but also places emphasis on the problem of political responsibility. Clearly, in any political system — be it presidential system, cabinet system or any other system — political responsibility is the most important.

The most significant change brought about by this political process was the emergence and formulation of new ideas for reform. The officially launched reform notion of "party-government integration" has formally reversed the idea of "separation of party and government", the guiding principle of the 1980s. This change will undoubtedly be a long process. There have already been efforts to implement "party-government integration" reform since the 14th party congress. As discussed earlier, the most obvious example was the formation of the "3 in 1" system at the highest level: the positions of party's general secretary, chairman of the central military commission and state president are to be concurrently held by one person. This meant that the president's role had transformed from a symbolic one to a position with substantive power. At the provincial level, the fact that the secretary of the provincial party committee is concurrently the director of the people's congress is also an institutional manifestation of party-government integration. However, the ruling party has never publicly declared its transformation from "separation of party and government" to "party-government integration". Despite its impracticality and the changes made, the "separation of party and government" is still an ideal political reform to many.

The biggest change to the reform theory after the 18th party congress is the official launch of the "party-government integration" reform theory. Wang Qishan has played a vital role in the formulation of this theory. During the anti-corruption campaign which Wang spearheaded, he discovered that corruption led to the waning of the party and to even more corruption. "Party building" thus became the most important issue in the party's reform agenda after the 18th party congress. The idea of "party-government integration" was initially embodied in Wang Qishan's concept of "the government in a broader sense (*guangyi zhengfu*)" raised on 5 March 2017 during the National People's Congress attended by Beijing delegates. This was reported by *Xinhua News Agency* in a news release titled, "Wang Qishan: building an anti-corruption system under the unified leadership of the Party: to upgrade the ability of governance and to improve the governance system".[15] However, this speech did not attract much attention, nor interest among Chinese academic and policy research circles. Nevertheless, it was obvious that Wang Qishan did not adopt the term causally but was referring to the construction of China's political system. This new political system, which stresses "internal division of labour among the three powers" based on the principle of the "party leading the government", is taking shape.

Wang Qishan also said "in the traditional history of China, the 'government' was always understood in a broader sense, and shouldered unlimited responsibility. Today, from the perspective of the masses, party organs, people's congress, administrative agencies, political consultative conference organs, courts and procuratorate are all part of the government. Under the leadership of the party, there is only labour division between the party and government, and there can be no separation. This must be clearly defined with a self-righteous attitude, and there must be unwavering confidence in the path of socialism with Chinese characteristics, theoretical confidence, institutional confidence and cultural confidence".[16]

Apparently, this was not the first time that Wang Qishan had spoken about his concept. In his meeting with former US Secretary of State Dr Kissinger at the end of 2016, he posited that to improve the supervision of the state is to supervise "the government in a broader sense", a full coverage of both the party organs and various governmental agencies. For instance, the deployment of inspection teams and disciplinary investigation teams to "leave no dead ends" echoes the idea of "the government in a broader sense". This was then merely regarded as

---

[15] *Xinhua News Agency*, 5 March 2017.
[16] *Xinhua News Agency*, 5 March 2017.

official jargon and did not attract sufficient attention because Wang Qishan was the secretary of the Central Commission for Discipline Inspection.[17]

Wang's concept went far beyond the discipline inspection system to encompass the entire Chinese political system. What the "government in a broader sense" hopes to resolve is the top-level design problem of the Chinese political system or of the party-government relationship. Specifically, as compared to the reform and opening up since the 1980s, there have been basic institutional changes in at least two aspects.

First, the concept has established the idea that the "party leads the government". "Party-government integration" is a realist concept, an admission to the fact that the "party" and "government" can never be fundamentally separated in the political system of China. Given the inseparability of the two, an alternative idea, which is "party-government integration", has been mooted. This new idea has been manifested in the reform plan for party and state institutions, and adopted by the National People's Congress in 2018.

This is the first time since the reform and opening up in the 1980s that the party and state institutions have been scheduled for reform. In the past, reforms had always been focused on state institutions, while the reform of party institutions had never been brought to the agenda. Evidently, government restructuring had reached its limit after the super-ministerial reforms and it will be difficult to continue without the reform of party institutions. From this perspective, party-government integration has provided possibility for genuine super-ministry reforms. The reforms will strive to achieve two goals. The first is to realise the principle of the "party leading the government" and the second is to improve the efficiency of governance through institutional integration.

This brings us to the second point on the system of the "internal division of labour among the three powers". It is difficult for those who adopt the Western concept of multi-party democracy to comprehend,

---

[17] *Xinhua News Agency*, 1 December 2016.

or even to accept, the idea of "party-government integration". In modern times, many political and intellectual elites including Dr Sun Yat-sen had been hoping to install the Western style of "checks and balances" via the "separation of executive, legislative and judicial powers" in China. For example, the "Five-Power Constitution" established by Dr Sun Yat-sen is a combination of the three powers from the West and the two Chinese traditional powers (examination system and supervision). Looking at Taiwan's experience, once the Western system of "separation of executive, legislative and judicial powers" has been established, the two Chinese traditional powers will be marginalised with no meaningful role to play. This is the current situation in Taiwan. In China, there is only one ruling party with no opposition and only one political process. In Western countries with a multi-party system, there can be a few simultaneous political processes; the ruling party and opposition parties can have their own political processes and politics is the replacement of one political process with another within one constitutional framework.

In China, with the power of supervision formally in place, the system of "internal division of labour among the three powers" (decision-making power, executive power and supervision power) is established. This will mean that though there is only one political process in this country, the process is divided into three components, or more specifically, the exercise of power will be split into three phases according to time. For China's institutions, the ones with policy decision-making power include the Central Committee, National People's Congress, Chinese People's Political Consultative Conference, social organisations and so on; the one with executive powers includes the state council, public security bureau, procuratorate, people's court, among others and the supervision committee holds the inspection power. Notably, there is a certain level of checks and balances in the "internal division of labour among the three powers" that avoids the phenomenon of the paralysis of power encountered in some Western countries. At the same time, the "internal division of labour among the three powers" also aims to effectively prevent corruption and assist in the construction of an uncorrupted government.

Challenges Ahead

From a grand historical perspective, the institutional building of China today is comparable to that of the Han dynasty. Although Emperor Qin Shihuang unified China, there was not much institutional building which resulted in a short-lived Qin dynasty. On the other hand, Han institutional building was successful as it survived the dynasty and had been around for more than 2,000 years until it was abolished by the late Qing dynasty. If the CCP manages to create an institutional system based on the "party leading the government" and the "internal division of labour among the three powers", a strong foundation for a secure and enduring governance system will be created.

Therefore, the construction of a system through political reform is an important and long-lasting project, with many huge challenges on the way.

The first challenge is how the "internal division of labour among the three powers" could make use of today's new political environment in the era of the social media. The "internal division of labour among the three powers" is a traditional elitist system with power shared between the emperor and the scholar-class. In today's world, people have developed a strong democratic consciousness, and possess the means and tools for political participation. Without considering society's democratic consciousness and its quests for participation, the construction of "internal division of labour among the three powers" will be very difficult.

The second is on how the division of labour and coordination among the "three powers" could proceed. Although the "three powers" are led by the party, they still need to draw clear boundaries for them to function normally.

The third is how to guarantee the democratic and scientific nature of decision-making power. For now, decision-making power comes under top-level policymakers who emphasise the centralisation of power. Elements of democracy will be needed to ensure scientific decision-making under the context of power centralisation. It will be difficult to achieve scientific decision-making if no democratic process is involved. In this aspect, how policy decision-making power can merge elements like openness, democratic, separation of power, the centralisation of power and so on needs to be considered.

The fourth is how to ensure the effectiveness of executive power. Executive power is sandwiched between policy decision makers and the inspectorate, which greatly hinders decision making or getting work done. To resolve this problem, both a trial-and-error institutional design and an executive responsibility institutional design are needed.

The last is with the limits of supervision power. This power is newly established. It will need a long time to explore the limits of its power and the methods for exercising them. If the power of inspection is left unchecked, a state of "internal opposition" such as "opposition only for the sake of opposition" may arise. In this case, it will lead to the mal-functioning of executive power.

In addition, "party-government integration" under the concept of "the government in a broader sense" is also plagued by the issue of establishing a boundary between both the government and market, and between the state and society. Without clear boundaries and effective methods to resolve the relationships, it will lead to ambiguous functions between them and their relations will be problematic. After all, the concept of "the government in a broader sense" did not mean that the entire country is the "government", with no market and society.

If these crucial issues are resolved, then the system of "internal division of labour among the three powers" can be established on the basis of "party leading the government" and with an enduring vitality. However, if it cannot be resolved, there is a possibility that the reform of the system may retreat to the model of the 1980s.

Chapter 7

Party Modernisation and Bureaucratic Reform in the Era of Xi Jinping

Kjeld Erik BRØDSGAARD[1]

Introduction

In his report to the 19th Party Congress Chinese President Xi Jinping put forward an ambitious development plan which he "called a journey to fully build a modern socialist China". This journey would take place in three stages. By the end of the first stage in 2020, China would realise the goal of turning the country into a moderately prosperous country. In the second stage from 2020 to 2035 China would basically realise socialist modernisation. Economic and technological strength would have increased significantly and the country would have become a global leader in innovation. The goal of building a beautiful China would basically have been attained. In the third stage of the journey from 2035 to the middle of the century China would develop into a "great modern socialist country that is strong, democratic, culturally advanced, harmonious and beautiful" and become a "global leader in terms of composite national strength and international influence" with a world-class military. This is the strategic

[1] Kjeld Erik BRØDSGAARD is Professor and Director of the China Policy Programme, Department of International Economics, Government and Business, Copenhagen Business School.

vision for developing socialism with Chinese characteristics in the new era — the strategic vision for Xi Jinping Thought.[2]

Xi Jinping underlined that the defining feature of socialism with Chinese characteristics is the leadership of the Chinese Communist Party (CCP). He called leadership of the CCP the greatest strength of socialism with Chinese characteristics. He also said that his Thought underlines the importance of political work and Party building.[3]

These formulations make it clear that the CCP will play a key role in the "journey to fully build a modern socialist China". The Party will be spearheading the modernisation drive and play an even stronger economic and political role than it does today. At the same time the CCP will undergo internal organisational modernisation and reform.

Xi Jinping's report to the 19th Party Congress emphasised that the Party leads everything. "The Party is the most exalted form of political leadership".[4] This was reiterated in the "Decision of the Third Plenum of the 19th Central Committee on Deepening Reform of Party and State Institutions" which underlined that the Party exercises overall leadership over all areas and in every part of the country.[5] The decision said that for the "Party, government, military, the people, education, the East, the West, the South, the North, and the Center, the Party is the leader of everything".

---

[2] Xi Jinping, "Secure a Decisive Victory in Building a Moderately Prosperous Society in All Respects and Strive for the Great Success of Socialism with Chinese Characteristics for a New Era", delivered at the 19th National Congress of the Communist Party of China, 18 October 2017, pp. 25–26.

[3] Xi Jinping, "Secure a Decisive Victory", pp. 17–18.

[4] "Full text of Xi Jinping's report at 19th CPC National Congress", *Xinhua News Agency*, available at <http://www.xinhuanet.com/english/download/Xi_Jinping's_report_at_19th_CPC_National_Congress.pdf> (accessed 15 November 2017).

[5] "Zhonggong zhongyang guanyu shenhua dang he guojia jigou gaige de jueding — 2018 nian 2 yue 28 ri Zhongguo gongchandang di shijiu zhongyang weiyuanhui di san ci quanti huiyi tongguo" (Decision of the Central Committee on Deepening reform of Party and State Institutions — Adopted at the Third Plenary Session of the 19th Central Committee of the Communist Party of China on 28 February 2018), available at <http://www.xinhuanet.com/politics/2018-03/04/c_1122485476.htm> (accessed 23 April 2018).

Commenting on the third plenum *Xinhua News* noted: "The Party's leadership should be strengthened over areas including deeper reform, the rule of law, economy, agriculture and rural work, disciplinary inspection and supervision, organisation, propaganda, theory and culture, national security, political and legal affairs, united front, ethnic and religious affairs, education, science and technology, cyberspace affairs, foreign affairs and auditing".[6]

As this is extremely comprehensive, not all areas will be covered in this article. I will focus on two main areas, namely, organisation and ideology. These are the areas that Schurmann famously said were holding China together.[7] I will also discuss what strengthened Party leadership in these areas means for Party-state relations.

Party Organisation

In the beginning of the 1980s, Deng emphasised the notion of "separation of Party and government" (*dangzheng fenkai*). In 1980 he said that "The Party organization neither equals the government nor the organs of state power. The method of the Party ruling everything is wrong".[8] Deng went on to state that it was necessary to pull the Party and its cadres out of daily administration in order "to strengthen the Party's leadership over the ideological and political fields".

The notion of separating Party from government became an important slogan during the 1980s. In 1987, the notion was a key part of Zhao Ziyang's work report to the 13th Party Congress.[9] According to Zhao, in the future, cadres should come under two categories, a political-administrative category (*zhengwu gongwuyuan*) and a professional work

---

[6] *Xinhua News*, "CPC Issues Decision on Deepening Reform of Party and State Institutions", 5 March 2018.

[7] Franz Schurmann, *Ideology and Organization in China*, Berkeley, California, University of California Press, 1968.

[8] See "A Speech of Deng Xiaoping for Restricted Use Only", *FBIS-CHI-86-117*, 18 June 1986, W1-2.

[9] Zhao Ziyang, "Yanzhe you Zhongguo tese de shehuizhuyi daolu qianjin" (Advance along the Road of Socialism with Chinese Characteristics), *Renmin ribao*, 4 November 1987.

category (*yewu gongwuyuan*). Only the former should be managed by the Party. The latter category should be managed by a newly formed Ministry of Personnel according to the relevant provisions of the constitution and be "subjected to supervision by the public". This bifurcation of the cadre corps also formed the basis for suggestions to establish a civil service system for state officials in China. In line with the "separation of Party and government" Zhao Ziyang also proposed abolishing Party groups in government ministries and agencies and managed to partly implement this initiative before he was ousted in 1989.

A key part of Deng's reforms in the 1980s was rejuvenating the cadre corps under the slogan of younger, more knowledgeable and professionally competent cadres. The reform was successfully implemented and within a few years the educational qualifications of cadres improved significantly and the average age of leading cadres was lowered.[10]

As part of the efforts to rejuvenate the cadre corps, Deng also introduced age limits for holding key offices. A limit of 65 was set for government ministers and 60 for vice ministers and department (*ju/si*) heads. Following a decision to abolish life tenure for leading positions, term limits for leading state positions were introduced. The tenure for state leaders was limited to two periods of five years each. Importantly, the imposed term limit also applied to the presidency.

After the Tiananmen incident in 1989 policies changed. "Separation of Party and Government" was taken off the agenda and though the notion reappeared at irregular intervals during the 1990s it never regained its former status. A number of Deng's bureaucratic reform measures such as the rejuvenation of the bureaucracy and term limits for holding high office remained. In 1997 they were supplemented by the introduction of the age limit of "67 up, 68 down" for appointment to the politburo and the politburo standing committee.

However, a number of other measures clearly contradicted the spirit of Deng Xiaoping's reforms. In 1993, Jiang Zemin took over the posi-

---

[10] Kjeld Erik Brødsgaard, "Management of Party Cadres in China", in Kjeld Erik Brødsgaard and Zheng Yongnian (eds.), *Bringing the Party Back In: How China is Governed*, Singapore, Eastern Universities Press, 2004, pp. 57–91.

tion as president and as he in 1992 had been reaffirmed as CCP general secretary and head of the central military committee, he then held all three top positions in the Chinese power hierarchy. In the 1980s, different Chinese leaders had held these positions. Hu Yaobang and Zhao Ziyang had served as CCP general secretary, Li Xiannian and Yang Shangkun as president and Deng Xiaoping as chairman of the central military commission. In this way the most important power centres were headed by different persons. This institutional arrangement changed in 1992-1993. An important reason for the change was to avoid the confusion that had happened in 1989 when the three power centres could not agree on how to solve a crisis. In 1992, Jiang Zemin also abolished the advisory commission, which was set up by Deng Xiaoping in 1982 to retire older cadres from top leadership positions. Members of the commission were active in criticising Hu Yaobang in 1986 as well as in toppling Zhao Ziyang in 1989 and in forming a fourth power centre. Jiang Zemin removed the advisory body to avoid potential criticism and interference in the leadership.

The Tiananmen debacle formed an important background for these measures of leadership consolidation. The new leaders believed that student demonstrations and the ensuing political crisis proved the necessity of strengthening unified Party rule. Another event that in the eyes of Chinese leaders led to the same conclusion was the collapse of the Soviet Union in 1991.

Immediately after the Tiananmen incident, Party groups were restored in government ministries and agencies.[11] Since then Party groups have been empowered in the institutions and organisations where they are located. In a ministry, for example, they are composed of the minister and a number of vice ministers and functional leaders who hold executive offices. If the minister is a Party member he/she will also serve as secretary of the Party group. This is where real power is located and if the minister is not a Party member, he/she will only

---

[11] Li Ling, "'Rule of Law' in a Party-State — A Conceptual Interpretive Framework of the Constitutional Reality of China", *Asian Journal of Law and Society*, vol. 2, Issue 1, 2015, pp. 1–20.

be a figurehead. In provincial governments party groups are composed of the governor, vice governors, head of the governor's office and most likely one assistant governor. The existence of Party groups prevents "separation of Party and government" since the Party is integrated in the key decision-making body of any ministry or governmental office.

In the late 1990s, in many localities the Party introduced a policy of overlapping positions. The Party secretary of a county would often also be appointed chairman of the local people's congress.[12] The system also expanded to higher levels so that the provincial Party secretary would concurrently serve as chairman of the provincial people's congress. In the Hu Jintao era this system spread to the business sector; the Party secretary of a state-owned enterprise (SOE) would also serve as chairman of the board, if the company had a board. The system became known as "double entry, overlapping positions" (*shuangxiang jinru, jiaocha zhiwu*).[13]

Incremental Bureaucratic Reform

However, the trend towards more centralised Party rule was ambiguous. A number of smaller bureaucratic reforms appeared to show the emergence of a more transparent and responsive Party organisation. In 2002 new regulations on the appointment of leading cadres introduced public nominations and open call for filling cadre positions.[14] They included the principle of secret voting among members of the recruitment committee. Other reform elements included supervision and democratic recommendation and consultation. This trend could also be observed at the highest level. Thus the filling of seats in the politburo

---

[12] Kjeld Erik Brødsgaard, "Governing Capacity and Institutional Change in China in the Reform Era", *The Copenhagen Journal of Asian Studies*, vol. 28, no. 1, 2010, pp. 20–35.

[13] Kjeld Erik Brødsgaard, "China's Political Order under Xi jinping: Concepts and Perspectives", *China: An International Journal*, vol. 16, no. 3, August 2018, pp. 1–17.

[14] "Dangzheng lingdao ganbu xuanba renyong gongzuo tiaoli" (Work Regulations for Selecting and Appointing Leading Party and Government Cadres), 23 July 2002, available at <http://www.people.com.cn/GB/shizheng/16/20020723/782504.html> (accessed 12 September 2018).

and the politburo standing committee in 2007 and 2012 was based on voting among 300 top level cadres.

Moreover, even though the three most important top positions were held by just one man, the general secretary of the CCP, his power was limited by the fact that each of his colleagues in the standing committee had authority over an important policy field or system. Thus in the Jiang Zemin era Ding Guangen headed the propaganda and ideology system, Li Peng and later Zhu Rongji was in charge of economics, Hu Jintao oversaw the personnel system and so on. In the Hu Jintao era this division of authority was deepened, resulting in near paralysis in the standing committee. Decisions had to be based on consensus and individual members of the standing committee had decisive power in matters relating to their own particular policy field.

This confusing mixture of incremental bureaucratic reform within the Party and strengthening of overall Party leadership changed when Xi Jinping came into power in 2012.

Bureaucratic internal Party "reform" continued during Xi Jinping's first five years in power. A flurry of new regulations has streamlined and strengthened how the Party organisation operates and what Party cadres are requested and allowed to do in relation to travelling, banquets, accommodation, reimbursement of expenses and so on.[15] There are also new regulations on housing facilities allocated by the Party as well as their working conditions in terms of office space. However all these regulations are about strictly governing and regulating the Party rather than about more transparency and more inner Party democracy. In October 2015 revised regulations were published concerning the various forms of sanctions and disciplinary punishment that will apply if cadres are not observing rules and regulations and are not behaving

---

[15] See "Shiba da yilai feng lian zheng jianshe he fan fubai fagui zhi huibian" (Collection of Documents on the Legal System in Relation to Building Party Work and Clean Government and Anti-corruption after the 18th Party Congress) Beijing, Zhongguo fangzhen chubanshe, 2014.

morally and ideologically correct.[16] Party members are even reminded that they are responsible for proper family affairs and according to new regulations on demotion and promotion, Party cadres whose wife is living permanently abroad cannot be promoted.[17] The publication of these documents shows that the anti-corruption campaign is about not only taking down corrupt officials, but also reinvigorating and improving the quality and morality of the cadre corps.

Regulations on selecting and appointing leading state and Party cadres have also been revised. The revisions include some changes compared to the previous regulations promulgated in 2002. The revised regulations no longer stipulate the possibility of voting in the democratic recommendation of candidates for leading positions.[18] In general, the Party group has a stronger role in identifying and recommending new leaders.

At the top level significant change has also taken place recently. In the run up to the 17th Party Congress in 2007 a poll among 300 Party leaders was conducted in order to select the lineup for new members of the politburo and the politburo standing committee. Xi Jinping received most votes and was therefore placed at the top of the list ahead of Li Keqiang who until this point had been considered the most likely person to succeed Hu Jintao as general secretary of the CCP. As a result of the poll, Xi Jinping was ranked higher than Li Keqiang in the new standing committee that was formed at the 17th Party Congress, indicating that he was scheduled to succeed Hu Jintao as general secretary of the CCP. In 2012 a similar procedure of voting among a select group

---

[16] "Zhongguo gongchandang jilu chufen tiaoli de tongzhi" (Notice on the Regulations Concerning CCP Disciplinary Punishment), 25 October 2015, <http://news.xinhuanet.com/politics/2015-10/21/c_1116897567.htm> (accessed 12 January 2016).

[17] See "Tuijin lingdao ganbu nenshang nengxia ruogan guiding (shixin)" (Trial Regulations for Promoting and Demoting Leading Cadres", 28 July 2015, <http://cpc.people.com.cn/n/2015/0728/c64387-27375493.html> (accessed 12 January 2016).

[18] "Dangzheng lingdao ganbu xuanba renyong gongzuo tiaoli" (Work Regulations for Selecting and Appointing Leading Party and Government Cadres), 15 January 2014, available at <http://renshi.people.com.cn/n/2014/0116/c139617-24132478-6.html> (accessed 10 September 2018).

of top officials was conducted in order to determine, who besides Xi Jinping and Li Keqiang, would make up the composition of the standing committee to be formally elected by the 18th Central Committee of the CCP.

However the selection process prior to the 19th Party Congress in October 2017 was conducted in a different way. It took place through face-to-face consultation rather than an internal selection based on voting. According to an official description of the selection process, Xi Jinping met personally with 57 senior current and retired Party leaders to seek their input for the final leadership line-up.[19] Apparently other members of the Politburo Standing Committee held similar meetings and a total of 258 ministerial level officials and senior military leaders were consulted.

The new way of selecting leaders was praised by *Xinhua News* which argued that both 2007 and 2012 had seen "reckless voting". Apparently purged Party leaders Bo Xilai, Sun Zhengcai and Ling Jihua had engaged in vote buying and other malpractices in order to win the elections. The new system was considered a better way of promoting inner-Party democracy.

However, one cannot escape the impression that the new system strengthens Xi Jinping's say in selecting new leaders. He was given the mandate to sum up the results of the face-to-face interviews and consultations and pass his impression to his colleagues in the Standing Committee of the CCP Politburo. He did this at a meeting on 27 September 2017. The Standing Committee approved Xi Jinping's recommendations and passed them to the Politburo which met on 29 September to review and approve the list.

From Xi Jinping's perspective the new method of selecting leaders was better and more efficient because it gave him a determining role in the whole selection process. Another advantage was that he would

---

[19] "Linghang xin shidai de jianqiang lingdao jiti" (Building a Strong Foundation for Strengthening the Leadership Collective in the New Era), *Xinhua News*, 3 July 2018, available at <http://www.xinhuanet.com/politics/19cpcnc/2017-10/26/c_1121860147.htm> (accessed 15 September 2018).

avoid any surprise results from voting. He knew that Li Keqiang had been Hu Jintao's favourite candidate in 2007 and if it had not been for the introduction of a voting procedure, he might not have been able to prevail.

Institutional Reform

Institutional reform in the spring of 2018 also showed that Party consolidation had reached a new level. The Party is no longer content with influencing government decision-making by way of embedded Party groups. It now wants important functions transferred to the Party.

This is done by way of a new round of institutional reform (*jigou gaige*). As part of the plan for institutional reform worked out by the central committee and adopted by the NPC, the Party currently is taking over functions that previously belonged to the state. These functions especially relate to personnel work and will, when implemented, dramatically increase the power of the CCP Central Organisational Department (COD).

This is not the first time institutional reform has been implemented. There had been seven previous rounds of institutional reform since 1982. The reform this time is different. In scope it is the most comprehensive since Zhu Rongji's reform in 1998. It is also different from previous rounds of reform in the sense that it explicitly not only serves to streamline the state apparatus, but also aims to increase the authority and power of the Party. The reform plan rationalises that it is needed to "resolutely preserve the authority and centralized and unified leadership of the Party Central Committee with Comrade Xi Jinping as the core, and to adapt to the new demands of developing socialism with Chinese characteristics in the new era". [20]

Firstly, the new institutional reform decided by the third plenary decision moved the bureau for civil servants (*guojia gongwuyuan ju*) to

---

[20] Zhonggong zhongyang (CPC Central Committee), "Shenhua dang he guojia jigou gaige fangan" (Draft Plan of Deepening Party and State Institutional Reform), *Xinhua News*, 21 March 2018.

the CCP's COD. It used to be a bureau of vice-ministerial rank within the Ministry of Human Resources and Social Security. The reason for having a ministry manage the civil servants was that most civil servants work in state organisations and institutions. Moreover almost half of the rank and file civil servants are not Party members, though almost all leading cadres are.

When the civil service system was established the intention was to separate it from the Party's personnel system. However, the Party was not too happy about this and during the 1990s and 2000s it often interfered in civil service work. For example, important rules and regulations concerning the civil service system were often issued jointly by the party's COD and the State Council or the Ministry of Personnel. In 2008 the administration and management of civil servants were formally placed under the newly formed Ministry of Human Resources and Social Security. However the recent plan for reform of the administrative structure takes the management of civil servants out of the state system and places it squarely on the CCP.

Secondly, in the era of Jiang Zemin and Hu Jintao and the first term of Xi Jinping's rule the Commission for *Bianzhi* Work (*bianzhi weiyuanhui*) was headed by the premier. Now it will be integrated into the COD. The importance of this cannot be underestimated. The *bianzhi* system is different from the nomenklatura system, though scholars often mix them up.[21] *Bianzhi* is about staff allocation and budget allocations, namely, institutional strength of mainly state ministries, bureaus and organisations. Nomenklatura is about appointing leaders and who have the authority to do so.[22] By both controlling the size and distribution of the bureaucracy (administrative *bianzhi*) as well as controlling leadership appointments, the Party, and especially the

---

[21] See, for example, Franz Schurmann, *Ideology and Organization in China*.

[22] See Kjeld Erik Brødsgaard, "Politics and Business Group Formation in China: The Party in Control?" *The China Quarterly*, vol. 211, September 2012, pp. 624–648; John Burns, "The Chinese Communist Party's Nomenklatura System as a Leadership Selection Mechanism", in Kjeld Erik Brødsgaard and Zheng Yongnian (eds.), *The Chinese Communist Party in Reform*, London, Routledge, 2006, pp. 33–58.

COD, will wield enormous power over the public sector. It is no coincidence that the COD is headed by Chen Xi, who is Xi Jinping's close confidante and former roommate at Qinghua University.

Thirdly, Chen Xi has been appointed president of the Central Party School, though he is not member of the Standing Committee. The new institutional reform plan stipulates that the Chinese Academy of Governance will be merged with the Central Party School thereby enhancing the Central Party School's role in high-level cadre training.

These are all clear examples of the expanding role of the Party in areas that used to belong to the state. These examples also illustrate a redefinition of the concept of institutional reform. All previous rounds of institutional reform focused on restructuring and reforming government institutions. The 2018 round of reform also involves Party institutions, a clear indication of the ongoing Party-government integration.

In addition, four leading small groups, namely, the central small leading groups for overall reform, for cyberspace affairs, for economic and financial affairs and for foreign affairs have been turned into commissions[23] headed by Xi Jinping. This change signals a stronger formal status for the small leading groups under the general secretary's control.

As for economic organisation and management, the Xi era has already seen a strong reassertion of the Party's exclusive rule. In 2016, in a Party document on Party work in SOEs, it was stipulated that all major issues pertaining to the company should first be discussed in the company's Party organisation before being decided at the company board and implemented by management.[24] The management style of "double entry, overlapping positions" (*shuangxiang jinru, jiaocha zhiwu*)

---

[23] "Dang he guojia jigou gaige fangan: Zhonguo caijing lingdao xiaozu wei weiyuanhui" (Party and State Institutional Reform: Economic and Finance Leading Small Group Will Be Changed to a Commission), *Xinhua News*, 21 March 2018, available at <http://finance.sina.com.cn/china/hgjj/2018-03-21/doc-ifyskeue2143575.shtml> (accessed 12 September 2018).

[24] Guoziwei "Guoqi zhongda juece xuhou you dangwei taolun hou dongshihui jueding" (Important Policies in State-Owned Enterprises Should Be Discussed by the Party

has been further strengthened. As a consequence all talk about "separating Party and business" has ceased.

Since 2015 it has also been strongly emphasised that in addition to the Party committee, enterprises should also have a Party cell (*dangzu*).[25] In fact, Party cells should be universally established even in private companies and non-governmental organisations (NGOs) — now only 53.1% of private firms and 41.9% of social organisations have such Party cells.

Party control of personnel management in the SOE sector also remains strong. The COD of the Central Committee controls leadership appointment in 49 of the largest central enterprises (*yang qi*), while State Assets Administration and Supervision Commission (SASAC) controls appointments in the rest of the central enterprises. A recent document issued by SASAC stipulates that in the future SASAC will recommend candidates for leadership positions and the appointment will be undertaken by the board. However, since the Party secretary and the board chairman of the enterprise is the same person, this does not imply a loosening of Party control.

The Party is also in charge of cadre rotation. In relation to the economy the circulation of business leaders is important. One fifth of all governors and vice governors in China have a business background. They include governors Ma Xingrui of Guangdong, Yuan Jiajun of Zhejiang and Zhang Guoqing, mayor of Tianjin. Some former business executives such as Zhang Qingwei managed to become provincial Party secretary. Others such as Guo Shengkun have made it to the Politburo and in the case of Zhou Yongkang even to the Politburo Standing Committee. Undoubtedly, this kind of *pantouflage* ("shuffling across") will continue to take place. Notably, five of the 25 new government

---

Committee before Being Decided by the Board), Caijingwang, 6 July 2016, available at <http://news.sohu.com/20160607/n453423303.shtml> (accessed 8 August 2016).

[25] See "Zhongguo gongchandang dangzu gongzuo tiaoli (shixing)" (The Chinese Communist Party's Working Regulations on Party Groups [trial use]), *Xinhua*, 16 June 2015, available at <http://www.gov.cn/zhengce/2015-06/16/content_2880383.htm> (accessed 2 August 2015).

ministers have a business background.[26] Relations between Party-state-and-business form an iron triangle that is at the heart of the Chinese power system. The recentralisation of Party rule makes the iron triangle even more important for the next phase of China's political development.

The centrality of the Party in economic work in China today is evidenced by the fact that Xi Jinping, the Party general secretary, and not Premier Li Keqiang, is heading the central economic and financial leading small group. In the past the director of this leading small group was always the premier.

Party Ideology

In the West it is often claimed that ideology in China is dead. It is claimed to be just a thin veneer on top of economic development. However as Christian Sorace points out in his book on the Wenchuan earthquake, Chinese leaders operate within a certain Marxist discourse which cannot be considered a formality or empty window dressing.[27] Discourse and ideology are not just instruments to achieve certain goals (e.g. career advancement). Ideology and discourse shape people's everyday life and habits of speech and disposition (their habitus in the language of Bourdieu). People do not stand outside of discourse, even when they manipulate it. A person who uses Party ideology and discourse to advance his own material interests "is still thinking in, assessing from, citing, and reproducing Party discourse".[28]

---

[26] They are the Minister of Science and Technology, Wang Zigang, former vice president of Sinopec; Minister of Emergency Management, Wang Yupu, former general manager of Petro China; Minister of Transportation, Li Xiaoping, who has served as chairman of Huaneng Power Corporation; and the Minister of Information Technology, Miao Wei, former general manager of Dongfeng Auto Corporation. The fifth minister, with a business background, is the Minister of Commerce, Zhong Shan, who was general manager of Zhejiang Zhongda Group Limited before shifting to government work.

[27] Christian Sorace, *Shaken Authority: China's Communist Party and the 2008 Sichuan Earthquake*, Ithaca, Cornell University Press, 2017.

[28] Christian Sorace, *Shaken Authority*, p. 11.

Under Xi, ideology and propaganda have become even more important. An interesting article by Jiang Shigong points out that since the 18th Party Congress, the Party centre has begun a process of merging Marxism with traditional Chinese culture. This means that the core values "of Socialism with Chinese Characteristics must be the blending of the core values of Marxism as represented by communism and the core values defined by China's traditional Confucian culture. Only in this way can we bring forth core values in accord with the spirit and character of the Chinese people and with the objective needs of modern society". Jiang continues, "Party rule and state law have become a modern version of the relationship between ritual and law in the Confucian system".[29] According to Jiang this blending will be even more pronounced in the next phase of China's development.

The institutional reform plan also signals a significant broadening of Party authority in the area of propaganda and ideology. The media has always been under Party supervision in China, but the CCP's control has been tightened as a result of the current round of restructuring. The State Administration of Press, Publication, Radio, Film and Television was disbanded and its functions divided among three new organisations. One of these, the new State Administration of Radio and Television, remains under the State Council, but the two other new administrations, one for Film, and one for Press and Publication, have now been placed under the CCP Publicity Department (Propaganda Department). The China Publishing Group, a state-owned publishing house, which was until 2018 under the State Council will also fall under the supervision of the Propaganda Department. This means that media content will increasingly be directly controlled by the CCP and the Party's narrative will become even more dominant in all media. Indeed, in official

---

[29] Jiang Shigong, "Zhexue yu lishi — cong dang de shijiuda baogao jiedu 'Xi Jinping shidai' (Philosophy and History: Interpreting the 'Xi Jinping Era' Through Xi's Report to the Nineteenth National Congress of the CCP), *Kaifang shida* (*Open Times*), no. 1, January 2018, pp. 11–31, at pp. 12–13.

documents the media sector is referred to as the 'ideological sector', implying the functionality the CCP sees in the media and its use for political means.

Separation of Party and Government

During the 1990s and early 2000s the concept of separation of Party and government continued to be stressed at irregular intervals. However, since Xi Jinping came into power policies have changed. This came to the fore on 5 March, on the opening day of the 2017 session of the National People's Congress when Wang Qishan met the delegation from Beijing. Here he stated his disagreement with Deng Xiaoping's views on the leading role of the Party in China. Although it signifies an important new policy line, Wang's reformulation has so far received little notice in Western news media.

During his meeting with the delegation from Beijing, Wang Qishan argued that the focus on the leading role of the Party did not mean "separation of Party and government" (*dangzheng fenkai*), but "division of labour between Party and government" (*dangzheng fengong*). The Party and government ministries and organs may perform different functions, but this is determined by the Party which is in complete control. He also said that Party organs, the organs of the People's Congress, the executive organs and the CPPCC organs are all governments in the eyes of the masses. Moreover the government is broad and bears unlimited responsibility.[30] This is Wang Qishan's concept of broad government (*guangyi zhengfu*). There can be no separation because government is unified with the Party at the centre. There can only be division of labour.

On 11 November 2017 Wang Qishan published a long article in the *People's Daily* where he discussed at length the CCP's rule of China and

---

[30] "Wang Qishan weihe fouding 'dangzheng fenkai'?" (Why Does Wang Qishan Negate "Separation of Party and Government?"), *Zaobao*, 6 March 2017, available at <https://www.zaobao.com.sg/realtime/china/story20170306-732633> (accessed 10 September 2018).

the future policy under the leadership of Xi Jinping.[31] He underlined that the CCP was the key to "the great rejuvenation of the Chinese nation" and argued that without the strong leadership of the CCP, the Chinese nation would be like loose sand. He reaffirmed that the idea of separating Party and government was wrong, maintaining that it would weaken Party building and undermine the leadership of the CCP.

Moreover control does not only imply setting the general direction and policy objectives, but also involves direct involvement in management affairs. This reformulation of the key relationship between Party and government in China, and the ongoing centralisation of political power in the hands of the CCP shows that Xi Jinping and his allies do not hesitate from breaking away from Deng's policy directions.

Wang Qishan's insistence that the relationship between Party and government should be regulated in terms of division of labour within the overall framework of Party dominance is a direct criticism of a basic policy line formulated by Deng Xiaoping and his reformist allies. Chinese media sources acknowledged the difference from the Deng era and argued that China's development trajectory has entered a new phase and Deng's formulations no longer apply. This important policy shift in the realm of Party-state relations is a sign that other breaks with the Deng era might follow. If it was possible to do away with what Deng had laid down in one area, it would also be possible to introduce changes in other areas. However, at the time the implications were not yet fully grasped among China observers.

When Xi decided to abolish the term limit for the presidency and vice presidency in China, many Chinese intellectuals supported the move by arguing that China was in a different historical trajectory from that of Deng and that it was necessary to fuse the Party and government to achieve a more unified governing system (a unitary governing system). This was for example underlined by Eric Li who

---

[31] Wang Qishan, "Kaiqi xin shidai, tashang xin zhengcheng" (Open a New Era, Embark on a New Journey), *Renmin Ribao,* 11 November 2017, available at <http://paper.people. com.cn/rmrb/html/2017-11/07/nw.D110000renmrb_20171107_1-02.htm> (accessed 5 September 2018).

often functions as a "spokesman" for the official Chinese line.[32] He said that the fusing of the Party and state would be the most far-reaching political transformation in Chinese governance. He also said that it was good for China "simply because the Party had developed into the most competent national political institution in the world today". Jiang Shigong went one step further to argue that the "separation of Party and government" was a reform of the political system with the intent of gradually weakening the leadership of the Party in order to bring about a "Western democratic system". The implication is that not only is Deng's policy of separating Party and government not applicable today, but it should in fact never have been implemented in the first place.[33]

There are dissenting voices in China concerning the need to fuse the Party and government, but they seem to be in the minority and often experience censorship from the authorities. An example of dissent is Xu Zhangrun, a professor at Qinghua, who posted a critical article on the website of Unirule Institute of Economics. The article titled "Our Current Fears and Expectations" was widely discussed on the social media before being censored. Xu argues that current policies of negating separation of Party and government may lead to a revival of totalitarianism in China. He is also extremely critical of lifting the term limit for the presidency, which in his mind will lead to a revival of one-man rule in China.

For a while it looked like criticism on the part of intellectuals in China such as Xu Zhangrun as well as brewing dissatisfaction among retired former Party leaders would weaken Xi Jinping's position. However, periodic absence from the front page of *People's Daily* is not tantamount to a lack of power and influence. This was the

---

[32] Eric Li, "Why Xi's Lifting of Term Limits is a Good Thing", *The Washington Post*, 2 April 2018, available at <https://www.washingtonpost.com/news/theworldpost/wp/2018/04/02/xi-term-limits/?noredirect=on&utm_term=.51cfefbac3eb> (accessed 10 May 2018).

[33] Jiang Shigong, "Philosophy and History: Interpreting the 'Xi Jinping Era' through Xi's Report to the Nineteenth National Congress of the CCP".

mistake made by demonstrating students in the spring of 1989, who thought that silence and long inaction (*wu wei*) on the part of Deng Xiaoping meant that he was no longer a political force to be reckoned with.

Four Stages of CCP History

Jiang Shigong periodises CCP history into four stages. The first stage was from 1921 when the CCP was founded, to 1949 when the People's Republic of China was established. The second period was from 1949 to 1978 in which the CCP led China to accomplish the transformation from "standing up" to "getting rich". The third phase was from 1978 and the policy of reform and opening to the 19th Party Congress when the Party had the courage to reform and open up and embark on the path of "Socialism with Chinese Characteristics". This accomplished the historical transformation from "getting rich" to "becoming powerful". The fourth period, the present period will extend from the 19th Party Congress to China's 100-year anniversary with the aim of realising and modernising socialism and a period of great revival of the Chinese nation. To realise this great strategic objective, the Party has developed Xi Jinping Thought on Socialism with Chinese Characteristics for a New Era. The indispensable instrument to carry out this mission and goal is the CCP.

Xi Jinping has focused a great deal of his writings and energy on governance. It is no coincidence that the two volumes of his writing are titled *The Governance of China*. In the section on "CCP leadership" in volume one, there is an excerpt from an interview dated 19 March 2013 in which Xi claims that governing a big country such as China is as delicate as frying a small fish.[34] In a *Xinhua* report he expands further on this notion and says that "ruling a large country is like cooking small fish, this must be the conduct of leaders". You fry it as a whole and don't

---

[34] Xi Jinping, "Governing a Big Country Is as Delicate as Frying a Small Fish", 19 March 2013, in Xi Jinping, *The Governance of China*, Beijing, Foreign Languages Press, 2014, pp. 457–459.

dissect it into parts".[35] This metaphor nicely illustrates Xi Jinping's leadership style and why he wants to be chairman of everything and not just parts of a Chinese building which still stands, held together by organisation and ideology.

Conclusion

It has become abundantly clear that notions of Party modernisation and Party reform in China cannot be understood from a Western perspective. Modernisation and reform are not about instituting political pluralism and multiparty elections. In the name of reform the Party is in fact consolidating its rule by way of top-level design, not grass-roots pressure. However, this does not mean that change is not taking place. The CCP is in fact streamlining and reforming its bureaucracy. New rules and regulations are adopted that call for accountability and transparency in governance. However, these bureaucratic reforms are initiated in order to strengthen Party control rather than loosen it.

This is all done by referring to the needs of a new era and that the challenges China are facing necessitate strong rule. In fact strong rule is necessary for breaking vested interests and other obstacles to reform. The centralising measures taken are clearly different from the reform measures advocated by Deng Xiaoping in the early 1980s. However, by placing a bracket around the Deng Xiaoping era in terms of the role of the CCP in government and business may question the legitimacy of the rule of the current leadership and open the door for criticism. Xu Zhangrun is an example of the kind of criticism that may be voiced.

What China and the world are witnessing is not a reversal to the Deng era after the weak rule of Hu Jintao and Wen Jiabao. It is in fact a centralisation and strengthening of Party rule which reaches back to

---

[35] Xi Jinping, "Lingdaozhe yao you 'zhi daguo ru peng xiao xian' de taidu" (Leaders Must Rule a Big Country as They Cook a Small Fish), available at <https://news.qq.com/a/20130320/000191.htm?pgv_ref=aio2012&ptlang=2052> (accessed 10 September 2018).

the 1950s and, with its synthesis of Marxism and Confucian elements, it reaches even further back in Chinese history. However, the project is also future-oriented and entails a number of development goals that will combine to create a modern socialist state with global political and economic influence and huge military might. To call this a small fish appears to be a bit of an understatement.

Chapter 8

Decline and Repositioning of the Communist Youth League in China

SHAN Wei and CHEN Juan*

Introduction

Throughout the thousands of years of Chinese imperial history, factions among political elites had always been perceived with negative connotations. As pointed out by Professor Wang Gungwu, "[f]actions could not become legitimate parties, no rights were gained in…any kind of sharing and grouping of political views".[1] Even today, factions have not vanished nor have they been eliminated from China's political arena. Studies on contemporary China are still able to find salient traces and effects of factional politics. The behavioural traits of factions, however, have been enduring debates among scholars. There are scholars who argue that factions among the top leadership have been consistently seeking to gain complete dominance of the Communist Party.[2] There are also others who believe that factions are capable of striking a balance

---

* SHAN Wei is Research Fellow at the East Asian Institute, National University of Singapore. CHEN Juan is Research Assistant at the same institute.
[1] Wang Gungwu, *The Chineseness of China: Selected Essays*, Oxford University Press, 1991. p. 178.
[2] Tang Tsou, "Prolegomenon to the Study of Informal Groups in CCP Politics", *The China Quarterly*, vol. 65, 1976, pp. 98–114.

among themselves and co-exist peacefully.[3] According to this second line of thought, no single faction can dominate.

This chapter observes that, after Xi Jinping came into power, power reshuffling at the upper echelon of the Chinese Communist Party (CCP) has manifested the tendency of Xi's faction to seek dominance. This supports views by the first group of scholars in the aforementioned debate. The factions including the Youth League faction and the princelings faction, which had been competing for power in Jiang Zemin's and Hu Jintao's eras, have been significantly weakened if not crumbled in Xi's time. To further support and illustrate this observation, this chapter studies how the Communist Youth League has been forced to reorganise and reposition itself after Xi assumed office, and how this affected the political prospects of the Youth League faction.

The Youth League faction (*gongqingtuan pai* or *tuanpai*) loosely refers to the informal political network of members with former work experience in the Communist Youth League (CYL) of China who are later accelerated to higher-ranking positions. Academic scholars define officials who once held leadership positions at the Central Committee of the CYL or the full/deputy secretary of the provincial CYL as *tuanpai* members.[4] Eminent members of *tuanpai* include former Party General Secretary Hu Jintao and current Premier Li Keqiang. Hu Jintao was the first secretary of the CYL Central Committee from 1984 to 1985. After securing his position as a Politburo Standing Committee member in 1992, he had promoted a great number of former colleagues or loyalists from the CYL to high official positions, constructing his own power base within the top echelon of the Party. *Tuanpai* thus came into form and gradually grew into one of the most influential blocs within the

---

[3] Andrew Nathan, "A Factionalism Model for CCP Politics", *The China Quarterly*, vol. 53, 1973, pp. 33–66.

[4] People who have work experience in the CYL are not necessarily loyalists or allies of Hu Jintao, Li Keqiang or other *tuanpai* top leaders. For instance, Han Zheng, Liu Yunshan and Li Zhanshu are recognised by many observers as protégés of either Jiang Zemin or Xi Jinping. Please see Li Cheng, "Hu's Followers: Provincial Leaders with Backgrounds in the Youth League", *China Leadership Monitor*, July 2002, <http://media.hoover.org/sites/default/files/documents/clm3_LC.pdf> (accessed 6 December 2017).

CCP. When Hu was general secretary (2002–2012), the number of top officials with CYL background further surged.[5]

The CYL is a national youth organisation under the Communist Party that identifies and grooms politically talented youths. Its members are mostly high school and university students aged 14 to 28. It functions as a link between the party and the youth across the nation. As one of the largest political organisations in China, the number of CYL members was about 88 million in 2015.[6] As CYL cadres are usually young and well educated, the League is a major source of recruitment for the party-state leadership. In its mission statement, the CYL also explicitly claims itself to be the "reserve army" of the Party.[7] Especially during the Hu era, the CYL was deemed as the cradle for high-flying political figures and a stepping stone to the pinnacle of power. Many ambitious college graduates competed for a position within the League.

By the time Hu Jintao stepped down in 2012, *tuanpai* had become the dominant faction in the 18th Politburo. Nine of the positions (out of 25)[8] were taken up by members with former experience at provincial CYL or above, though not all could be labelled as *tuanpai*.[9] Under Hu, the number of *tuanpai* leaders with top provincial-level posts increased from five in 2002 to 13 in 2005 and 21 in 2010.[10]

Since President Xi Jinping came into power in 2012, *tuanpai* has begun to encounter its greatest challenge in decades. Xi has barely

---

[5] Please see Appendix for a list of top leaders with CYL background.

[6] "Xinhua Insight: China Youth League reforms to reinforce CPC leadership", *Xinhua News Agency*, 3 August 2016, <http://news.xinhuanet.com/english/2016–08/03/c_135561349.htm> (accessed 4 September 2017).

[7] Li Cheng, "Hu's Followers".

[8] Li Keqiang, Liu Yunshan, Liu Yandong, Liu Qibao, Li Yuanchao, Wang Yang, Hu Chunhua, Li Zhanshu and Han Zheng.

[9] For instance, Li Zhanshu had former experience in the CYL, but he is a loyal ally to President Xi.

[10] "Analysis: China's Next Inner Circle", Reuters, 4 March 2013, <http://www.reuters.com/article/us-china-factions/analysis-chinas-next-inner-circle-idUSBRE9220GJ20130303> (accessed 7 September 2017). Top provincial-level posts refer to secretary of Provincial Party Committees and provincial governor.

concealed his discontentment with the *tuanpai* and adopted a series of measures to crack down on the *tuanpai* and the CYL. Media reports suggested that Xi was moving towards reducing the power of the *tuanpai* so as to appoint people from his own faction into the decision-making body during the 19th National Congress of the CCP in 2017.[11] This argument gained ground when members elected to the 19th Politburo are mostly Xi's former colleagues. This was nearing the end of his first term as president. Once influential, the "Youth League faction" has nearly disappeared after the 19th Party Congress. A number of cadres with Youth League background, once the rising stars, now face dim prospects in their political career.

The series of crackdowns show that Xi has not only suppressed the *tuanpai* faction by restraining the political power and career prospect of *tuanpai* leaders, but also penalised and weakened the CYL organisationally and financially. To suppress *tuanpai* leaders, Xi has weakened the power of Li Keqiang by usurping the power of the State Council. He also took advantage of the fall of Ling Jihua to purge Ling's allies, many of whom are *tuanpai* members. Xi has also disrupted the routine promotion of several *tuanpai* members and diminished their chances of reaching high positions in the future. Among them is the most promising superstar of *tuanpai*, Guangdong's former party chief Hu Chunhua who failed to enter the 19th Politburo Standing Committee. It implies that Xi is reluctant to accept another supreme leader with CYL background.

The CYL has been under heavy denunciation and pressure to streamline its organisation and restrict its scope of activities. It lost the channel of nurturing its own talents when the Central School of CYL was forced to terminate its degree education. It also saw a 50% cut in funding and lost the stock ownership of two large listed companies that were its financial sources. Under such unprecedented pressure from the top, the CYL has to seek a way out and re-position itself within the

---

[11] "Exclusive: Xi Set to Consolidate Power in China by Curbing Communist Youth League", Reuters, 30 September 2016, <http://www.reuters.com/article/us-china-politics-league-exclusive/exclusive-xi-set-to-consolidate-power-in-china-by-curbing-communist-youth-league-idUSKCN1200OL> (accessed 4 September 2017).

party-state system. A number of provincial CYL have transformed themselves into "pivotal social organisations" to assist the Party in the control and surveillance of non-governmental organisations. The CYL is also working on guiding and mobilising Chinese youth in cyberspace. By attracting millions of followers to their social media accounts, the CYL is able to guide public opinions or even create agendas to wage internet fights in defence of the regime. Other programmes, including setting up of dating events for singles and business incubators for young entrepreneurs, are also put in place.

In the short run, the political prospects of CYL and its members remain gloomy as the League will continue to be restructured and weakened financially and organisationally. In the long run, however, CYL leaders may return to the centre of the political stage. The CCP would still need the organisation to connect and guide the younger generation. With generally better education and younger in age, CYL leaders may still gain a foothold in the future.

Suppression of Youth League Leaders

Xi's bitterness against the CYL could be traced back to the 2000s when Li Keqiang was his top rival for the Party's general secretary position. As the leading figure of the new generation of *tuanpai* after Hu Jintao, Li Keqiang and his second-ranking position in the Party was a possible threat to Xi's power.

Xi's first move to shave the influence of the *tuanpai* was to weaken the power of Li Keqiang. He created a number of small leading groups to extract power from party-state establishments. Two of them, the Deepening Reform Small Leading Group and the Central Finance and Economy Small Leading Group, have worked extensively in policy-making for economic and social issues, which were previously within the authority of Premier Li and his State Council.[12] By chairing the two leading groups, Xi has successfully curtailed Li's power. Such efforts

---

[12] Shan Wei, "Xi Jinping's Leadership Style", *EAI Background Brief,* no. 1120, East Asian Institute, 17 March 2016.

were so successful that *The Economist* has forthrightly pointed out that "Li Keqiang is the weakest Chinese prime minister in decades".[13] Many observers believe that Li's role resembles that of an assistant to Xi or an implementer of Xi's decisions.[14]

The Ling Jihua Incident gave Xi a great opportunity to further suppress *tuanpai* personnel in the party. Ling had risen from his career in the CYL to become the principal political adviser to Hu Jintao. During this period he used his influence to advance the interests of a number of senior officials and establish a network that was later charged with conspiracies against Xi's leadership. Shortly after Ling's 23-year-old son was killed in a Ferrari accident in 2012, an embarrassing event for the party elites, he was politically sidelined and later convicted on charges of taking bribes and abuse of power. [15] At the same time, all members in Ling's network were either purged or politically marginalised. Since many of them are also *tuanpai* members, the purge was a damaging blow to the *tuanpai*.

A number of previously rising stars from the *tuanpai* who have not been purged have stalled in their career ladder. Li Yuanchao, former Central Organisation Department chief, vice state president and Politburo member, lost his position in the Central Committee and all leadership roles at the 19th Congress. Zhou Qiang, chairman of the Supreme Court and once a leading figure among the post-1960 generation of *tuanpai* (born after 1960), failed to enter the 19th Politburo. Yang Yue, vice governor of Jiangsu province, an alternate member of the 18th Central Committee and one of the youngest provincial-level

[13] "A Very Chinese Coup", *The Economist*, 15 October 2015, <https://www.economist.com/news/ china/21674793-li-keqiang-weakest-chinese-prime-minister-decades-very-chinese-coup> (accessed 25 October 2017).

[14] Barry Naughton, "Shifting Structures and Processes in Economic Policy-Making at the Centre", in Sebastian Heilmann and Matthias Stepan (eds.), *China's Core Executive: Leadership styles, structures and processes under Xi Jinping*, Merics Papers on China, June 2016.

[15] Ling Jihua was placed under investigation in December 2014 by the Communist Party Central Commission for Discipline Inspection; he was later sentenced to life imprisonment in July 2016 for corruption, illegal possession of state secrets and abuse of power.

leaders in the country,[16] lost his position as an alternate member of the Central Committee at the 19th Congress. In 2018, he was reappointed as the head of the United Front Work Department of Jiangsu province, a rather marginalised political position.[17]

Hu Chunhua, former party chief of Guangdong, the country's richest province, was *tuanpai*'s most promising superstar and one of the youngest members of the Politburo. Many observers believed he would be a top leading figure among the next generation of party leadership, or even become Xi's successor. After the 19th Congress, however, Hu failed to enter the all-powerful Politburo Standing Committee. Although he remains in the Politburo, he was appointed in 2018 as vice premier in charge of poverty reduction. This indicated that his chances of moving up to the Party general secretary position after Xi's term have become much slimmer. By blocking Hu's promotion Xi frustrated *tuanpai*'s attempt to control the top echelon of the Party.

Since the early 1980s, all outgoing first secretaries of the Central CYL were transferred to provincial-ministerial level positions (such as the provincial party chief, governor or minister) after their service in the CYL. As they are generally younger than other party-state leaders of the same rank, they enjoyed better chances of being promoted to the central leadership. This routine practice was broken during Xi's term. The then first secretary of the Central CYL, Qin Yizhi, was demoted to the position of deputy director of the General Administration of Quality Supervision, Inspection and Quarantine, a vice-ministerial position in a marginal bureau within the party-state system. He also lost his position in the 19th Party Central Committee. The incoming first secretary, He Junke, is only an alternate member of the 19th Central Committee, while his predecessors were usually guaranteed a full membership in the Central Committee. At the provincial level,

---

[16] Yang Yue was born in 1968.

[17] "Yang Yue Appointed as Head of United Front Work Department of Jiangsu Province (yangyue ren jiangsu shenwei tongzhanbu buzhang)", *Xinhua News Agency*, 10 April 2018, <http://www.xinhuanet.com/2018-04/10/c_1122657425.htm> (accessed 28 May 2019).

former first secretary of Zhejiang CYL Committee and the youngest rising star at the time, Zhou Yan, was reassigned the position of deputy director of Geological Exploration Bureau in Zhejiang province. These appointments indicate that the affected officials would have very low chance of rising to high posts in the future. Their marginalisation is meant to demonstrate that the CYL is no longer a guaranteed expressway to top political positions.

Penalisation of the Organisation

The onslaught of public criticisms and corruption arrests has dampened CYL's reputation and legitimacy. They provide justification for reform plans to limit the activities of CYL and structurally restrict the promotion of its members. Xi Jinping's harshest criticisms of the CYL were reportedly made during a conference on improving the operation of mass organisations back in July 2015. Xi sternly warned the CYL against turning into a "quadriplegic" (*gaowei jietan*) organisation that detaches itself from the youth and engages in unproductive works.[18] Xi's remark led to a round of disciplinary inspections from 30 October to 29 December 2015. The party's disciplinary inspection team, upon completing the assessment, openly condemned the CYL for its "formalism, unnecessary bureaucracy, aristocracy and a focus on entertainment".[19]

Synchronised voices from the state media constantly reinforced the denunciations of CYL. For example, *Xinhua News Agency* and its affiliated magazine *Outlook Weekly* (*liaowang*) published an article in July 2016 that elaborated on the organisational problems of CYL pointed

---

[18] "Communist Youth League Entering the 'Reform Period' (gongqingtuan jinru 'gaige shijian')", *Xinhua News Agency*, 31 July 2016, <http://news.xinhuanet.com/politics/2016-07/31/c_129191786.htm> (accessed 25 October 2017).

[19] "The Second Central Inspection Group Feedback to Communist Youth League Central Committee Regarding the Inspection Situation (zhongyang dier xunshizu xiang gongqingtuan zhongyang fankui zhuanxiang xunshi qingkuang)", People.cn, 4 February 2016, <http://politics.people.com.cn/ n1/2016/0204/c1001-28111955.html> (accessed 25 October 2017).

out earlier by Xi and the disciplinary inspection team.[20] With the purge of Ling Jihua and his allies from the *tuanpai*, Xi was able to extensively launch reform policies aimed at the CYL as a whole and tightened control of the organisation.

Financially, the CYL received a 50% cut in their allocated fund in 2016 from RMB624 million in 2015 to RMB306 million.[21] Xi also took away the CYL's internal sources of finance. In early December 2017, two listed companies, China CYTS Tours Holding and Cachet Pharmaceutical Co Ltd, announced the transfer of their stock ownership from the CYL to a state-owned company.[22] CYTS is one of the country's top three travel agencies with a listed market value of around RMB14 billion in mid-December 2017. Cachet is the largest chain pharmacy in Beijing, with a market value of RMB7.3 billion during the same period.[23] The two companies were created by the Central CYL and had been a major financial resource of the League. The transfer of stock ownership dealt a heavy blow to the CYL, severely weakening its functioning.

Organisationally, the CYL was also under pressure to reform. On 2 August 2016, the General Office of the Communist Party published the "CYL Central Committee Reform Plan (*gongqingtuan zhongyang gaige fangan*)", demanding the reform of the organisational structure and management by trimming the top/leadership level and expanding the lower/cadres level. It also proposed the restricting of CYL scope of activities to merely connecting with youth at the grass-roots level. There is a view that this plan is to cripple CYL's privileged platform of sending

---

[20] "Communist Youth League Entering the 'Reform Period'", *Xinhua News Agency*.
[21] "2016 Departmental Budget of the Communist Youth League Central Committee (gongqingtuan zhongyang 2016 nian bumen yusuan)", Youth.cn, 15 April 2016, <http://www.ccyl.org.cn/notice/201604/t20160415_757233.htm> (accessed 25 October 2017).
[22] "The Communist Youth League Suffers Another Purge, Two Large Financial Sources Removed (Gongqingtuan zaizao zhonggong zhengsu, liangda caiyuan bei wuchang zhuanzou)", DW News, 6 December 2017, <http://news.dwnews.com/china/news/2017-12-06/60028062.html> (accessed 6 December 2017).
[23] Market values sourced from Sina Finance (finance.sina.com.cn).

officials to high-ranking positions in the Party and government.[24] Months before the proposed reforms, a trial had started in the Shanghai provincial committee of CYL to recruit youths from outside CYL as trainees and part-time deputy secretaries.[25] Such measures have been claimed to help increase the diversity and vigour of the CYL and to better connect with the youth. In reality, these measures could dilute internal solidarity, prevent faction formation and clamp down on elitism within CYL.

In April 2017, the Medium- and Long-Term Youth Development Plan (*zhongchangqi qingnian fazhan guihua*) for the period 2016–2025, the first-ever national plan for youth development in China, was published. The plan serves as a specific guideline for the job scope and tasks of CYL. The guidelines are in line with the broader national development plan of improving education, encouraging entrepreneurship and assisting youths in marriage, among others. In effect, it also signifies the exerting of tighter control over CYL and reducing their manoeuvrability in terms of activities.

In May 2017, the CYL lost its channel of nurturing talents. The China Youth University of Political Studies (*zhongguo qingnian zhengzhi xueyuan*), commonly known as the Central School of CYL, announced the termination of its undergraduate programme. A large part of the university has been absorbed into the Chinese Academy of Social Sciences and renamed as the University of Chinese Academy of Social Sciences. Although the Central CYL still keeps part of the school, its activities are restricted to cadre training.[26]

---

[24] He Qinglian, "The Reform of the Communist Youth League AIMS to Restructure the Organisation Line (gongqingtuan gaige yizai gaibian zuzhi luxian)", Voice of America, 6 August 2016, <https://www.voachinese.com/a/heqinglian-china-youth-league-20160805/3452486.html> (accessed 7 September 2017).

[25] "Reform of Shanghai Mass Organisations (shanghai quntuan gaige)", People.cn, 11 May 2016, <http://cpc.people.com.cn/n1/2016/0511/c64387-28340249.html> (accessed 25 October 2017).

[26] "CCP's High-pressure Reform, Suspension of Main Financial Source (zhonggong gaoya zhenggai gongqingtuan, zhuyao caiyuan tingpai)", DN News, 21 November 2017, <http://news.dwnews.com/china/news/2017-11-21/60024949.html> (accessed 22 November 2017).

Reforms at the provincial level include the termination of the degree programmes in 2015 of the Chongqing League School and the Shanghai League School, which used to be a vocational school and a management personnel training school for the youth respectively. The two schools have since served as training bases for local League cadres and think tanks for the local governments.[27]

Struggling for New Roles

With *tuanpai* leaders losing their influence and chances of gaining political power, the CYL as an organisation has to closely align itself with the Party under the leadership of President Xi Jinping. Echoing Xi's criticisms, Chinese Vice President Li Yuanchao, a former member of the Secretariat of CYL Central Committee, has called on the CYL to support and implement decisions and policies made by the Party.[28] Similarly, the Secretariat of CYL Central Committee had also published an article in *People's Daily* to reflect on its areas for improvement and to show its awareness that if nothing has been done to deal with its problems, "the organisation may lose the value of its existence".[29] Such display of loyalty, apart from being political formality, is a struggle for survival by the CYL as it earnestly tries to re-position itself within the party-state system.

---

[27] "Will the China Youth University of Political Studies still Exist after Reform? (zhongyang tuanxiao gaige hou, zhongguo qingnian zhengzhi xueyuan haihui cunzai ma?)", Sina News, 21 November 2017, <http://news.sina.com.cn/c/2017-11-21/doc-ifynvxeh5566345.shtml> (accessed 6 December 2017).

[28] "Li Yuanchao: Carrying out Work Arrangements Made by the Party Central Committee, the Communist Youth League Must Lead at the Front (li yuanchao: guanche zhongyang quntuan gongzuo bushu gongqingtuan yao zouzai qiantou)", Youth.cn, 23 October 2015, <http://news.youth.cn/gn/201510/t20151023_7236063.htm> (accessed 25 October 2017).

[29] "Secretariat of the Communist Youth League Central Committee: Actively and Steadily Deepen the Reform of the Communist Youth League (gongqingtuan zhongyang shuji chu: jiji wentuo di shenhua gongqingtuan gaige)", People.cn, 9 October 2015, <http://dangjian.people.com.cn/n/2015/1009/c117092-27675377.html> (accessed 25 October 2017).

Parenting non-governmental organisations

In recent years, Beijing leaders have revived the traditional Leninist style of non-governmental organisation (NGO) control by placing NGOs under direct party surveillance or turning them into grass-root cells of the Party. NGOs are grouped according to their respective fields and "pivotal organisations" (*shuniu xing shehui zuzh*i) are put into these groups to act as party-state apparatus overseeing the NGOs in their respective fields.[30] These pivotal organisations are usually traditional Party-led mass organisations such as the CYL, Women's Federation and Federation of Trade Unions.[31] The government buys services from, outsources projects to, or offers funds to these pivotal groups which commission the projects or distribute funds to their subordinate organisations. Through these pivotal groups the government is able to regulate and supervise various organisations which become their subordinates at the grass-roots.

Earlier in 2012, Guangdong CYL had already begun to transform itself into a pivotal organisation. It established an "incubation base" for NGOs targeting at youth,[32] which aims to nurture and develop organisations that help tackle problems faced by youth, and promote youth participation in public affairs. In the following year, Zhongshan city of Guangdong also started a trial cooperation effort between Guangdong, Macao and Hong Kong to bring social workers and volunteers together to improve their social services.[33]

---

[30] "What is Pivotal Social Organization (shenme shi shuniu xing shehui zuzhi)", Chinese Ministry of Civil Affairs, <http://www.mca.gov.cn/article/mxht/mtgz/201310/20131000536410.shtml> (accessed 6 December 2017).

[31] Interview, Zhuhai, July 2013.

[32] "Guangdong Communist Youth League Promotes Construction of Social Organisations Hub (Guangdong gongqingtuan litui shuniu xing zuzhi jianshe)", *China Youth Daily*, 24 December 2012, <http://zqb.cyol.com/html/2012-12/24/nw.D110000zgqnb_20121224_2-01.htm> (accessed 26 October 2017).

[33] "Guangdong Zhongshan to Build Pilot 'Social Workers + Volunteers' Cooperation in Guangdong, Macao and Hong Kong (guangdong zhongshan shi nijian yuegangao 'shegong+yigong' hezuo shiyanqu)", *China News*, 6 December 2013, <http://www.chinanews.com/ga/2013/12-06/5589607.shtml> (accessed 26 October 2017).

The CYLs in Beijing and Shanghai adopted a different approach. They have attempted to establish networks for existing youth organisations and put them under direct surveillance. In Beijing, the CYL has gathered about 9,000 NGOs as its subordinate organisations, while the CYL in Shanghai has connected over 500 influential youth organisations. In addition to overseeing daily operation, the CYLs provide NGOs with facilities and accommodation for activities, as well as services such as coordinating various NGOs in a large-scale event.[34]

"Youth Leader" in cyberspace

The CYL has been active on various Chinese social media platforms, especially those frequented by youngsters. It has set up official accounts at the largest social media applications like WeChat and Weibo, and reached out to platforms patronised by youth, including Bilibili, Zhihu and NetEase Cloud Music,[35] tapping on hot topics to attract readers. Eventually, the CYL is able to accumulate increasing number of followers on their different online portals,[36] which then serve as channels for the CYL to launch and publicise other programmes.

China has adopted a two-prong approach to internet control: screening online content through the Great Firewall, establishing control of web companies and other ways of censorship, and proactively guide online public opinion through governmental commentators and pro-government netizens. The CYL has taken a lead role in the latter approach, seeking to guide and mobilise Chinese youth.

---

[34] Wang Peng, "Constructing Pivotal Social Organizations from a State-Society Relations Perspective (guojia yu shehui guanxi shijiao xia de shuniu xing zuzhi jiangou)", *Journal of China Youth University for Political Sciences* (*zhongguo qingnian zhengzhi xueyuan bao*), vol. 5, 2013, pp. 33–39.

[35] Bilibili is a website that shares videos on cartoons, anime and games; Zhihu is a Chinese question-and-answer website an equivalent to Quora; and NetEase Cloud Music provides music and video streaming service.

[36] For instance, the Youth League Central Committee's Weibo account had accumulated 8.88 million followers as of May 2019 and was ranked by *People's Daily* as the second most influential Weibo account on state affairs in 2017.

The League has successfully mobilised a group of young people known as the "Little Pinks" (*xiao fenhong*) who are patriotic and ready to defend the government in cyberspace.[37] The Little Pinks, mostly born in the 1990s, belong to a generation that witnesses China becoming the second largest economy and its "Made in China" products sweeping every corner of the world. They hold a highly positive view of the "China Model" and development path, taking pride in the regime's achievements and deprecating Western political values.[38] They constitute a remarkable group on the Chinese internet, taking collective action in social media to attack people who have slighted China. In January 2016, when Tsai Ing-wen, the pro-independence leader, was elected Taiwan's president, tens of thousands of Little Pinks waged a "memes war" (*biaoqingbao dazhan*). They skirted the Great Firewall and bombarded Tsai's Facebook page with various memes and pro-China messages.[39]

The Central CYL and many provincial/local CYL have set up official accounts on China's largest twitter-like site, Weibo.com, that has

---

[37] The term "Little Pinks" originated from an online forum in Jinjiang Literary City for users to share original writings. As the background of the website was pink and users are mostly female, the nickname of "Little Pinks" was given to refer to the female majority and in reference to the pink background of the homepage of the forum. There is a hidden section on the site for political discussions. The dominant group in the discussion is "patriots" who argue against anyone who holds a negative view of the Chinese government. With time, the patriotic group migrated to other websites to defend the government and the term Little Pinks began to gain ground nationwide. The term now has been generally used on young netizens who have a pro-government political stance and are likely to argue with anyone who disagree with them. Please see <https://finance.yahoo.com/news/face-chinese-nationalism-135154262.html> and <http://www.economist.com/news/china/21704853-online-mobs-get-rowdier-they-also-get-label-east-pink> (accessed 15 December 2017).

[38] "The Release of Big Data on 'Little Pinks' (Xiaofenhong' dashuju fabu)", *Caijing*, 30 December 2016, <http://m.caijing.com.cn/api/show?contentid=4219057&winzoom=1> (accessed 15 December 2017).

[39] "Taiwan President-Elect's Facebook Page Flooded by Chinese Users despite Ban", ABC News, 21 January 2016, <http://www.abc.net.au:80/news/2016-01-21/chinese-facebook-users-flooding-taiwan-president-elect-account/7105228> (accessed 15 December 2017).

attracted millions of followers. Acting as the leaders of Chinese youth, these accounts publicly praised Little Pinks' attack on Tsai's Facebook page and encouraged them to do more for the "motherland". In a recent report, the CYL has defined its Weibo followers as Little Pinks.[40]

The CYL also creates agenda for the Little Pinks to wage internet fights. In July 2016, the CYL's Weibo accounts accused Chinese director Zhao Wei of casting Taiwanese actor Leon Dai, a supporter of Taiwanese Independence, as a lead in her movie. The League's posts ignited Little Pinks' rage, who lashed out at Zhao on the Chinese internet and condemned her as a traitor.[41] Ten days later, Zhao gave in and apologised, promising to remove Dai from the movie cast even though the movie had completed filming.[42] In another case when South Korea decided to deploy the American anti-ballistic missile defence system in 2017, the Little Pinks saw this as an infringement to China's security, and called out for the boycott of the South Korean supermarket chain store Lotte on various social media platforms.[43] The CYL of Jiangxi province added to the tension by releasing on its Weibo account a list of five Lotte departmental stores and 114 Lotte supermarkets all over China, hinting netizens to go on strike in front of the stores.[44] In May 2019 when the Sino-American trade tension was brewing, the CYL released an editorial on its official newspaper *China Youth Daily*, calling all Chinese youths to be united and commenting

---

[40] "The Release of Big Data on 'Little Pinks' (Xiaofenhong' dashuju fabu)", *Caijing*, 30 December 2016, <http://m.caijing.com.cn/api/show?contentid=4219057&winzoom=1> (accessed 15 December 2017).

[41] "Zhao Wei's New Film Provoked Controversy (Zhao Wei xinpian re zhengyi)", BBC, 15 July 2016, <http://www.bbc.com/zhongwen/simp/china/2016/07/160715_zhaowei_film> (accessed 15 December 2017).

[42] "Being Accused of Pro-Independence, Zhao Wei Changed the Lead Actor in her New Movie (zao jubao taidu zhaowei huan xinpian nanzhujue dailiren)", TVB News, 15 July 2016, <https://news.tvbs.com.tw/china/664140> (accessed 2 January 2018).

[43] Discussion threads were created on Weibo.com calling for boycott. Please see <https://www.weibo.com/p/100808e8c877e980461f66175b6e4608fe7551/super_index> (accessed 11 July 2018).

[44] <https://www.weibo.com/ttarticle/p/show?id=2309404080445556924889&sudaref=www.google.com&display=0&retcode=6102> (accessed 28 April 2019).

that the trade friction raged by the United States would only make Chinese youths more confident with their country's independent innovation.[45] This article was reposted on the social media accounts of CYL and stimulated a wave of patriotic sentiments among the followers.

Social services

To further penetrate the daily lives and address the personal concerns of youths, the provincial CYL committees have also begun to organise dating events for them. In May 2016, the Zhejiang provincial branch of CYL began to organise speed dating events for singles, attracting more than a million participants.[46] The Zhejiang CYL has since officially adopted this as part of its work by establishing a "marriage division (*hunlian shiye bu*)". It also organises smaller scale speed dating events in different parts of the province, and even provides dating and marriage courses for youth. The initiative was so successful that CYL branches in other provinces also soon began to organise similar events for youth in their respective region.

In April 2017, CYL collaborated with Suning Commerce Group to construct a Youth Entrepreneurship Park in Nanjing, Jiangsu province.[47] The park is to serve as a training ground and business incubator for young entrepreneurs interested in start-ups related to e-commerce, cultural innovation, video making and more.

The range of social services that the CYL engages in correspond with China's problem of ageing population, the revised two-child policy, youth unemployment and industrial upgrading, indicating CYL's efforts to serve as a more effective support for the national development

---

[45] <https://www.weibo.com/ttarticle/p/show?id=2309404377261317957301> (accessed 30 May 2019).

[46] <http://www.inewsweek.cn/news/special/1275.html> (accessed 4 September 2017).

[47] "The Official Opening of Suning Youth Entrepreneurship Park (suning qingchuangyuan zhengshi kaiyuan 2020 nian shixian fuhua xiangmu chao 200 jia)", *China News*, 10 April 2017, <http://www.chinanews.com/it/2017/04-10/8195511.shtml> (accessed 26 October 2017).

strategy. Meanwhile, CYL as an official organisation is able to utilise its credibility and publicity to attract participants. This could also be seen from the CYL's increasing role among NGOs.

Political Prospects of the Youth League

Since the reform and opening up in the late 1970s, the CYL has never encountered such a crisis that challenges its very "value of existence".[48] *Tuanpai* leaders have fallen from their peak within such a short period. This demonstrates the capricious and precarious side of Chinese elite politics. For observers and researchers on China, when making predictions on the basis of factional politics, this has to be accounted for. Before Xi came to power some observers argue that there would be a de facto bipartisanship dominating Chinese politics because there were two political coalitions balancing one another at the top. One of the coalitions was the *tuanpai* and the other was the leaders from Shanghai and the princelings.[49]

According to this bipartisanship argument, the two dominant factions will end the "vicious power struggle and zero-sum game in which a winner takes all" in that neither side "is willing to, or capable of, defeating the other".[50] What has happened since 2012 has falsified this argument. The CYL faction has been mercilessly shoved away by Xi and his allies now constitute the only dominant faction in the Politburo.

The political prospects of the CYL, in the short run, will be gloomy. It will remain under severe denunciations and continue to be restructured into an organisationally and financially weaker body. Its struggle to find a new role in the party-state system will continue. The *tuanpai*

[48] "Secretariat of the Communist Youth League Central Committee: Actively and Steadily Deepen the Reform of the Communist Youth League" (Gongqingtuan zhongyang shujichu: jiji wentuo di shenhua gongqingtuan gaige)", People.cn, 9 October 2015, <http://dangjian.people.com.cn/n/2015/1009/c117092-27675377.html> (accessed 25 October 2017).

[49] Li Cheng, "One Party, Two Factions: Chinese Bipartisanship in the Making?" (2 November 2005), <http://carnegieendowment.org/files/li.pdf> (accessed 6 December 2017).

[50] Li Cheng, "One Party, Two Factions".

will stay insignificant at least during Xi's office terms. At the top leadership level, the few officials with CYL background can no longer constitute a faction. They have to show, at least apparently, their loyalty to Xi. At the lower level, cadres with CYL experience risk demotions, not to mention enjoy any promotion prospects.

In the long term, however, cadres with CYL experience may return to the centre of the political stage. The CCP still needs the CYL to connect and guide the youth. The rapid economic development has brought value changes among the younger generation.[51] Hence, maintaining support from the youth and co-opting, guiding and controlling the youth will be crucial for regime survival. In this aspect, the CYL can play an important role. As CYL leaders are normally better educated and younger than average cadres, even without the current promotion prospects, they still have their competence and advantage in age. Once the Party relaxes its lash over the League, it stands in good stead to lead again.

---

[51] Shan Wei, "How China's Post-1980 Generation Is Politically Different", *EAI Background Brief*, no. 1279, East Asian Institute, 7 September 2017.

Appendix

List of Chinese Leaders with Former Posts in the Communist Youth League (CYL) (Provincial level and above, 1979–2018)

Name	Highest Position in the Party/State	Highest Position in CYL
Bagatur	Head of State Ethnic Affairs Commission	Secretary of Inner Mongolia, 1986–1992
Bayanqolu	Party secretary of Jilin	Executive secretary of Central Committee Secretariat, 1998–2001
Cai Wu	Minister of Culture	Member of the Central Standing Committee, 1983–1995
Chen Haosu	Vice minister, Ministry of Radio, Film and Television	Member of Central Committee Secretariat, 1981–1983
Chen Xunqiu	Deputy secretary of the Central Political and Legal Affairs Commission	Secretary of Hubei, 1992–1993
Cui Bo	Deputy Party secretary of Ningxia	Member of Central Committee Secretariat, 2001–2003
Du Qinglin	Member of 18th Politburo Secretariat and vice chairman of 11th–12th CPPCC	Deputy secretary of Jilin, 1979–1984
Erkenjan Turahun	Head of the Hubei United Front Work Department	Member of Central Committee Secretariat, 2003–2008
Feng Jun	Head of Tibet Organisation Department	Member of Central Committee Secretariat, 1985–1991
Gao Zhanxiang	Director of the State Ethnic Affairs Commission	Member of Central Committee Secretariat, 1978–1982
Han Changfu	Minister of Agriculture	Director of the Central Committee Youth Peasantry Department, 1990–2001
Han Ying	Party secretary of Shanxi	General secretary, 1978–1982

(Continued)

(Continued)

Name	Highest Position in the Party/State	Highest Position in CYL
Han Zheng	Member of 19th Politburo Standing Committee	Secretary of Shanghai, 1991–1992
He Guangwei	Director of the National Tourism Administration	Member of Central Committee Secretariat, 1981–1986
Hu Chunhua	Member of 18th–19th Politburo and Party secretary of Guangdong	General secretary, 2007–2008
Hu Jintao	General secretary of 16th–17th CPC Central Committee	General secretary, 1984–1985
Hu Qili	Member of 13th Politburo Standing Committee and vice chairman of Ninth CPPCC	Member of Central Committee Secretariat, 1978–1980
Hu Wei	Deputy director of the General Administration of Customs	Member of Central Committee Secretariat, 2001–2005
Huang Danhua	Deputy head of the State-owned Assets Supervision and Administration Commission	Member of Central Committee Secretariat, 1997–2001
Huang Shuxian	Minister of Civil Affairs and deputy secretary of Central Commission for Discipline Inspection	Secretary of Jiangsu, 1985–1989
Ji Bingxuan	Vice chairman of 12th NPC Standing Committee	Member of Central Committee Secretariat, 1993–1995
Ji Lin	Chairman of the Beijing CPPCC	Secretary of Beijing, 1995–1998
Jia Chunwang	Procurator-General	Member of the Central Standing Committee, 1982–1983
Jiang Daming	Minister of Land and Resources	Member of Central Committee Secretariat, 1993–1998
Keyoumu Bawudong	Deputy Party secretary of Xinjiang	Member of Central Committee Secretariat, 1981–1983
Li Bing	Deputy director of the State Information Office	Head of the Worker, Farmer and Youth Department, 1978–1989

Li Gang	Deputy head of the State Overseas Chinese Affairs Office	Head of the Central Committee International Liaison Department, 1984–1993
Li Haifeng	Vice chairman of 12th CPPCC	Member of Central Committee Secretariat, 1978–1985
Li Keqiang	Premier	General secretary, 1993–1998
Li Liguo	Minister of Civil Affairs	Deputy secretary of Liaoning, 1985–1990
Li Ruihuan	Chairman of the 9th CPPCC	Member of Central Committee Secretariat, 1979–1981
Li Yuanchao	Member of 17th-18th Politburo and vice president	Member of Central Committee Secretariat, 1983–1990
Li Zhanshu	Member of 19th Politburo Standing Committee and director of the National Security Commission General Office	Secretary of Hebei, 1986–1990
Ling Jihua	Vice chairman of 12th CPPCC	Director of Central Propaganda Department, 1994–1995
Liu Binjie	Director of the General Administration of Press and Publications	Member of the Central Standing Committee, 1990–1994
Liu Hui	Deputy head of State Ethnic Affairs Commission	Secretary of Ningxia, 1995–1998
Liu Peng	Director and Party secretary of the State General Administration of Sports	Member of Central Committee Secretariat, 1993–1997
Liu Qibao	Member of 18th Politburo, director of the Party Central Publicity Department	Member of Central Committee Secretariat, 1985–1993
Liu Wei	Deputy Party secretary of Shandong	Secretary of Anhui, 1994–1995
Liu Weiming	Vice governor of Guangdong	Member of Central Committee Secretariat, 1978–1982
Liu Yandong	Member of 17th-18th Politburo and vice premier	Executive secretary of Central Committee Secretariat, 1982–1991

(Continued)

(Continued)

Name	Highest Position in the Party/State	Highest Position in CYL
Liu Yunshan	Member of 18th Politburo Standing Committee	Deputy secretary of Inner Mongolia, 1982–1984
Losang Jamcan	Deputy Party secretary of Tibet	Secretary of Tibet, 1986–1992
Lu Hao	Governor of Heilongjiang	General secretary, 2008–2013
Lu Yongzheng	Deputy director of the State Administration of Civil Service	Member of Central Committee Secretariat, 2005–2013
Luo Baoming	Party secretary of Hainan	Secretary of Tianjin, 1985–1992
Luo Zhijun	Party secretary of Jiangsu	Member of the Central Standing Committee, 1990–1995
Meng Xuenong	Deputy secretary of Work Committee for Departments under CPC Central Committee	Deputy secretary of Beijing, 1983–1986
Qian Yunlu	Vice chairman and secretary-general of 11th CPPCC	Secretary of Hubei, 1982–1983
Qiang Wei	Party secretary of Jiangxi	Secretary of Beijing, 1987–1990
Qin Guangrong	Party secretary of Yunnan	Deputy secretary of Hunan, 1984–1987
Qin Yizhi	Deputy director of the General Administration of Quality Supervision, Inspection and Quarantine	General secretary, 2013–2017
Shen Yueyue	Chairman of the All-China Women's Federation	Secretary of Zhejiang, 1991–1993
Song Defu	Party secretary of Fujian	General secretary, 1985–1993
Song Xiuyan	Vice chairman of the All-China Women's Federation	Secretary of Qinghai, 1983–1989
Sun Jiazheng	Vice chairman of 11th CPPCC	Secretary of Jiangsu, 1978–1983
Sun Jinlong	Deputy Party secretary of Xinjiang	Executive secretary of Central Committee Secretariat, 2001–2003

Name		
Wang Jiangong	Deputy Party secretary of Heilongjiang	Member of Central Committee Secretariat, 1981–1983
Wang Lequan	Member of 16th-17th Politburo, deputy secretary of the Central Political and Legal Affairs Commission	Deputy secretary of Shandong, 1982–1986
Wang Minsheng	Deputy director of the Jiangsu Provincial People's Congress Standing Committee	Member of Central Committee Secretariat, 1978–1982
Wang Rulin	Party secretary of Shanxi	Secretary of Jilin, 1987–1991
Wang Sanyun	Party secretary of Gansu	Secretary of Guizhou, 1990–1992
Wang Xiao	Vice governor of Qinghai	Executive secretary of Central Committee Secretariat, 2009–2013
Wang Yang	Member of 19th Politburo Standing Committee and vice premier	Deputy secretary of Anhui, 1983–1984
Wang Zhaoguo	Member of 16th-17th Politburo and vice chairman of 11th NPC Standing Committee	General secretary, 1982–1984
Wu Aiying	Minister of Justice	Deputy secretary of Shandong, 1982–1989
Yang Chuantang	Minister of Transport	Secretary of Shandong, 1987–1992
Yang Jing	Member of 18th Politburo Secretariat; secretary-general of State Council	Secretary of Inner Mongolia, 1993–1996
Yang Yue	Head of United Front Work Department of Jiangsu	Executive secretary of Central Committee Secretariat, 2005–2008
Yuan Chunqing	Deputy head of Central Committee Leading Small Group for Rural Work	Member of Central Committee Secretariat, 1992–1997
Zhang Baoshun	Party secretary of Anhui	Member of Central Committee Secretariat, 1985–1991

(Continued)

(*Continued*)

Name	Highest Position in the **Party/State**	**Highest Position in CYL**
Zhang Jinan	Director of the Central Institutional Organisation Commission General Office	Deputy secretary of Tianjin, 1987–1991
Zhang Qingli	Vice chairman and secretary-general of 12th CPPCC	Deputy head of the Worker, Farmer and Youth Department, 1983–1986
Zhang Xiaolan	Vice chairman of the All-China Women's Federation	Member of Central Committee Secretariat, 2003–2008
Zhao Shi	Deputy director of the State Administration of Press, Publication, Radio, Film and Television	Member of Central Committee Secretariat, 1993–1996
Zhao Yong	Deputy director of the General Administration of Sports	Member of Central Committee Secretariat, 1998–2005
Zhi Shuping	Director of the State Administration of Quality Supervision, Inspection and Quarantine	Secretary of Shanxi, 1990–1994
Zhou Qiang	President of the Supreme Court	General secretary, 1998–2006

Note: Only those who held positions at the level of deputy secretary of provincial CYL or above and those who held positions at the Central CYL are included in the list.

CPPCC stands for Chinese People's Political Consultative Conference.

Sources: Compiled from official resumes, chinavitae.com, wikipedia.org and baike.baidu.com.

Chapter 9

Indigenous Technology as Chinese Modernity

ZHAO Litao*

Over 40 years ago, Wang Gungwu wrote the first history of post-1949 China, a book titled *China and the World since 1949: The Impact of Independence, Modernity and Revolution*. As the subtitle suggests, modernity is one of the key themes for understanding the People's Republic of China and its relationship with the world. Specifically, Wang noted:

> *In Asia, this modernity meant imitating the West, or Westernisation, and many leaders of smaller, economically dependent countries have this in mind when they want to modernize. Thus the Chinese remain in an ambiguous position. They do not deny the modernity of Western technology and may concede the higher economic growth and standard of living produced by superior technology, but seek to avoid subordinating themselves by mere imitation. Part of their fervent quest for independence spills over into the search for the scientific progress which would not require them to acknowledge the superiority of other peoples but only the objective criteria for attaining a higher stage of history. This ambiguity towards the West also derives from China's history, from its perception of its cultural superiority for twenty centuries.*[1]

---

* ZHAO Litao is Senior Research Fellow at the East Asian Institute, National University of Singapore.
[1] Wang Gungwu, *China and the World since 1949: The Impact of Independence, Modernity and Revolution*, New York, St Martin's Press, 1977, pp. 4–5.

China today is moving closer to "a higher stage in history" than any time in modern history. Wang's statement on the Chinese attitude towards modernity remains valid and relevant. The belief in technology as a measure of modernity is the same for the Chinese as for other peoples. Yet the quest for technology has another motivation for the Chinese. Superior technology is also a measure for regaining its lost status, which had been taken for granted for "20 centuries" prior to China's painful encounters with the West since the mid-19th century.

Through the 20th century, this motivation — or "ambiguity towards the West", in Wang's words — did not bother the world very much. China as a technological laggard did not warrant much serious consideration. The late 2010s, however, was a turning point. The quest for technology has not only set the Chinese on the way to realising their dream of national rejuvenation, but also put them on a collision course with hardliners in the United States who come to see the Chinese aspiration to regain their lost status as a threat to American dominance in general and superiority in technology in particular. US measures, in whatever form, are unlikely to see the Chinese backing down in their quest for superior technology, a pursuit they believe could re-claim their lost centrality in the world order.

A Centennial Dream

The Chinese dream of national rejuvenation is widely known as the core agenda for the Xi Jinping leadership. It serves as a rallying call for mobilising the Chinese towards a common goal of restoring China's superior status in the world by the mid-21st century. This dream is widely shared between the Chinese Communist Party (CCP) leadership and the population. In fact, it is a dream of the past, dating back to the mid-19th century as a response to the humiliating encounters with the Western powers.

The earliest thinking was centred on Zhang Zhidong's idea of Chinese learning as the foundation and Western learning for practical use. The emphasis was still on Confucian learning. The decisive shift in favour of Western learning was driven by the shock of defeat in the

Sino-Japanese War of 1894–95. Thereafter "China could no longer maintain even the pretense of its ancient superiority as the center of the East Asian world".[2] With the abolition of imperial examination in 1905 and the imperial system in 1911, the rush to study abroad commenced, in the hope that the cultural and educational models borrowed from Japan, Europe and especially the United States would lead to national salvation.

The dominant approach sought to modernise China by modelling after the systems of the United States and other western powers. The rush to create a new China through this liberal approach, however, had provoked backlashes. The idealistic faith in the Western model had been hard hit when victorious western powers at the end of World War I decided to transfer Germany's special concessions in Shandong province to Japan. The disillusionment with the uncritical imitation of Western ideas and institutions took different forms. Cultural conservatives such as Liang Shuming lashed out that the old is not necessarily bad and the new is not necessarily good. Young Marxists such as Mao Zedong were critical of the growing divide in education between the elite and the mass. Even pro-American liberals such as Tao Xingzhi came to emphasise the need to adapt Western learning to the needs of Chinese society.[3]

The Chinese could not come to a consensus on which part of the Western model and how much of it should be learned and adopted. Competing ideologies are part of the reason. Those holding culturally conservative views are more sceptical of Western learning than those subscribing to the ideas of progress and modernisation. A more fundamental reason, as Wang pointed out, is that the Chinese "seek to avoid subordinating themselves by mere imitation". This attitude towards Western learning is deeply rooted in the Chinese perception of their "cultural superiority for 20 centuries", regardless of their political ideologies in the 20th century.[4]

[2] Suzanne Pepper, *China's Education Reform in the 1980s: Policies, Issues, and Historical Perspectives*, Institute of East Asian Studies, University of California at Berkeley, 1990, p. 10.

[3] Suzanne Pepper, *China's Education Reform in the 1980s*.

[4] Wang Gungwu, *China and the World since 1949*, p. 5.

Seen in this light, the Chinese understanding of modernity has both a consensual component and an ambiguous one. The consensual component is the view on the importance of science and technology for achieving and measuring modernity; the ambiguous component is the way to achieving superior technology and modernity. In this sense, achieving superior technology through the Chinese way or indigenous efforts is much preferred than mere imitation or technology transfer.

Throughout the 20th century, China was lagging behind the technologically advanced nations. Achieving parity with the latter was a distant dream; achieving superior technology through indigenous efforts was more of an inspiration than a practical goal. Into the 21st century, the Chinese have begun to see the hope of a catch-up. In some of the emerging technologies, the chance for China to make a breakthrough is real. This has revived the Chinese dream of national rejuvenation, popularised by Xi Jinping after he became secretary general of the CCP in late 2012.[5] An explicitly stated goal for this Chinese dream is to have a fully developed China by 2049, the 100th anniversary of the founding of the People's Republic. Technology is central to this Chinese dream, for the importance not only in itself, but also to economic and military strengths.

If there is a crucial difference between the Chinese dream in the first half of the 21st century and the one in the 20th century, it has to be the higher demand on "indigenous innovation" for the 21st century Chinese dream. The Chinese have become confident of advancing from a "follower" in technology to a "parallel runner", and further to a "forefront runner" in the world by the mid-21st century. Xi on many occasions has highlighted the importance of "indigenous innovation" on the road to a leading innovation power status. The new development suggests that the Chinese are becoming less ambiguous about Western

---

[5] Xi made his first rejuvenation speech in November 2012, soon after he took power from Hu Jintao. During a high-profile visit to a historical exhibition called "Road to Rejuvenation" at China's National Museum, he explicitly stated that the Chinese dream is to achieve national rejuvenation. See <http://www.xinhuanet.com//politics/2017-11/29/c_1122031311.htm> (accessed 27 May 2019).

learning and the modernity of Western technology. They aspire to achieve superior technology through indigenous efforts rather than mere imitation. In this way, the Chinese can talk about the modernity of *Chinese* technology and the Chinese dream of national rejuvenation can be said to be truly *Chinese*.

This updated Chinese dream faces a growing challenge, not internally but externally. China's pursuit of superiority in emerging technologies is increasingly seen by the United States as a national security threat. The reaction of the Trump administration has broadened and intensified. Not surprisingly, Huawei, China's most globally competitive high-tech company, has become the target of the most severe attacks orchestrated by the Trump administration. If there is no turn around, a prolonged battle in technology between the United States and China is well under way, with profound implications for geopolitics and the global innovation network.

Evolving Approaches to Technology

Despite a strong desire for advanced technology, the state was simply too weak to make substantial and sustained technology effort either in the Qing or Republic period. After the CCP came into power in 1949, there was renewed commitment to technology catch-up. While low- and lower-middle income countries typically expend less than one per cent of GDP (gross domestic product) on research and development (R&D), China's spending was unusually high, averaging 1.4% of GDP from the late 1950s through 1978.[6]

In the 1950s, the Soviet Union was China's technology patron. Through arguably the largest international transfer of technology in world history, China not only gained industrial and military technologies from the Soviet Union, but also reorganised the national innovation system after the Soviet model. Notably, research was separated from teaching. Following the Soviet model, China set up the Academy

---

[6] Barry Naughton, *The Chinese Economy: Adaptation and Growth*, the second edition, Cambridge, Massachusetts, The MIT Press, 2017, p. 368.

of Sciences to undertake natural science research, leaving teaching largely to colleges/universities. Universities were also reorganised. With the exception of a few, most American-style comprehensive universities were split and reorganised by disciplines. Specialisation took precedence over broad-based education in order to produce needed manpower for state-led industrialisation as quickly as possible. The Soviet-inspired thought reform was also carried out to remove the Western/American orientation of Chinese intellectuals.

After the death of Stalin in 1953, the CCP leadership began to problematise over-reliance on the Soviet Union. Premier Zhou Enlai's speech in January 1956 was illustrative. Acknowledging that "China's science and technology are still very backward", Zhou stressed that "we must first discard all servile thinking, which shows a lack of national self-confidence". He separated a right and wrong way to learn from the Soviet Union. The wrong way was "to seek a solution from the Soviet Union to every question, large and small, that arises and to send mostly secondary school graduates rather than scientists, to study in the Soviet. The result would be to remain forever in a state of dependence and imitation". By comparison, the right way was "to make an overall plan that distinguishes between what is essential and urgent and what is not … and to systematically use the latest achievement of Soviet science so as to bring ourselves abreast of Soviet levels as quickly as possible".[7]

After the Sino-Soviet split in the late 1950s, China was forced to turn from dependence on the Soviet Union to *technology autarky*, an approach that lasted into the 1980s. During this period, China tested its first atomic bomb in 1964 and hydrogen bomb in 1967, and successfully launched its first satellite in 1970. The "Two Bombs, One Satellite" project brought much pride to the Chinese. The CCP also used it to legitimise technology autarky. In particular, the practice of "concentrating resources to accomplish great things" (*jizhong liliang ban dashi*) was promoted as an intrinsic advantage of Chinese socialism, while the role of Soviet technology assistance was deliberately downplayed.

---

[7] Cited in Suzanne Pepper, *China's Education Reform in the 1980s*, pp. 43–44.

Despite huge technology effort and remarkable achievement in nuclear and missile technologies, the autarky approach did not work for China. Overall, the gap between China and technological leaders widened. To worsen matters, China was not able to sustain large technology effort with the transition to a market oriented economy. Its government R&D expenditure dropped from about 1.5% of GDP in 1979 to the lowest point of 0.6% in 1994, at or even below the level a low-income country would spend.[8]

From the 1980s through the mid-2000s, China tried different approaches to seek technology from foreign companies. In the 1980s, China sought to acquire technology through *centralised, massive purchases* of industrial machinery. After this expensive approach was abandoned, China turned to *direct negotiation* with multinational corporations (MNCs) for technology transfer. MNCs which are willing to share advanced technologies would enjoy privileged access to China's market. This was essentially a market for technology approach. Overall, it did not work well either.[9]

After Deng Xiaoping's 1992 southern tour, the CCP adopted a much more liberal and *open approach to FDI* (foreign direct investment). The entry of multiple technology suppliers gave China a wider choice of partners and put it in a better bargaining position for technology transfers. More importantly, MNCs played an instrumental role in knitting China into global production networks of high-technology products.[10] Still, China's policymakers were not satisfied. The best expression of the unhappiness was a lament by a former minister of commerce that China must export 100 million shoes or 800 million shirts in exchange for the value of a Boeing aircraft.[11] Into the 2000s, China began to rethink its approach to technology. By this time, the Chinese economy had become much

---

[8] Barry Naughton, *The Chinese Economy*, p. 369.
[9] Barry Naughton, *The Chinese Economy*, p.374.
[10] Barry Naughton, *The Chinese Economy*, p.374.
[11] Taco C R van Someren and Shuhua van Someren-Wang, *Innovative China: Innovation Race between East and West*, Heidelberg, Springer, 2013.

larger and more diversified; its college/university enrolment had overtaken that of the United States to top the world.

China's approach to technology and innovation was about to change again with the leadership succession from Jiang Zemin-Zhu Rongji to Hu Jintao-Wen Jiabao in 2003. The shift was manifested in the Medium- and Long-Term Plan (2006–2020) for Science and Technology Development (MLP), unveiled in 2006 with a clear stated focus on "indigenous technology". This plan signalled the *renaissance of techno-nationalism* in China.[12] Evidently, it was not a return to the autarky approach of the 1960s and 1970s, but a shift towards state activism in the hope of moving up the value chain in the global production networks.

After two decades of retreat from state interventions, China was determined to nurture strategic and emerging industries through government interventions. Starting in 2006, China for the first time had a techno-industrial policy since it embarked on the market-oriented reform in the late 1970s. The MLP designated 16 megaprojects for government priority funding.

State activism in technology accelerated during the global financial crisis of 2008–2009. China announced a plan in 2010 to promote strategic emerging industries (SEIs). Targeting 20 industrial sectors, this SEI programme had significant sectoral overlap with the MLP. Nevertheless, it was more focused on emerging industries with no entrenched technological leaders, motivated by the desire for leapfrog development into the technological frontier. During the global financial crisis of 2008–2009, developed countries including the United States also rolled out their plans to promote certain emerging industries, such as renewable energy and electric vehicles, making China a direct competitor to developed countries in the innovation race.[13]

---

[12] Andrew B Kennedy, "China's Search for Renewable Energy: Pragmatic Techno-nationalism", *Asian Survey*, vol. 53, no. 5, 2013, pp. 909-930.
[13] Barry Naughton, *The Chinese Economy*, p. 382.

Techno-nationalism versus techno-globalism

China's rapid advancement in technology catch-up has aroused growing concerns among foreign companies, business associations and governments. The accusation is focused on the role of the Chinese state in nurturing technologies and industries. Such a role has often been described as techno-nationalism, an approach to technology catch-up and innovation through state intervention and protection. Since China's WTO (World Trade Organisation) accession in 2001, an oft-heard complaint is that of the Chinese government intervening unfairly to nurture national champions at the cost of foreign competitors.[14]

In East Asia, China is not the first nation to be associated with techno-nationalism. In fact, Japan took the lead in industrialising the economy and achieving technology catch-up through state activism, followed by Korea, Taiwan and Singapore. Widely seen as a hallmark of East Asian developmentalism, techno-nationalism features the extensive use of state policies to nurture strategic industries and foster national competitiveness against foreign rivals. The underlying belief is that technology as a fundamental element in national security and power has to be indigenised and nurtured.[15]

In practice, techno-nationalism can take many forms, particularly in relation to FDI. Technology autarky as practised by China in the 1960s and 1970s is an extreme form of techno-nationalism caused by international isolation. There are less extreme variants. Japan and Korea in the 1950s to the 1970s restricted incoming FDI while fostering domestic capabilities. By comparison, the more pragmatic variant combines state activism with openness towards high-technology FDI. Scholars

---

[14] The term "techno-nationalism" was coined in a 1987 article for *The Atlantic* by Robert Reich. He used the term to describe a shift in the American approach to technology, from more global-oriented to more nationalistic, in the 1980s, driven by the need to "protect future American technological breakthroughs from exploitation at the hands of foreigners, especially the Japanese". Robert Reich, "The Rise of Techno-nationalism", *The Atlantic*, May 1987, p. 62.

[15] Richard J Samuels, *Rich Nation, Strong Army: National Security and the Technological Transformation of Japan*, Ithaca, N Y, Cornell University Press, 1994.

have used terms such as "pragmatic techno-nationalism"[16] or "open techno-nationalism"[17] to describe the combination of nationalistic and liberal policies for technology catch-up.

After the 1997 Asian Financial Crisis, the appeal of the developmental state model has dwindled. The advent of globalisation, particularly the emergence of global governance regimes in trade, investment and intellectual property rights, has made it more problematic and difficult for nation-states to nurture strategic industries by manipulating tariffs, restricting market access, forcing technology transfers and providing subsidies.[18] Meanwhile, as global production networks and value chains have emerged to shape how and where innovation occurs and diffuses, techno-globalism has become increasingly fashionable in the media as well as the academic world. From the perspective of techno-globalism, globalisation reduces the effectiveness of national policies for organising and fostering technological advance, and hence the relevance of techno-nationalism.[19]

Techno-globalism and techno-nationalism are not necessarily mutually exclusive. However, the emergence of techno-globalism creates a new set of dynamics and conditions to which the pragmatic or open variant of techno-nationalism has to adapt. This is where China has run into problems in recent years. After Xi Jinping became the CCP's general secretary in November 2012 and the country's president in March 2013, there have been lopsided references to "indigenous innovation", even though China's high-tech companies have

---

[16] Andrew B Kennedy, "China's Search for Renewable Energy: Pragmatic Techno-nationalism".

[17] David Kang and Adam Segal (2006), "The Siren Song of Techno-nationalism", *Far Eastern Economic Review*, vol. 169, Issue 2, 2006, pp. 5–11.

[18] Toby Carroll and Darryl S L Jarvis (eds.), *Asia after the Developmental State: Disembedding Autonomy*. Cambridge, UK, Cambridge University Press, 2017.

[19] Daniele Archibugi and Jonathan Michie, "The Globalisation of Technology: A New Taxonomy", *Cambridge Journal of Economics*, vol. 19, 1995, pp. 121–140; Sandro Montresor, "Techno-globalism, Techno-nationalism and Technological systems: Organizing the Evidence", *Technovation*, vol. 21, 2001, pp. 399–412.

benefitted from foreign partners in joint ventures and/or the integration into global supply chains.

Xi has talked about science and technology (S&T) innovation on many occasions. The Central Committee of the Communist Party of China's Party Literature Research Office (*Zhongyang Wenxian Yanjiu Shi*) has even edited and published a Chinese book titled, "Excerpts of Xi Jinping's Remarks on Science and Technology Innovation". To him, technology and the Chinese dream of national rejuvenation are closely linked. In July 2013, a few months after he became state president, Xi visited the Chinese Academy of Sciences. He urged Chinese scientists to serve the homeland and to benefit the people, to apply their scientific results to the modernisation of the country and to combine their own aspiration with the Chinese dream — the rejuvenation of the country.

On 30 September 2013, the Politburo of the 18th CCP Central Committee held its ninth group study session at Beijing's Zhongguancun Science Park, the first ever held outside the CCP's Zhongnanhai headquarters. Xi reflected on why China was defeated many times in modern history. He pointed to scientific backwardness as an explanation for Western and Japanese domination over China. Xi reiterated this point when he addressed the National Conference on Science and Technology in June 2014. He noted that while the Qing emperor Kangxi invited Jesuit missionaries to lecture on astronomy, mathematics and other subjects, the interest was not sustained in subsequent generations. He further added, "Science and technology are the foundation of national strength and prosperity, and innovation is the soul of national advance. In a certain sense, scientific and technological strength determines changes in the world's balance of political and economic power, and determines the fate of every nation".[20]

Xi is not the first Chinese leader to promote the idea of indigenous innovation. What is remarkable is that his emphasis on indigenous innovation has gone hand in hand with his aspiration for China playing

---

[20] Cited from Chris Buckley, "Xi Urges Greater Innovation in 'Core Technologies'", 10 June 2014, <http://sinosphere.blogs.nytimes.com/2014/06/10/xi-urges-greater-innovation-in-core-technologies/?_r=0> (accessed 31 May 2016).

a bigger role in setting rules and standards for global S&T innovation. At the 2014 National Conference on Science and Technology, Xi emphatically pointed out, "On the traditional competition field of international development, the rules were set by other people. To seize the great opportunities in the new scientific-technological revolution and industrial transformation, we must enter early while the new competition field is being built, or even dominate some of the competition field construction, so we become a major designer of the new rules of competition and a leader in the new field".[21]

Evidently, Xi prefers the approach of "top-level design" (*dingceng sheji*) and the practice of "concentrating resources to accomplish great things". In his speech at the 2014 National Conference on Science and Technology, Xi stressed that China "should accelerate the top-level design for the innovation-driven development strategy, and should have a roadmap and timetable for important tasks".[22] Addressing the 2016 National Conference on Science and Technology, he said, "Our biggest advantage is that we, as a socialist country, can pool resources in a major mission".[23]

Policy-wise, Xi has inherited Hu-Wen's active state intervention approach, albeit on a much larger scale. A new wave of techno-industrial policies has been rolled out since 2015. The most prominent and the most disliked by the United States is "Made in China 2025". This plan seeks to upgrade China's manufacturing industry and create globally competitive "smart factories".[24] Made in China 2025 was inspired by the industrial West. In particular, Germany's

---

[21] Chris Buckley, "Xi Urges Greater Innovation".

[22] <http://news.xinhuanet.com/politics/2016-02/29/c_128761312.htm> (accessed 31 May 2016).

[23] <http://www.chinadaily.com.cn/china/2016-05/31/content_25542620.htm> (accessed 31 May 2016).

[24] Made in China 2025 is a comprehensive plan that targets 10 key technologies: new-generation information technology, high-end computerised machines and robots, space and aviation, maritime equipment and high-tech chips, advanced railway transportation equipment, new energy and energy-saving vehicles, energy equipment, agricultural machines, new materials, and biopharma and high-tech medical devices.

"Industry 4.0" and America's "Industrial Internet" have provided the conceptual framework for Made in China 2025.[25]

It is the Chinese way of pursuing "smart manufacturing", "industry 4.0" or "industrial internet" that worries the Western governments and business associations. The level of state backing in other countries is nowhere near that of China. To support Made in China 2025, China has established Advanced Manufacturing Fund (*guojia xianjin zhizao chanye jijin*). The central government, state-owned investment corporations, state-owned banks and local governments have provided RMB20 billion to the fund. By comparison, the German government has provided only about €200 million (about RMB1.5 billion) for its Industry 4.0 programme. China has also set up other funds for the development of smart manufacturing technologies. National IC Fund (*guojia jicheng dianlu chanye touzi jijin*) and the Emerging Industrial Investment Guidance Fund (*guojia xinxing chanye chuangye touzi yindao jijin*), with RMB139 billion and RMB40 billion respectively at their disposal, overshadowing even Advanced Manufacturing Fund in terms of capital size.[26]

Made in China 2025 has not only strong state backing, but also a strong emphasis on "indigenous innovation". An explicitly stated goal is to raise the domestic market share of Chinese suppliers for "basic core components and important basic materials" to 70%.[27] Understandably, the aim of substituting Chinese technology for foreign technology is a big concern for Western governments and MNCs. Overall, techno-nationalism as a particular approach to technology has been further strengthened. Under Xi, techno-industrial policies have proliferated

---

[25] The Chinese Academy of Engineering borrowed ideas and concepts from Germany's Industry 4.0 Strategy when drafting its "Manufacturing Superpower" report in 2013. The report served as a scientific foundation for the formulation of Made in China 2025. Chinese leaders including Xi Jinping and Li Keqiang have shown strong interest in Germany's Industry 4.0. See Jost Wubbeke, Mirjam Meissner, Max J Zenglein, Jaqueline Ives and Bjorn Conrad, "Made in China 2025: The Making of a High-Tech Superpower and Consequences for Industrial Countries", *MERICS Papers on China*, no. 2, Mercator Institute for China Studies, Germany, 2016.

[26] Wubbeke *et al.*, "Made in China 2025", p. 23.

[27] Wubbeke *et al.*, "Made in China 2025", p. 20.

and government funding for technology catch-up and innovation have reached an unprecedented level, making the motivation of technology substitution amply clear.

The US Reaction

Prior to the Trump administration, most trade and investment-related disputes between the United States and China had been settled through negotiations and compromises without escalating into a crisis. The current US President Donald Trump takes a different approach, often dealing blows to Chinese exports and companies in ways that Chinese leaders had not expected. He has used the threat of tariff hikes and sanctions to coerce concessions from the Chinese side since 2018. Remarkably, the threat has become real in many cases. Trump's leadership style aside, US-China relationship has entered a new era. Hawkish voices now dominate the Trump administration and the US congress to portray China as the top rival in the high-technology race and more broadly, in global affairs and the world order.

To Trump, trade and technology issues should be dealt with together. In particular, he singled out Made in China 2025, arguing that the plan unfairly disadvantages US companies. Trump has explicitly stated that the proposed US tariffs are designed to impede Made in China 2025.[28] From the US perspective, China has forced US companies operating in China to transfer technologies and intellectual property, and stolen American trade secrets. Made in China 2025 further disadvantages US companies in advanced manufacturing as their Chinese counterparts have the support of massive government investment and subsidies that would help the country leapfrog from "Industry 2.0" to "Industry 4.0".[29]

---

[28] <https://www.washingtonpost.com/news/monkey-cage/wp/2018/05/03/what-is-made-in-china-2025-and-why-is-it-a-threat-to-trumps-trade-goals/?noredirect=on&utm_term=.a2793e5c326f> (accessed 28 September 2018).

[29] "Industry 1.0" refers to the first industrial revolution in the late 18th century, characterised by mechanical production driven by steam and water power; "Industry 2.0" denotes the second industrial revolution in the late 19th century, featuring electrification of machines and mass production; "Industry 3.0" represents the third industrial revolution

From a comparative perspective, using state intervention to nurture strategic industries is not unique to China. East Asian developmental states had extensively used it before, so did the industrial West, including the United States, which had used state intervention and protectionist policies to grow infant industries at the early stages of development.[30] Countries worldwide are rolling out industrial and innovation policies. United Nations Conference on Trade and Development (UNCTAD) World Investment Report 2018 concludes that "industrial policies have become ubiquitous". Over the past decade, at least 101 economies across the developed and developing world (accounting for more than 90% of global GDP) have adopted formal industrial development strategies. The trend has accelerated in the past five years.[31]

Trump takes issues with Made in China 2025 not because techno-industrial policies are unique to China. The real concern, as some analysts point out, is that "China is becoming less complementary to the United States and more directly competitive".[32] Behind Trump's threat and actual use of tariff hikes and sanctions is the concern that the United States is losing its technological edge to China, even though such a concern seems to have seriously underestimated US innovation capability while exaggerating the extent of the Chinese threat.

Citing national security as the reason, the Trump administration is considering rules that would bar companies with 25% or more Chinese

---

in the 1970s, featuring industrial robots, programmable logic controllers and IT-based production management. The forthcoming "Industry 4.0" is characterised by the combination of automation and digitisation in industrial production and organisation. See Wubbeke *et al.*, "Made in China 2025".

[30] <https://www.washingtonpost.com/news/monkey-cage/wp/2018/05/03/what-is-made-in-china-2025-and-why-is-it-a-threat-to-trumps-trade-goals/?noredirect=on&utm_term=.a2793e5c326f> (accessed 28 September 2018).

[31] UNCTAD, *World Investment Report*, New York and Geneva, United Nations, 2018. <https://unctad.org/en/PublicationsLibrary/wir2018_en.pdf> (accessed 28 September 2018).

[32] <https://www.bloomberg.com/news/articles/2018-04-10/how-made-in-china-2025-frames-trump-strade-threats-quicktake> (accessed 28 September 2018).

ownership from acquiring US firms with "industrially significant technology". Chinese students in American universities, US-based scientists/scholars participating in China's talent schemes and programmes of academic cooperation and exchanges will also undergo stricter national security scrutiny. The US National Intelligence Council warned that these programmes serve to "facilitate the legal and illicit transfer of US technology, intellectual property and know-how" to China.[33] US-China Economic and Security Review Commission has made suggestions to prohibit participants in the programme from "receiving future federal support in terms of grants, loans or other assistance" and require universities receiving federal support to "report on any cooperative research programs or exchanges in the science and technology arena with Chinese-funded entities".[34]

Sanctions through technology ban are a preferred approach adopted by the Trump administration. In April 2018, US Commerce Department banned ZTE, China's second largest telecom equipment manufacturer after Huawei, for seven years from purchasing components from American suppliers. The ban forced ZTE to suspend major operations within weeks. Evidently Trump did not want to go that far as he directed Commerce to work out a deal that would allow ZTE to stay in business. In June 2018, the ban was lifted, but ZTE had to pay a US$1 billion fine (plus US$400 million in escrow in the event of future violations), replace the entire board of directors and establish a special compliance unit onsite. The deal sent a strong message that the United States has the ability to deter its competitors from violating US rules. As US Commerce Secretary Wilbur Ross remarked in a statement, the settlement sets a "new standard for the protection of American technology" as "removal of the directors and executives will have a deterrent

[33] <https://www.bloomberg.com/news/articles/2018-06-22/china-s-thousand-talents-called-key-in-seizing-us-expertise> (accessed 28 September 2018).
[34] Michael Wessel, "Prepared Testimony before the joint Oversight and Research and Technology Subcommittees House Science, Space and Technology Committee", 11 April 2018, <https://docs.house.gov/meetings/SY/SY21/20180411/108175/HHRG-115-SY21-Wstate-WesselM-20180411.pdf> (accessed 28 September 2018).

effect on other individuals at ZTE and elsewhere, by showing that violative behavior has consequences for the individuals involved".[35]

The target of sanction in 2019 shifted to Huawei, the World's No.1 telecom supplier and No. 2 smart phone maker. On 15 May, Trump declared a national emergency over threats against American technology. The executive order led the US Commerce Department to add Huawei and its affiliates to the Bureau of Industry and Security (BIS) Entity List, effectively blocking the Chinese telecom giant from accessing components and services that contain critical US technologies.[36] This move was preceded by a series of other measures against Huawei. With varying degrees of success, the Trump administration had urged allies around the world not to adopt Huawei's 5G network technology, citing cyberespionage of the Chinese government as the reason. Complying with Trump's executive order, chipmakers Intel, Qualcomm, Xilinx and Broadcom decided to cut off their supply to Huawei; Google followed suit by blocking Huawei from using Android operating system and apps in its devices; chip designer Arm, the SD Association and Wi-Fi Alliance subsequently joined to sever links with Huawei.

In sharp contrast to ZTE's full compliance with US demands, Huawei took a different approach. It denied US accusation that it is controlled by the Chinese government, military or intelligence services. It also rejected the allegation of intellectual property theft. In an interview conducted in late May 2019, Huawei founder Ren Zhengfei highlighted a two-year lead Huawei has built over its competitors in the 5G technology. He was quoted as saying, "The US has not developed that technology, so from where should I steal it? We are leading the US. If we were behind, Trump would not need to make so many efforts to

---

[35] <https://www.wsj.com/articles/zte-replaces-board-to-push-trump-deal-closer-1530281683> (accessed 28 September 2018).

[36] The US Commerce Department issued a temporary general licence on 20 May for Huawei and other affected companies to deal with Trump's executive order. The licence, to last until 19 August 2019, would also give the US Commerce Department sufficient time to assess its future measures.

attack us".[37] In this interview, Ren stressed that "there is no need for negotiation". Instead, Huawei's plan was to either ramp up its chip supply or find alternatives to stay ahead in smartphones and 5G.[38]

The ZTE Way or the Huawei Way?

The two cases involving China's two largest telecom companies represent two different ways of dealing with US demands. The ZTE case suggests that disputes can be settled. To the United States, it is a perfect model of dispute resolution. It shows that sanctions really work to bring about the intended changes. To the satisfaction of the Trump administration, "the most powerful man at ZTE" now is a former US Federal Prosecutor dispatched by the US Department of Commerce on 24 August 2018 as the special compliance coordinator, who has "sweeping authority over the business" of ZTE.[39] To ZTE, the new deal allows it to operate without the threat of further sanction. The key to this pattern of dispute resolution is ZTE's full compliance with US demands.

The Huawei case represents a totally different way. Huawei denies US accusations and does not see any need for negotiation. US sanctions fail to win Huawei's concession, but if success is measured by the disruption of Huawei's technology supply, Trump's executive order certainly has achieved immediate results. The future of Huawei looks more uncertain than ZTE. US technology ban may prove devastating for Huawei, or that Huawei will survive or even thrive by rolling out its own technology and reconfiguring the supply chain.

---

[37] <https://www.channelnewsasia.com/news/business/huawei-founder-ren-zhengfei-oppose-chinese-retaliation-apple-11567966?cid=h3_referral_inarticlelinks_24082018_cna> (accessed 29 May 2019).

[38] <https://www.channelnewsasia.com/news/business/huawei-founder-ren-zhengfei-oppose-chinese-retaliation-apple-11567966?cid=h3_referral_inarticlelinks_24082018_cna> (accessed 29 May 2019).

[39] <https://www.scmp.com/tech/enterprises/article/2163938/meet-legal-watchdog-whos-keeping-zte-line-us-export-control-laws> (accessed 14 September 2018).

Which way the CCP leadership is likely to take in dealing with the US-China relationship? Undoubtedly, the ZTE way is too subservient to be acceptable as a national strategy. It would lead to an unequal power relationship, which the Chinese aspiration for national rejuvenation will seek to avoid in the first place. By comparison, the Huawei way combines indigenous innovation with an open attitude towards non-US technology supply. Essentially, the Huawei way epitomises the model of pragmatic/open techno-nationalism.

By all signs, Xi is in favour of the Huawei way. On 26 April 2018, 10 days after US Commerce Department banned ZTE from buying American components, Xi Jinping toured a chip manufacturing plant and other high-tech firms in Wuhan. Stressing that "core technologies should be in our own hands", he urged Chinese scientists to "discard illusions, and rely on our own efforts".[40] One week later, China announced a second round of fund-raising — up to RMB150-200 billion — for the National Integrated Circuit Investment Fund, more than doubling the overall size of the fund.[41] During this visit, Xi reiterated the advantage of socialism for innovation, which is the ability to "concentrate resources to accomplish great things". His stance did not soften amidst the escalating trade war, even though the State Council was preparing to cut import tariffs on a wide range of goods including machinery, paper, textiles and construction materials.

On 20 May 2019, within one week of Trump's executive order targeting Huawei, Xi toured one of China's major rare earths mining and processing facilities in Jiangxi province, and paid respect to a monument in Yudu, a county in Jiangxi, marking the start of the CCP's Long March 85 years ago. He was accompanied by Vice-Premier Liu He, China's top trade negotiator with the United States. Xi's visit was highly symbolic, sending a strong message that the "Long March" spirit of

---

[40] <http://cjrb.cjn.cn/html/2018-05/01/content_72028.htm> (accessed 1 October 2018).

[41] See Barry Naughton "Economic Policy under Trade War Conditions: Can China Move beyond Tit for Tat?" 2018, <https://www.hoover.org/research/economic-policy-under-trade-war-conditions-canchina-move-beyond-tit-tat> (accessed 28 September 2018).

endurance is needed amid the heightened trade and technology tensions, and inviting speculations that China can use rare earths as a bargaining chip in the technology stand-off with the United States. Indeed, Xi reiterated the importance of technology self-reliance. Reportedly he said, "Technological innovation is the root of life for businesses. Only if we own our own intellectual property and core technologies, then can we produce products with core competitiveness and [we] won't be beaten in intensifying competition".[42]

China-US relationship is a state-to-state one. It is fundamentally different from the relationship between a Chinese firm — ZTE or Huawei — and the US Commerce Department. Nonetheless, Xi's (indirect) response to US sanctions on ZTE in 2018 and on Huawei in 2019 illustrates that the CCP leadership does not accept any deal that would subject China to an inferior position in the newest wave of high-tech race. In this light, China is unlikely to take the ZTE way, even though it surely leads to a quick dispute resolution. The Huawei way is full of uncertainties, but it upholds the principle of independence. To the CCP leadership, no deal is better than an unequal deal.

A Looming Large Clash

History does not provide clues to the future of the China-US relationship. However, by drawing lessons from the past, it is clear that US policymakers have an entrenched view of superior technology as the foundation of national security. This view led the United States to a fierce race in space technology with the former Soviet Union and massive investment in education and innovation in response to the "Sputnik crisis", triggered by the Soviet's launch of Sputnik 1 in October 1957, the world's first artificial satellite. It also led the United States to see Japan as the top rival in the 1990s, even though Japan has been a US ally since the post-World War II period. The Clinton

---

[42] <https://www.scmp.com/news/china/politics/article/3011388/xi-jinping-calls-self-reliance-china-grapples-long-term-us> (accessed 29 May 2019).

administration was unusually harsh on Japan in the first term.[43] By the late 2010s, China had become the top rival.

The US-Soviet rivalry ended with the collapse of the Soviet Union and unambiguous triumph for the United States. The US-Japan rivalry was not only much more limited, but also short-lived. Japan continued to depend on the United States for security guarantee; its economy entered a prolonged recession — in fact, the worst since the 1920s — after the bursting of the country's asset bubbles in the late 1980s. Japanese woes amplified in the 1990s. Its telecom industry bet wrongly on "competency enhancing" technologies and fell behind in developing the burgeoning "disruptive" technologies.[44] By contrast, the United States regained confidence by leading the internet revolution and trailblazing the information and communication technologies. Amazons and Google were founded, and Apple was reborn. US fear of losing to Japan dissipated. Japan began to fade from the radar screen of American policymakers, starting from the second term of the Clinton administration.[45] US-Japan rivalry was settled when the United States dominated the new international technological order in the 1990s.

How will the US-China rivalry play out? It is unlikely to be a replication of the US-Soviet rivalry. Today's China is not another Soviet Union in the Cold War era. Despite Xi's repeated references to "self-reliance" and "indigenous technologies", China has more options other than autarky, a prevailing approach to technology in the 1960s and 1970s when China was cut off from international suppliers of technology. China has learned to adapt "techno-nationalism" to the new trend of "techno-globalism" since the 1990s. Unlike the former Soviet Union, China's quest for "indigenous technologies" is motivated by national security and renaissance rather than hegemonic domination.

---

[43] John Kunkel, *America's Trade Policy Towards Japan: Demanding Results*, London and New York, Routledge, 2003.

[44] Robert E Cole, "The Telecommunication Industry: A Turnaround in Japan's Global Presence", in D Hugh Whittaker and Robert E Cole (eds.), *Recovering from Success: Innovation and Technology Management in Japan*, Oxford, Oxford University Press, 2006, pp. 31–46.

[45] John Kunkel, *America's Trade Policy Towards Japan*.

Its economy is much more diversified in terms of ownership, much less reliant on heavy industries and defence industries, and more integrated into the world economy; its society is much more entrepreneurial. A replication of the US-Soviet rivalry is least likely to occur.

Where high-tech race is concerned, a replication of the US-Japan rivalry cannot be ruled out. This scenario depends on the United States emerging from the current wave of techno-industrial revolution as a clear winner. Its confidence level hinges on how its research labs and high-tech firms perform in emerging technologies such as artificial intelligence (AI), 5G, big data analytics and so on. If China's breakthrough is limited to some niche technologies while the United States can replicate its earlier success, the US fear of losing to China will dissipate. For the US-China high-tech rivalry to resemble the US-Japan one, the new international technological order has to re-establish the United States as the unrivalled leader.[46] This scenario, while preserving the status quo, is not particularly inspiring for the Chinese. They desire for much broader successes and breakthroughs.

Another scenario, suggested by some analysts, is that the United States and China head towards disengagement as a result of the escalating trade and technology war. As far as technological relationship is concerned, the United States and China are never closely engaged. The United States has never been a wholehearted supporter of China's technology catch-up. China has always been blocked from access to core technologies protected by the United States and its allies. In fact, the only disengagement China had gone through is the Sino-Soviet split that occurred in the late 1950s. Prior to this split, China had gained much-needed military and industrial technologies from the Soviet Union. However, the relationship between the two went sour and the largest technology transfer in world history ended. Without alternative suppliers, China turned to autarky in the 1960s and 1970s. In comparison, the US-China technological relationship has never

---

[46] China of course differs from Japan in important aspects. China's technological gap with the United States is much larger than the Japan-US gap in the 1980s. By and large China is still a country of "industry 2.0". See Jost Wubbeke *et al.*, "Made in China 2025".

been as close as the Sino-Soviet one in the 1950s. Without engagement in the first place, the China-US high-tech rivalry is heading for more trouble, but not disengagement.

The most desired scenario, from the Chinese perspective, is to achieve superior technology through its own efforts. The Chinese dream of national rejuvenation requires the attainment of Chinese supremacy in technology. US sanctions and technology ban will create a less accommodative innovation environment for the Chinese, but will not stop the Chinese from pursuing superior technology. Building on the remarkable progress made in technology catch-up in the past decades, the Chinese will continue to "concentrate resources to accomplish great things". Of course, competition at the technological frontiers is different from technology catch-up. In this regard, the Chinese innovation system has yet to prove itself, despite the roadmap set to move China from the position of a "follower" to a "frontrunner" in the next 30 years.

Chapter 10

The Use of History in Divided China: Diverging Reappraisals of the Kuomintang in Mainland China and Taiwan

QI Dongtao and Ryan HO*

"The oneness of China is the norm. Periods of division are aberrations. This is how Chinese thinkers, leaders, and ultimately the majority of Chinese people have regarded Chinese politics and history for more than 2,000 years".

Wang Gungwu (2007)[1]

Introduction

Professor Wang Gungwu, a historian with both a local and international reputation, has written extensively and contributed greatly to the study of Chinese history in general. Three of Professor Wang's scholarly works have inspired our research, which focus on the diverging reappraisals of the Kuomintang's (KMT) history in mainland China and in Taiwan. Firstly, in *The Use of History* (1968), Professor Wang high-

* QI Dongtao is Research Fellow at the East Asian Institute, National University of Singapore. Ryan HO is Research Assistant with the same institute.
[1] Wang Gungwu, "Preface to the Second Edition" in *Divided China: Preparing for Reunification 883–947*, Singapore, World Scientific Publishing, 2007, p. 1.

lighted that imperfect historical data could be presented in the form of propaganda and subject to different interpretations as it is easy to make history sound simple as well as emotionally appealing.[2] The use of history as propaganda for political purposes has been prevalent in both the Chinese Communist Party's (CCP) reappraisal of the KMT's history in mainland China and the Democratic Progressive Party's (DPP) reappraisal of KMT's history in Taiwan. Secondly, Professor Wang's concept of restoration nationalism in China in *Another China Cycle: Committing to Reform* (2014) also draws our attention to Taiwan's *Qujianghua* (De-Chiang Kai-shek) movement since the 1990s, which has been an important component of both the reappraisal of the KMT and Taiwanese nationalism. Professor Wang argues that the most common face of China's restoration nationalism concerns questions of polity and stresses the recovery of sovereignty, unification of divided territory and national self-respect. Therefore, the Taiwan issue, or in other words, the divided-China issue, is central to the idea of restoration nationalism. The rise of Taiwanese nationalism, as manifested partly by *Qujianghua* and reappraisal of the KMT in Taiwan, does not identify itself with China and poses a threat to the Mainland's version of nationalism. Finally, in *Divided China: Preparing for Reunification 883–947,* Professor Wang argued that "the ability to restore the civilizational idea of an undivided norm is still the key to legitimacy, which is why issues like uniting Taiwan with the mainland today have become new kinds of dominant symbols".[3] This chapter posits that mainland China's reappraisal of the KMT's history in China, especially its contribution alongside the CCP during the war against Japan, is one of the ways the current government in Beijing is using to restore the civilisational idea of an undivided China. A case study of the diverging reappraisals of the KMT's history in mainland China and Taiwan, which embodies Professor Wang's arguments in these three works, would be the focus of this chapter.

---

[2] Wang Gungwu, *The Use Of History*, Ohio, Ohio University Centre for International Studies, 1968, p. 5.
[3] Wang Gungwu, "Preface to the Second Edition", in *Divided China*, p. 1.

The Chinese Communist Party's View of KMT Wartime History from 1949 to the 1980s

After winning the civil war and the establishment of the People's Republic of China (PRC), the CCP sought to remove all vestiges of the KMT in China. For a long time, KMT history and its leadership were portrayed in a very bad light in China. However, following the coming into power of the pro-independence DPP in Taiwan since the 2000s, the CCP has taken the bold step of officially reappraising certain aspects of KMT's history on the Mainland that fits the party's official narrative. The reappraisal is to emphasise the national unity between the KMT and the CCP during the war. It has reduced the decades of hostility between the KMT and the CCP, paving the way for the rehabilitation of the relationship between the two parties in recent times.

The CCP's portrayal of the KMT in its official history can be classified into a few distinct phases.[4] From 1949 to the late 1970s, the KMT was viewed as an enemy of the Chinese people and its wartime role against Japan was downplayed. However, starting from the 1980s, KMT's role in the war against Japan had been presented in a more positive light. During the Mao era, a Marxist-Leninist view of history was propagated. The focus on modern Chinese history in the 20th century was portrayed as a 'class struggle' led by the CCP against the KMT, in which the CCP represented the working class, farmers and all the other exploited and repressed classes, while the KMT represented the capitalists and all the other exploitive and repressive ones.

Of the few official commentaries that were on the war against Japan, all tended to portray the CCP as pioneers of the war effort. Chiang Kai-shek, the KMT leader, was depicted as an enemy of the people (*renmin gongdi jiang jieshi*) and the KMT was labelled as a running dog of the American imperialists (*meidi de zougou*). In the mid-1980s, the

---

[4] Zhang Qiang and Robert Weatherly, "Owning up to the Past: The KMT's Role in the War against Japan and the Impact on CCP Legitimacy", *The Pacific Review*, vol. 26, no. 3, February 2013, p. 221.

CCP began its first steps to modify its official historiography of the KMT. KMT General Zhang Zizhong who died fighting the Japanese at Yichang in 1940 was posthumously awarded the title of 'revolutionary martyr' in 1982.[5] General Li Zongren was also acknowledged by the CCP for his leading role in the victorious 1938 Battle of Taierzhuang. However, both cases were just symbolic steps in the reappraisal of KMT history by the CCP as both Zhang and Li were not within the inner circle of the KMT and Chiang Kai-shek. The CCP continued to place Chiang and the central leadership of the KMT in a bad light in its official party history.

CCP's Partial Reappraisal of KMT's Wartime History during Hu and Xi

In recent years, the evaluation of the KMT and its central leadership by the CCP has changed markedly. Former Chinese President Hu Jintao and his successor Xi Jinping have officially acknowledged KMT's role in the war against Japan, in contrast to the widely held party line that only stressed the contributions of the CCP and downplayed KMT's role in the war. At the 2005 China Victory Day Parade, CCP leader Hu Jintao affirmed that the war against Japan was led by KMT leader Chiang Kai-shek. Hu also asserted that the KMT and the CCP worked hand in hand during the war. While the KMT army faced the Japanese army in large-scale battles in Shanghai, Xuzhou and Wuhan, the CCP engaged the Japanese army in occupied areas.[6] Since then, high school history textbooks have undergone a revision, attributing the victory against Japan to KMT-CCP cooperation, with the former leading in "front line battles" and the latter in "enemy occupied areas".

---

[5] Arthur Waldron, "China's New Remembering of World War II: The Case of Zhang Zizhong", *Modern Asian Studies,* vol. 30, Issue 4, October 1996, p. 945.

[6] "Hu Jintao Affirms the Positive Role of the KMT in the Major Battles during the Anti-Japanese War" (Hu Jintao kending Guomindang kangri zhengmian zhanchang gongxian da), <http://news.sina.com.cn/c/2005-09-07/04516878935s.shtml> (accessed 3 April 2018).

After Xi Jinping assumed office, the recognition of KMT's role in the war against Japan has gone even further. In 2013, the Chinese government announced that KMT veterans of the war would be eligible to collect pensions. In 2014, the Ministry of Civil Affairs released a list of 300 newly acknowledged martyrs in the war, one third of whom were reportedly former KMT soldiers.[7] In 2015, the invitation to attend the China Victory Day Parade was extended to KMT veterans. For many decades in China, KMT veterans were not recognised for their efforts in World War II (WWII) due to the political conflict between the KMT and the CCP. Many of these veterans had also participated in anti-communist campaigns of the KMT during the 1930s and sided with the KMT during the Chinese Civil War (1946–1949). This symbolic act by Beijing in 2015 marked a dramatic turn from decades of non-recognition by the Chinese government. On 17 January 2018, four days after the 30th anniversary of the passing of former KMT leader Chiang Ching-Kuo (Chiang Kai-shek's son), spokesman of the Taiwan Affairs Office of the State Council of the PRC Ma Xiaoguang praised the younger Chiang as a leader who "firmly opposed Taiwanese independence and worked for national reunification".[8] This was one of the clearest signs of a CCP re-evaluation of KMT history and its past leadership.

However, not all aspects of KMT's history have been rehabilitated in China. The various anti-communist campaigns of the KMT during the 1920s and 1930s are still portrayed in a bad light in CCP's official history records. Xi Jinping's speech at the 90th anniversary of the birth of the People's Liberation Army (PLA) largely followed the party's official history that the KMT betrayed the revolution and slaughtered

---

[7] "Xi Jinping as Historian: Marxist, Chinese, Nationalist, Global", The Asan Forum, <http://www.theasanforum.org/xi-jinping-as-historian-marxist-chinese-nationalist-global/> (accessed 3 April 2018).

[8] "News Conference of the Taiwan Affairs Office of the State Council of the PRC" (Guotaiban xinwen fabuhui jilu), 17 <January 2018, http://www.gwytb.gov.cn/xwfbh/201801/t20180117_11894595.htm> (accessed 5 April 2018).

CCP comrades in 1927.[9] The movie "Founding of a Republic" (*jianguo daye*) commissioned in 2009 also attributed the civil war to Chiang Kai-shek and the KMT. The movie "Founding of the Red Army" (*jianjun daye*) commissioned in 2017 detailed the betrayal of Chiang Kai-shek and the KMT for their role in initiating the April 1927 massacre of communists in Shanghai. The two movies were produced with the backing of the CCP and were made by the state-owned China Film Group, clearly showing that the rehabilitation of KMT history of China is only partial at best.

The KMT: From Enemy to Ally

Although informal contacts between the KMT and the Mainland existed during the Cold War era, the first official meeting between the two sides occurred only in 1992 with the conclusion of the "92 consensus". Official reappraisal of KMT's wartime history in China from the 2000s has paved the way for the reconciliation between the parties in the last decade (see Appendix 1 for the list of KMT-CCP high-level meetings since 2005).

President Hu Jintao's affirmation of KMT's role in the war against Japan in 2005 was the first-ever official recognition of KMT's wartime contributions by the Chinese leadership. Coupled with Lien Chan's earlier visit, Taiwan President Ma Ying-jeou claimed that KMT-CCP party-to-party relations had improved markedly.[10] The positive reinterpretation of KMT's wartime history in China and the emergence of the pro-independence DPP in Taiwan have seen KMT-CCP relations strengthened. KMT Chairman Lien Chan met President Hu in China

---

[9] "Xi Jinping's Speech at the Commemoration Parade of the 90th Anniversary of the Founding of the PLA" (Xi Jinping: zai qingzhu zhongguo renmin jiefangjun 90 zhounian dahuishang de jianghua), <http://www.xinhuanet.com/politics/2017-08/01/c_1121416045.htm> (accessed 3 April 2018).

[10] "Hu Jintao Confirms Kuomintang's Role in the War against Japan, Ma Ying-Jeou Claims It Leaves a Lasting Impression" (Hu Jintao kending guomindang kangri Ma Yingjiu cheng duici yinxiang shenke), *Sina News*, 11 September 2005, <http://news.sina.com.cn/c/2005-09-11/08516913749s.shtml?from=wap> (accessed 10 April 2018).

in 2005. This marked the first meeting between the top leaders of the two parties since the Chinese Civil War.

Since then, KMT chairpersons have visited the Mainland to strengthen party-to-party relations and reaffirm their adherence to the "92 consensus".[11] In May 2008 and May 2009, KMT Chairman Wu Po-hsiung met Hu. In February and June 2013, President Xi met KMT honorary chairmen Lien Chan and Wu Po-hsiung. In 2015, KMT Chairman Eric Chu visited Xi in Beijing. The last meeting between the KMT and CCP leadership was in November 2016 when KMT Chairman Hung Hsiu-chu met Xi to reiterate their commitment to a "One China Principle" and to oppose Taiwanese independence. In addition to high-level party-party interactions, a Cross-Strait Economic, Trade and Culture Forum, also known as KMT-CPC Forum, has been set up after 2005 to promote cross-strait economic, trade and cultural exchanges. Since 2006, 11 forums had been held between two parties, with the latest forum from 2 to 3 November 2016 in Beijing.

The thawing of tension between the two parties after decades of hostility was most notably represented in the Xi Jinping-Ma Ying-jeou meeting in Singapore in November 2015. The positive reinterpretation of KMT history in mainland China has arguably played a role in facilitating this transformation. Despite improved KMT-CCP relations in recent years, Ma Ying-jeou urged the CCP not to distort the history of wartime China during a speech at the July 2015 Special Exhibit on the Historical Truths of the War of Resistance against Japan.[12] In August 2015, during the 70th anniversary celebrations of the end of WWII in Taipei, Ma also criticised China for its false representation of wartime history. This was because China's wartime leader Chiang Kai-shek was

---

[11] "The 10 Meetings between KMT and CCP Leadership since the Founding of New China" (Pandian Xinzhongguo chengli yilai guogong liang lingdaoren de shici huiwu), 2 November 2016, <http://news.sohu.com/20161102/n472071057.shtml> (accessed 9 April 2018).

[12] "Ma Ying-Jeou Urges the CCP Not to Distort Historical Truths" (Ma Yingjiu xu zhonggong bie cuangai kangri lishi zhenxiang), *Voice of America*, 7 July 2015, <https://www.voachinese.com/amp/taiwan-ma-20150707/2851772.html> (accessed 10 April 2018).

omitted from the poster of the CCP-backed wartime movie "1943 Cairo Conference" in favour of CCP Chairman Mao Zedong. Ma thus expressed his sarcasm by labelling the movie "a great joke".[13]

Some KMT veteran soldiers in Taiwan are also suspicious of the sincerity of China in its re-evaluation of the KMT's wartime history. Taiwan's defence ministry urged KMT war veterans not to attend the 2015 Victory Day military parade in Beijing, stating that the CCP's narrative of China's wartime history was distorted.[14] In an interview with the BBC in July 2015, Hau Pei-Tsun, ex-premier of Taiwan from 1990 to 1993 and a retired army general of the Republic of China, felt that despite the CCP's reappraisal of KMT's wartime history, China's wartime history remains skewed towards the CCP. Hau insists that the CCP still owes old KMT wartime veterans an apology for its continued version of "distorted history".[15]

Increasing Public and Academic Interest in KMT's History in China

The CCP's reappraisal of KMT's wartime history in recent times has given rise to a phenomenon of *Guofen*, which refers to increasing public interest and support for Republican China (the KMT-era from 1927 to 1949). The *Guofen* believes that the Republic was much more vibrant,

---

[13] "Ma Ying-Jeou Attends Commemoration Event on the 70th Anniversary of the End of WWII, Criticises Mao Zedong's Poster on the Movie 'Cairo Conference' as a Big Joke" (Ma Yingjiu chuxi jinian kangzhan shengli huodong, piping <<kailuo xuanyan>> Mao Zedong haibao shi daxiaohua), 20 April 2015, <https://www.rfa.org/mandarin/yatai-baodao/gangtai/hx1-08202015111955.html> (accessed 10 April 2018).

[14] "Taiwan Military Tells Veterans to Avoid China's World War II Parade", *The Straits Times*, 28 August 2015, <http://www.straitstimes.com/asia/east-asia/taiwan-military-tells-veterans-to-avoid-chinas-world-war-ii-parade> (accessed 10 April 2018).

[15] "Hau Pei-Tsun: The CCP Still Owes Us an Apology for Saying That They Were the Pioneers During the War Against Japan" (He Bocun: Zhonggong zicheng shi kangzhan "zhongliu dizhu" youqian gongdao), *BBC*, 2 July 2015, <http://www.bbc.com/zhongwen/trad/china/2015/ 07/150702_hao_bocun_japan_war> (accessed 9 April 2018).

successful and open than previously propagated by the overwhelmingly negative CCP narrative.[16]

Flags of the Republican period (especially Republic of China flag of the Blue Sky, White Sun and Red ground/*qingtian bairi mandihong qi*) have been used by *Guofen* in their online profile pictures, while the KMT emblem has also been part of their monikers, all of which are in open defiance of Chinese web censors. Douban.com, Renren.com and Weibo are examples of popular social networking sites that host several Republican interest groups, with topics of discussion ranging from Republican politics to society and culture.[17]

The relatively relaxed political climate on KMT history in mainland China has also led to a flurry of scholarly works on KMT history in recent times. According to Wang Chaoguang of the Chinese Academy of Social Sciences (CASS) in 2008, the KMT period (1927–1949) had been the most dynamic and productive field in Chinese history studies.[18] In 2011, CASS compiled and published a landmark 36-volume history of the Republic. Prominent CASS historian Yang Tianshi, author of many scholarly articles and monographs on KMT leader Chiang Kai-shek, published a book in 2002 titled, 'The Truth about Chiang Kai-Shek and His Secret Files ', which was based on excerpts from Chiang's diaries.

However, a year thereafter, Yang was accused by an anonymous open letter on the internet to have elevated Chiang to a national hero in his book,[19] a departure from the Party's interpretation of KMT history, which has often referred to Chiang as a war criminal for his role in the Chinese Civil War. CASS reviewed the allegations made against Yang's book and concluded in its report to the central government that Yang's

---

[16] Robert Weatherly and Zhang Qiang, *History and Nationalist Legitimacy*, London, Palgrave Macmillan, 2017, pp. 154–155.

[17] Robert Weatherly and Zhang Qiang, *History and Nationalist Legitimacy*, pp. 154–155.

[18] Wang Chaoguang, "Recent Research on Chinese Republican History", *Journal of Modern Chinese History*, vol. 2, no. 1, p. 89.

[19] "Yang Tianshi: The Truth You Don't Know About Chiang Kai-Shek", 29 October 2010, <http://history.people.com.cn/GB/205140/13082300.html> (accessed 9 April 2018).

book was a piece of 'solid academic research'.[20] Academic research on certain aspects of KMT history hence remains as a controversial topic if it challenges the legitimacy of the CCP despite the recent CCP reappraisal of KMT history.

The Politics behind the Selective Rehabilitation of KMT History

As both the KMT and the CCP adhere to the "One China Policy", the acknowledgement of the KMT's wartime contribution is part of a wider effort by the CCP to improve relations with them in the face of the rise of pro-independence movements in Taiwan from the late 1980s. In particular, with the election of pro-independence DPP into power in Taiwan since the 2000s, the emphasis on the wartime united front between the KMT and the CCP is a way of building a common consensus with the KMT and promoting cross-strait reunification. The timing of the reappraisal of KMT history in mainland China (from the 2000s) also hinted of a response to the series of moves by the DPP and other pro-independence groups to expose the brutality of Taiwan's authoritarian past and to remove Chiang Kai-shek and authoritarian-era monuments from the public sphere in Taiwan (*Qujianghua*).

However, suspicions remain within the KMT leadership on the CCP reappraisal of KMT's wartime history. This is still a sticking point in the relations between the two parties, as seen from the 2015 Victory Day celebrations in China when Taiwan's defence ministry called on KMT war veterans not to attend the event despite the invitation. As the long-term objective of the CCP is reunification with Taiwan, the reappraisal of KMT history as a tool to promote its national unity with certain segments of the Taiwanese public who are pro-KMT will continue. However, there is a limit to the CCP reappraisal of KMT history, as rehabilitating certain aspects of KMT's wartime history could severely damage CCP's legitimacy.

---

[20] Robert Weatherly and Qiang Zhang, *History and Nationalist Legitimacy*, London: Palgrave Macmillan, 2017, pp. 154–155.

Qujianghua and the Transitional Justice Bill

In Taiwan, the reverse has taken place with the reappraisal of the KMT. In recent years, the KMT in Taiwan has been vilified for its authoritarian excesses and there has been a movement to rid the Taiwanese landscape of the legacies of former KMT leader Chiang Kai-shek, known as *Qujianghua*.

On 5 December 2017, Taiwanese lawmakers voted to pass the Transitional Justice Bill, which mandates the removal of tributes to Chiang Kai-shek. The renaming of streets and schools which bear his name has been made mandatory for the first time under Taiwanese law. This is one of the latest attempts to remove the image of Chiang from the public sphere as part of *Qujianghua*. In fact, the erosion of Chiang's public profile began as early as Chen Shui-bian's DPP administration from 2000 to 2007.

This new bill also calls for a full investigation of Chiang's "White Terror", the purge of his political opponents from 1949 to 1975. This "Transitional Justice Bill" detailed the formation of a "Transitional Justice Promotion Committee" consisting of nine members nominated by the premier and subject to legislative review and confirmation. The committee has four missions: retrieve KMT party archives for future research, remove remnants of Taiwan's authoritarian rule, redress judicial injustices and produce a report on the history of the authoritarian period.

As the legacy of Chiang Kai-shek is highly contested in Taiwan, the passing of this bill has generated huge controversy. Although the KMT has apologised for the 2.28 Incident and the excesses of Chiang's "White Terror" (*baise kongbu*) in recent years, it still holds its former leader[21] as the "eternal leader" (*yongjiu zongcai*), with many still regarding him as a hero for taking on the communist forces and fighting the Japanese during WWII.

---

[21] The 2.28 was an anti-government uprising in Taiwan (Republic of China) on 28 February 1947 that was violently supressed by KMT troops. The White Terror was the suppression of political dissidents from 1949 after the KMT had retreated to Taiwan following the loss of mainland China to the Chinese Communists.

On the other hand, the DPP and pro-independence groups deem Chiang as a stain on the history of Taiwan's democracy; Chiang had clamped down on pro-democracy and pro-independence activists during the "White Terror", imprisoning or executing them. The DPP portrays the passing of the bill as "a bridge of reconciliation" that would be a "comfort and compensation" to the 2.28 victims and their families. However, as Chiang embodies the historical memory of the KMT, which has long been the source of its legitimacy, the KMT regards the bill as a political attack.[22]

Origins of *Qujianghua*

During the authoritarian KMT rule in Taiwan from 1949 to 1992, an officially sanctioned cult of Chiang was created. The celebration of Chiang Kai-shek was a major part of post-war reordering of the Taiwanese landscape as Chiang's face appeared as portraits and statues in parks, schools and government offices. Chiang's official name in Chinese, *Zhongzheng* was also applied to names, streets and institutions. With the passing of his son Chiang Ching-Kuo in 1988, new instances of the elder Chiang's commemoration began to slow, with many statues of Chiang Kai-shek removed by local authorities and portraits withdrawn from classroom walls. These efforts were led by the reformist sections of the KMT under the then President Lee Teng-Hui and at the local level under the DPP.

This was the beginning of a programme by the DPP and other pro-democracy activists since the 1990s to remove references to Chiang Kai-shek from public life. The term *Qujianghua* was first used by the Taiwanese media in the 1990s. *Qujianghua* involves the taking down of road names, signages and infrastructures bearing the name of *Jieshi/Zhongzheng* in the Taiwanese landscape, and the alteration of sites or objects which had been built to honour Chiang in the earlier years.

---

[22] Vladimir Stolojan, "Transitional Justice and Collective Memory in Taiwan: How Taiwanese Society is Coming to Terms with its Authoritarian Past", *China Perspectives*, Issue 2, 2017, p. 31.

The scope of *Qujianghua* has since expanded to include denunciations of Chiang Kai-shek, particularly on his involvement in the 28 February 1947 massacre in Taiwan. The authoritarian excesses of the "White Terror" perpetrated by the KMT regime in Taiwan have also been subject to re-evaluation and criticism by the ruling DPP. In 1994, the DPP took control of Taipei after winning the local elections, with Chen Shui-bian taking over the mayoralty of the city where there were many sites associated with Chiang Kai-shek. In 1996, one of the *Qujianghua* steps taken by the DPP was to rename Jieshou Road (or literally, 'Road of Chiang Kai-shek's Longevity') which ran directly in front of the Presidential Palace to Ketagalan Boulevard (named after a Taiwanese aboriginal tribe). The move was one of the clearest intentions of the DPP to remove Chiang from the face of the Taiwanese public.

As early as in the 1990s under Lee Teng-hui, the 'twenty-foot photographs and paintings of Chiang' which covered public structures on public holidays in the 1960s were no longer visible. In 1996, the Taiwanese media also classified the DPP's opening of Chiang Kai-shek's former home in northern Taipei, the Shilin Official Residence (*shilin guandi*), to the public as another instance of *Qujianghua*. Following the opening of Chiang's residence at Shilin to the public, the Chung Hsing Guesthouse, Chiang's summer residence and the Grass Mountain Chateau, the occasional residence of Chiang, were opened to the public in 1998 and 2003 respectively. According to the DPP, it was to 'return' those spaces previously monopolised by Chiang and the people at the top echelons of the ruling KMT to the people.[23]

Qujianghua during Chen Shui-bian's and Tsai Ing-wen's Presidencies

After Chen Shui-bian was elected president in 2000, *Qujianghua* continued at both the central and regional levels. The Chen adminis-

---

[23] Chen Shui-bian, "Shizhang Xu" (Mayoral Preface), in Li Dequan (ed.), Shilin Guandi Daolan (Guidebook to the Shihlin Official Residence), Taipei 1996, p. 4.

tration replaced the Jieshou Hall (*jieshouguan*) sign that hung over the entrance to the Presidential Office with a new sign that simply reads "Presidential Office". The Ministry of National Defence also removed references to Chiang on the facilities under its control in 2001. In 2006, the Executive Yuan of the Chen Shui-bian administration approved the renaming of the Chiang Kai-Shek International Airport as Taiwan Taoyuan International Airport. The Chen administration under the auspices of the Ministry of Education in 2007 also renamed Chiang Kai-shek memorial hall in the Zhongzheng district of Taipei as National Taiwan Democracy Hall and replaced the inscription on the gateway (*dazhongzhizheng*), which means "great neutrality and perfect uprightness of Chiang", with "Liberty Square" (*ziyou guangchang*). It was only until the return to power of the KMT under President Ma Ying-Jeou in 2008 that Chiang's name was restored to the memorial hall. Other instances include the renaming of "Zhongzheng Cultural Centre" to "Gaoxiong Cultural Centre" and the removal of the bronze statues of Chiang Kai-shek by the then DPP mayor of Gaoxiong city Chen Chu.

After the DPP under Tsai Ing-wen took power in 2016, a new offensive targeting the legacy of former KMT leader Chiang Kai-shek was renewed. In early 2017, the DPP announced that the Chiang Kai-shek memorial hall would stop selling souvenirs depicting him and references to him will also be removed from the galleries. With the passing of the "Transitional Justice Bill" on 5 December 2017, statues of Chiang throughout the island will be taken down. There have also been plans to print new Taiwan 200-, 5- and 1-dollar notes without Chiang's image on them.

Implications behind the DPP's Promotion of *Qujianghua*

The Chen Shui-bian and Tsai Ing-wen administrations have promoted *Qujianghua* for political reasons. According to the DPP, *Qujianghua* was to remove the personality cult of Chiang Kai-shek which had been cultivated by the ruling KMT during the authoritarian era. From the

DPP's perspective, Chiang Kai-shek stands for everything the DPP is against. Chiang is a symbol of Chinese nationalism and authoritarianism, an enemy of Taiwanese nationalism and democracy that the DPP has been promoting since the 1980s.

Chiang is a symbol of Chinese nationalism in both the historical and cultural sense. After its defeat in the Chinese Civil War, the KMT had viewed its time in Taiwan as temporary and a base for counterattacking the Mainland (*fangong dalu*). Chiang and the KMT also never sought to 'Taiwanise' their regime. Chinese culture was promoted at the cost of alienating local Taiwanese culture. In the 1960s, mainland China was engulfed in the Cultural Revolution, but Taiwan under Chiang Kai-shek sought to defend traditional Chinese culture. Chiang Kai-shek and his son also abided by the "One China Policy" throughout their term, viewing Taiwan as part of China. The legacy of Chiang Kai-shek and the mainlander faction of the KMT represented a cultural and historical link with the Mainland that the DPP tries to play down. Chiang Kai-shek also stood for authoritarianism. During the White Terror, many of his political opponents who had pro-independence and pro-democracy sentiments were suppressed. As such, the DPP equates *Qujianghua* to the elimination of Taiwan's authoritarian past, which has no relevance in the context of today's Taiwanese democracy. Like the wave of Eastern European nationalist movements where states sought to remove all references of the communist period in their country after the end of the Cold War, the promotion of *Qujianghua* can be viewed as a form of Taiwanese nationalism which excludes its authoritarian past.

Presently, the scope of *Qujianghua* has widened to include investigations into Chiang's "White Terror" involvement. The 2.28 incident and the excesses of KMT's authoritarian rule are tools that the DPP is using to attack the historical legitimacy of the KMT.[24] As a major part of the "Transitional Justice Bill" serves to expose the wrongdoings of Chiang's "White Terror" in Taiwan, the legacy of Chiang in Taiwan is set to worsen.

---

[24] Jeremy E Taylor "Discovering a Nationalist-Heritage in Present-Day Taiwan", *China Heritage Quarterly*, vol. 17, March 2009, <http://www.chinaheritagequarterly.org/articles. php?searchterm=017_taiwan. inc&issue=017> (accessed 23 April 2018).

Qujianghua is also an extension of the "De-Sinification/*Quzhonghua*" trend in the wake of a strengthening Taiwanese consciousness. This strengthening of Taiwanese consciousness is a reaction to the Republic of China-themed national narratives promoted by the mainlander faction of the KMT under Chiang Kai-shek and his son Chiang Ching-Kuo since 1949, which largely sidelined local Taiwanese culture.[25] As Chiang Kai-shek was also the leader of both China and Taiwan in the 20th century, *Qujianghua* is a subtle attempt to erase the cultural and historical linkages between Taiwan and China, a move which China sees as a step towards Taiwanese independence.[26]

Local Reactions to *Qujianghua*

Among the Taiwanese public, Chiang Kai-shek's image is still controversial. Some view him as a great leader, yet some segments of the public view him as a dictator. The Mainlanders (*waishengren*) who retreated to Taiwan with the KMT after 1949 do not approve of *Qujianghua* as they feel that it is a lack of respect for the late KMT leader. Chiang Kai-shek's image as the president of the ROC and chairman of the KMT still stands strong for this group.

The pro-independence and pro-democracy groups which had been repressed during the authoritarian era have been the most outspoken supporters of *Qujianghua*. According to the Taiwanese media, anti-Chiang activists have been destructing and vandalising Chiang's statues throughout the island. In one case, red paint was sprayed over Chiang's statue to form the word "Butcher" (*tufu*) to refer to Chiang's perceived role in the 28 February incident. Some of Chiang's statues also had their heads, arms and legs cut off by angry activists. Very often, the destroyed statues were sent to a museum in the northern city of Taoyuan

---

[25] Katherine Tseng Hui-Yi, "Taiwan's Nationalist Party (II): The Taiwanese Identity", *EAI Background Brief*, no. 1341, East Asian Institute, National University of Singapore, 10 April 2018, p. 1.

[26] "News Conference of the Taiwan Affairs Office of the State Council PRC" (Guotaiban yiyue shiqiri lixing xinwen fabuhui), *Phoenix News*, 17 January 2018, <http://news.ifeng.com/a/20180117/55198932_0.shtml> (accessed 23 April 2018).

where they are left on the grounds of the Cihu Mausoleum of Late President Chiang. The number of discarded statues there is expected to increase with the passing of the "Transitional Justice Bill". Even in school compounds, the statues of Chiang Kai-shek have also been subject to vandalism and destruction. On 28 February of every year, public statues of Chiang Kai-shek have been targeted for vandalism and destruction by anti-Chiang activists. On 28 February 2018, pro-independence activists took their "anti-Chiang protests" one step further by spraying red paint on Chiang Kai-shek's coffin in the Cihu Mausoleum and planting a banner that called for Taiwan's independence.[27]

For segments of the public, particularly among the older generation who lost their families or relatives during the "White Terror", *Qujianghua* represents an opportunity for them to seek redress from the state for losses suffered during the authoritarian period. The "Transitional Justice Bill" passed recently by the DPP will go some way towards redressing the losses of this group.

On the other hand, the legacy of Chiang Kai-shek has not been totally wiped out. Chiang's legacy has been commercialised as tourist attractions to cater for mainland tourists. This is particularly so during the Ma Ying-Jeou administration when Taiwan enjoyed warm relations with China and tourism thrived between the two sides.

In 2008, a "Chiang Cultural Park" was created in Taoyuan by local authorities to attract curious mainland Chinese visitors to Taiwan.[28] Chiang Kai-shek's former home was brought to life and aspects of his domestic life were recreated for mainland visitors. The Chiang Kai-shek Memorial Hall, the Shilin Official Residence and the Grass Mountain Chateau are popular sites for mainland visitors. Some public sites in

---

[27] "Chiang Kai-Shek's Coffin Gets Splashed Red Paint on the Anniversary of the 71st February 28 Incident" (Ererba jinianri, cihu Jiang Zhongzheng lingjiu beibo hongqi[ying], CNA, 28 February 2018, <www.cna.com.tw/news/firstnews/201802285002-1.aspx> (accessed 23 April 2018).

[28] "Taipei and Taoyuan Team up to Promote the Chiang Cultural Tour to Attract Mainland Visitors" (Taibei he Taoyuan cujin jiang gong shenghuo you, xiying bushao dalu youke), RFA News, 30 June 2008, <https://www.rfa.org/cantonese/news/taiwan_tourist-06302008120336. html?encoding=simplified> (accessed 30 April 2018).

Taiwan that have references to Chiang Kai-shek are also preserved on the initiative of the public. Where mainland visitors could not find references to Chiang Kai-shek in China, they could find them in Taiwan. A visit to Taiwan is hence the only way for the Mainlanders to know more about the life of this former leader of the Republic of China. The ongoing reappraisal of KMT history in China has also played a part in this interest. After the passing of the Transitional Justice Bill, it remains unclear how the removal of sites associated with Chiang Kai-shek would impact the tourism industry and whether non-governmental attempts to preserve and commercialise sites associated with Chiang Kai-shek will continue.

KMT's Responses to *Qujianghua*

The KMT views *Qujianghua* as an attempt by the DPP and pro-independence groups to destroy its legacy by tarnishing the image of its former leader. KMT's declining legitimacy in Taiwanese society, as seen from the local elections in 2014 and presidential and legislative elections in 2016, has rendered the KMT powerless in responding to the *Qujianghua* phenomenon. All it could do is to defend Chiang's contributions to Taiwan, particularly his role in protecting the island against the Mainland's invasion and linking the island's economic success to the leadership of both Chiang Kai-shek and Chiang Ching-Kuo.

Former KMT Chairman Ma Ying-Jeou who was a staunch supporter of Chiang's China-centric narrative of history had made high-profile appearances at the 70th anniversary commemorations of the end of WWII in Taipei. On many occasions, Ma had also sought to defend Chiang's legacy, particularly Chiang's leadership of China in WWII and his role in protecting Taiwan from communism.[29] KMT Chairman Wu Den-Yih has also spoken out against the DPP's *Qujianghua* recently; he has called for an objective view of the legacy

---

[29] "Ma Ying-Jeou: Cannot Whitewash Chiang Kai-Shek's Contribution to Taiwan", Sohu News, 3 March 2015, <http://news.sohu.com/20150303/n409309300.shtml> (accessed 23 April 2018).

and contributions of Chiang Kai-shek in Taiwan.[30] Wu acknowledged the complicity of Chiang and the KMT leadership in the 28 February incident, but stated that the injustices had been redressed.[31]

However, due to the weakening position of the KMT in Taiwanese politics, it could not counter the DPP-sponsored *Qujianghua*. KMT's response to the DPP's offensive has been the mere issuing of strongly worded remarks, but nothing substantial has been achieved to reverse the process of *Qujianghua*. Ironically, as Chiang and the KMT are slowly being rehabilitated in China, the image of Chiang has worsened in Taiwan with the portrayal of Chiang as a dictator and a "butcher of democracy and Taiwanese independence".

Impact on Cross-Strait Relations

Interestingly, the CCP condemns *Qujianghua* in Taiwan even though it had embarked on the same process after the Chinese Civil War. For decades, the CCP has sought to remove Chiang Kai-shek's personality cult in China and portrayed the KMT in a very bad light. It was only in recent years that the CCP has begun to reappraise the legacy of Chiang Kai-shek and the KMT leadership more objectively, highlighting the leader's positive role in the war against Japan and for the adherence to a "One China Policy".

The CCP links *Qujianghua* to the plot by the DPP and pro-independence groups to promote Taiwanese independence. Chiang Kai-shek was considered as an enemy to pro-independence groups during his rule as he had insisted on a "One China Policy" during the confrontation with mainland China and suppressed pro-independence dissidents. He was also the leader of the ROC during its rule on the mainland and in Taiwan during the 20th century. Hence, the *Qujianghua* movement supported by the pro-independence administration in

---

[30] "Wu Den-Yih: I Cannot Take the DPP's Qujianghua Anymore", Phoenix News, 9 April 2017, <http://news.ifeng.com/a/20170409/50908641_0.shtml> (accessed 23 April 2018).

[31] "Wu Den-Yih: I Cannot Take the DPP's Qujianghua Anymore", Phoenix News.

Taiwan contains a subtle political tone which strengthens pro-independence voices. The CCP also views *Qujianghua* as a subtle attempt to strengthen Taiwanese consciousness. By embarking on *Qujianghua*, Taiwan will shed some of its cultural affinities and historical links with the Mainland, which could lead to creeping Taiwanese independence.

Qujianghua during Chen Shui-bian's administration had added to the already strained relations between China and Taiwan from 2000 to 2007, not to mention the frosty relations since the election of DPP's Tsai Ing-wen into power in 2016. *Qujianghua* has widened the distrust between Beijing and Taipei. However, mainland Chinese authorities remain positive about the prospects of reunification. The spokesman of the Taiwan Affairs Office of the State Council of the PRC Ma Xiaoguang asserted that though the "majority of the Taiwanese people are against independence",[32] the PRC will continue to seek to "unite the Taiwanese compatriots who are against Taiwanese independence".[33]

Conclusion

The use of history as propaganda for political purposes has been practised in both the CCP's reappraisal of the KMT's history in mainland China and the DPP's reappraisal of KMT history in Taiwan. Both the CCP and the DPP have sought to use history to further their diverging political agenda: pro-unification for the CCP and pro-independence for the DPP. While the CCP has reappraised the KMT's history more positively to build closer relations with the KMT and Taiwan, the DPP has tried to lead Taiwan towards an opposite direction through *Qujianghua*, an important component of a boarder movement of *Quzhonghua* (de-sinicization). Both *Qujianghua* and *Quzhonghua* have been fuelled by growing nationalism in Taiwan, a reaction to

---

[32] "News Conference of the Taiwan Affairs Office of the State Council of the PRC" (Guotaiban yiyue shiqiri lixing xinwen fabuhui), Phoenix News, 17 January 2018, <http://news.ifeng.com/a/20180117/55198932_0.shtml> (accessed 23 April 2018).

[33] "News Conference of the Taiwan Affairs Office" (Guotaiban yiyue shiqiri lixing xinwen fabuhui), Phoenix News.

ROC-themed national narratives promoted by the mainlander faction of the KMT since 1949. The *Qujianghua* movement can also be viewed as a form of Taiwanese nationalism which embraces its democratic culture and excludes its authoritarian past.

Professor Wang Gungwu mentioned that in Chinese history, separation did not last for too long before the norm of reunification avails. However, the situation of present-day mainland China and Taiwan may be seen in a different light. Taiwan has been separated from the Mainland for over 100 years from 1895 to 1945, and once again from 1949 to the present. As a result of this long period of separation, Taiwan underwent a different historical experience from that of mainland China. It developed its own national identity and culture, which was unprecedented as during previous periods of separation in Chinese history, the idea of the "oneness of China" was still maintained. The richest soil for the growing Taiwanese identity has been Taiwan's historical path to democratisation, a reason why the democratic culture is strongly cherished by Taiwanese society. However, Taiwan's democratic culture is alien to Chinese traditional culture, the bonding force between Taiwan and mainland China. This democratic culture has also underpinned the DPP's reappraisal of KMT history, which has contributed to the KMT's declining popularity in Taiwan. The real challenge for the CCP in promoting unification is how to embrace the Taiwanese identity and at its root, Taiwan's democratic culture.

The CCP's more positive reappraisal of the KMT history indicates that it has made progress in embracing one of Taiwan's major political forces. However, it is the DPP and not the KMT that is the representative of Taiwan's democratic culture. From the perspective of pro-democracy groups in Taiwan, the reconciliation between the CCP and the KMT is an alliance between two authoritarian forces, which might endanger Taiwan's democracy. Notably, the DPP does not share any common historical experience with the CCP, unlike the KMT. In its future efforts for unification with Taiwan, the CCP would need to be much more creative in its strive to engage the DPP and the pro-democracy groups, and to embrace Taiwan's democratic culture.

Appendix 1 Top-Level KMT-CCP Meetings From 2005

Date of Meeting	KMT leader present at meeting	CCP leader present at meeting	Key agreements made after the meeting
29 April 2005	Lien Chan (chairman)	Hu Jintao (general secretary)	Affirm the '92 consensus' Pledge to increase interactions between China and Taiwan
28 May 2008	Wu Po-Hsiung (chairman)	Hu Jintao (general secretary)	Set the stage for the implementation of the "3 links" (*dasantong*)
26 May 2009	Wu Po-Hsiung (chairman)	Hu Jintao (general secretary)	Pledge to strengthen China-Taiwan economic partnership and hasten the signing of an agreement on economic partnership Set the stage for the signing of the Economic Cooperation Framework Agreement between China and Taiwan in June 2010
13 June 2013	Wu Po-Hsiung (honorary chairman)	Xi Jinping (general secretary)	Affirm the '92 consensus' Oppose Taiwan independence
18 February 2014	Lien Chan (honorary chairman)	Xi Jinping (general secretary)	Affirm 'China Taiwan is one family' Affirm 'China-Taiwan relations are not state-to-state relations'

4 May 2015	Eric Chu (chairman)	Xi Jinping (general secretary)	Affirm the '92 consensus' and oppose Taiwan independence as the basis for peaceful China-Taiwan relations
3 September 2015	Lien Chan (honorary chairman)	Xi Jinping (general secretary)	Agree that the victory in WWII was the first ever total victory against foreign aggression Affirm the sacrifices of Taiwanese compatriots in China's WWII victory Affirm the '92 consensus' and oppose Taiwan independence
7 November 2015	Ma Ying-Jeou (president of the ROC)	Xi Jinping (general secretary)	Pledge to maintain the '92 consensus' Oppose Taiwan independence and Promote peaceful development
1 November 2016	Hung Hsiu-chu (chairman)	Xi Jinping (general secretary)	Affirm 'One China principle' Oppose any form of Taiwan independence

Source: Qi Dongtao and Ryan Ho, "China's Partial Reappraisal of Kuomintang History and Its Impact", *EAI Background Brief*, no. 1355, East Asian Institute, National University of Singapore, 23 May 2018.

Chapter 11

Cross-Strait Relations in the Wake of Taiwan's January 2016 Election: Taiwan's Narratives

John F COPPER*

Introduction

Since the present government in China was established in 1949, the Taiwan Strait has been one of the world's most dangerous flashpoints — flashpoint being defined as a site where a conflict involving two or more major world powers might occur with each employing weapons of mass destruction.

In this case, there are two protagonists, the United States and China. The "Taiwan issue" or Taiwan's status, whether an independent nation-state or a part of China, has widely been seen as the fuse. It is the only non-negotiable issue between China and the United States. This situation remains.[1]

The salience of this tinderbox situation is currently underscored by another reality — the United States is the world's superpower and its status quo power, and China is the sole fast rising power and challenger

---

* John F COPPER is the Stanley J Buckman Professor (Emeritus) of International Studies at Rhodes College in Memphis, Tennessee.
[1] See Bernard D Cole, *China's Quest for Great Power: Ships, Oil, and Foreign Policy*, Annapolis, Naval Institute Press, 2016, p. 168.

to the United States (and to the status quo). Many observers thus subscribed to the belief, based on Thucydides' classic book, *The Peloponnesian War*, that war between the United States and China is inevitable.[2]

Recent history is also telling. Tension between the United States and China over Taiwan was high in the 1950s with two near outbreaks of conflict. The two also engaged in serious face-offs in 1995 and 1996 precipitated by a national election in Taiwan, the first popular election of its president and a sign of Taiwan pursuing popular sovereignty. After that, President Lee Teng-hui provoked China with statements seen to constitute advancing Taiwan's independence.[3] Cross-Strait tensions continued at a high pitch to the end of Lee's presidency and worsened throughout the presidency of Chen Shui-bian (2000 to 2008).

The Taiwan Strait stress subsided during the Ma Ying-jeou presidency (2008–2016) accompanied by markedly improved cross-Strait relations.

However, in late 2015 and early 2016 Taiwan became once again a major source of cross-Strait tension during a national election campaign. It was also arguably a deciding factor in who won and who lost in the January 2016 election. Tsai Ing-wen, the then opposition Democratic Progressive Party's (DPP) candidate, won handily and her party the DPP grabbed a majority in the legislature for the first time ever, helped by anti-China populism and local fear of Taiwan losing its sovereignty.[4]

Post-election cross-Strait relations deteriorated as Beijing sought to diminish President Tsai and the DPP.[5] After the 19th Chinese

---

[2] See Graham Allison, *Destined for War: Can America and China Escape Thucydides's Trap?* New York, Houghton Mifflin Harcourt, 2017.

[3] For details on this face-off, see John F Copper, *Playing with Fire: The Looming War with China Over Taiwan,* Westport, CT, Praeger, 2006 and John W Garver, *Face Off: China, the United States, and Taiwan's Democratization,* Seattle, University of Washington Press, 1997.

[4] See John F Copper, *Taiwan at a Tipping Point: The Democratic Progressive Party Returns to Power,* Lanham, MD, Lexington Books, 2018, chapter 3.

[5] John F Copper, *Taiwan at a Tipping Point,* pp. 186–93.

Communist Party Congress in October 2017 Beijing changed its Taiwan policy from "promote unification" to "oppose independence".[6]

China's Taiwan strategy consisted of three elements or "legs": economic, political (mainly diplomatic) and military. Beijing's preference was (and is) to employ them in that order — with economic pressure being not only first but also its preferred policy. The others would follow depending on the situation cum need, though there was no reason for China not to employ all three at the same time.[7] Meanwhile Beijing raised the volume of both its appeals and its threats.

After the election, President Tsai and her party chose four arrows in their quiver of narratives to deal with China. All of them promised to cope with the "China threat" though none of them was without difficulties, even problems, insofar as turning them into policies resulted in confusion and contradictions.

In the following pages the author will examine the unease and mistrust between Beijing and Taipei following the January 2016 election looking at both the "theory" (better said to be the assumptions, goals and political forces at work) and events behind deteriorating relations between the two. The focus will be on Taiwan's policies and its actions vis-a-vis China, in particular its accounts on that subject.

National Identity in Taiwan

The Tsai administration's first narrative was to underscore trends in Taiwan residents' views on the matter of their national identity.[8] Plainly the majority of Taiwan's population was shifting away from a Chinese-defined identity to a Taiwanese one. There was also a decline in Chinese/Taiwanese (or both) identity.

---

[6] Qi Dongtao, "China's Reactive Taiwan Policy", *EAI Bulletin*, vol. 19, no. 2, p. 5.

[7] John F Copper, *Taiwan at a Tipping Point*, p. 186.

[8] For a detailed study of Taiwan's national identity see Alan M Wakeman, *Taiwan: National Identity and Democratization*, Armonk, NY, M E Sharpe, 1994. A more recent work is Shirley Lin Syaru, *Taiwan's China Dilemma: Contested Identities and Multiple Interests in Taiwan's Cross-Strait Economic Policy*, Stanford, Stanford University Press, 2016.

These trends were pronounced and appeared to be gaining momentum. The numbers are revealing. In the early 1990s nearly 25.5% of the island's residents considered themselves Chinese. This number fell to 10.6% in 2001 and to only three per cent in 2016. Those who considered themselves Taiwanese rose from 17.6% in 1992 to 41.6% in 2001 and 59.3% in 2016. The percentage of those who saw themselves as both Chinese and Taiwanese dropped from 46.4% to 33.6% during this same period.[9] This seemed clear proof that Taiwan was heading towards independence.

However, the matter was not as simple as it looked. First, the term Chinese is ambiguous since it may imply either, sometimes alternating, between a cultural or ethnic meaning as opposed to a political one. In the former case the term may also have either a broad or narrow meaning. In the latter case it depends largely on one's definition of the nation-state and its origins.[10]

Furthermore, events affect Taiwan's national identity. Changing trends were no doubt partly a product of the Tiananmen Incident and events that followed. China's rise and its high visibility in Taiwan and elsewhere in Asia in subsequent years likewise created blowback and fear of its encroachment on the region's freedom of action. This development was more salient to Taiwan because Taiwan is especially vulnerable and needs an outside actor's protection, the United States, to survive.[11]

Residents' fear of Taiwan losing its sovereignty was amplified after 2008 because President Ma overreached in building close relations with China, in particular pushing (at least in the minds of many Taiwanese)

---

[9] Jiang Yi-huah, "Taiwan's National Identity and Cross Strait Relations", in Lowell Dittmer (ed.), *Taiwan and China: Fitful Embrace*, Berkeley, University of California Press, 2017, pp. 23–25.

[10] Jiang Yi-huah, "Taiwan's National Identity and Cross Strait Relations", pp. 21–23. There are two views about the nation-state that affect one's perspective on this matter. The "primordial" view is that nationhood is based on shared history, myth, genealogical relations and religious beliefs that preexist the modern state. The "modernist" position is that the nation-state is based on decolonisation and democratisation. China favours the former position; Taiwan espouses mainly the latter.

[11] Lin, *Taiwan's China Dilemma*, p. 2.

unification with China. Ma's feud with Kuomintang (KMT) Legislative Speaker Wang Jin-pyng strengthened the trend towards a Taiwanese identification even among KMT members (the two holding quite different views on the subject).[12] Towards the end of Ma's presidency, Hung Hsiu-chu who supported an even more assertive unification stance became the KMT's presidential nominee for the coming 2016 election. However, many potential voters rejected her (according to various polls) based on the national identity issue. Eric Chu, mayor of New Taipei, replaced her as the KMT's standard-bearer, but not before she caused the national identity issue to further divide voters thereby abetting Tsai Ing-wen and the DPP to win the election.[13]

However, an argument that raises questions about this is that national identity is not the real issue; instead it is the matter of there being one China (and Taiwan being part of China), or not.[14] This better reflects one's view of Taiwan's future. Yet none of the choices, unification with China, independence or "neither", offers an actionable path for Taiwan.[15]

When queried about the choices most residents of Taiwan, both in the past and the present, respond that they favour the status quo (60% in 2016).[16] This, of course, may be seen as tantamount to avoiding a decision or wanting to have one's cake and eating it too, insofar as this answer suggests that most want economic ties with China but not political ties which would inevitably follow. In other words, maintaining the status quo is not a solution.

Thus, it can be argued that the trends in national identity will persist for a long time and resolve nothing.[17] This likely view on national

---

[12] John F Copper, *Taiwan at a Tipping Point,* pp. 47–48.

[13] See Jean-Pierre Cabestan, "Changing Identities in Taiwan under Ma Ying-jeou", in Dittmer (ed.), *Taiwan and China,* pp. 42–60.

[14] Both Jiang and Cabastan, cited in the preceding footnotes, so argue.

[15] John F Copper, "Three Sbcenarios for Taiwan's Future — Really?" *Eurasia Studies Quarterly,* no. 2 2018 (in Chinese).

[16] Jiang, "Taiwan's National Identity and Cross-Strait Relations", in Dittmer (ed.), *Taiwan and China,* p. 23.

[17] Dittmer suggests that it will be the last issue to be resolved regarding Taiwan's status. See Lowell Dittmer, "Conclusion", in Dittmer (ed.), *Taiwan and China,* p. 298.

identity will fluctuate as time passes both in terms of respondents' answers to polls and as a political issue.

In any event, the debate about one China morphed into a discussion of the 1992 Consensus during the 2016 election campaign. President Tsai, cognisant of the problem this presented in terms of keeping the loyalty of her DPP base while needing to maintain economic and other ties with China that are critical to Taiwan, adopted a policy of supporting the status quo. What she said was that she would "push for the peaceful and stable development of cross-Strait relations in accordance with the will of the Taiwanese people and the existing ROC constitutional order".[18] This won her the presidency without her endorsing the 92 Consensus.

However, Tsai's stance was at best unclear. Whether the will of the Taiwanese people was to be measured by their national identity (which supposedly implied they wanted independence) or their support of the status quo was uncertain. The "ROC constitutional order" could be taken to mean that China could not be split but that the government in Beijing (which Tsai admitted she wanted to deal with) was illegitimate. This is an out of date view and in the present context is confusing to say the least.

Members of her party, not to mention, of course, KMT leaders, assailed her policy as being imprecise and even vacuous. Some DPP leaders said it was Ma's policy and/or that it said nothing. Tsai was thus "walking a tightrope" between seeking to improve ties with China (that she had promised during the campaign) and separation from China (which her party base demanded and linked to its support of her). Tsai arguably had no choice but to be elusive. Yet not making a policy would eventually lead to difficulties.

President Tsai no doubt fully understands that Taiwan's economy is integrated with China's to the degree that breaking these ties would cause a profound hit to Taiwan's gross domestic product (GDP) growth because a whopping 40% of Taiwan's trade is with China and 80% of its foreign investment goes to China. There are also more than 100,000

---

[18] Dittmer (ed.), *Taiwan and China*, p. 31. The ROC means the Republic of China, Taiwan's official, Constitutional name.

Taiwan-owned enterprises operating in China.[19] In short, the economic bonds are too extensive to break without causing Taiwan extreme harm. She may also have understood that it would even have a negative impact on the pursuit of independence.[20]

Tsai had to face two special problems that were beyond the realm of theory or which represent the intersecting of theory and practice. One was the attraction of Taiwan's youth to China in terms of finding good paying jobs and attaining experience with global companies. Another was Tsai's campaign to shift Taiwan's economic ties from China to Southeast Asia, a goal she has pursued as president.

On the first, there are around half a million young people from Taiwan working in China, most of them with an undergraduate college degree or higher. China's government encourages this and offers incentives to welcome Taiwan's youthful residents to go to China, calculating that for them financial benefits trump national identity. There is little Taiwan can do about this other than speak out against it, which has not been very effective.[21] Thus, while Taiwan's youth more than other age groups support Tsai, the DPP and independence, they do not behave that way. This is a clear contradiction for the Tsai administration.

The second problem is the matter of immigrants (including foreign workers) in Taiwan. The Tsai administration has encouraged more immigrants to juice the economy and promote "progressive" policies of inclusion. Southeast Asia is the favourite source of arrivals as their presence in Taiwan also comports with the idea that Taiwanese are not Chinese but rather a mixed race (of Chinese and Aboriginal people that came from or are related to the current population of Southeast Asia).[22]

---

[19] Lowell Dittmer, "Taiwan and the Waning Dream of Reunification", in Dittmer (ed.), *Taiwan and China*, p. 288.

[20] Wu Yu-shan, "Pivot, Hedger, or Partner: Strategies of Lesser Powers Caught between Hegemons", in Dittmer (ed.), *Taiwan and China*, p. 208.

[21] Nicola Smith, "Taiwan is Suffering from a Massive Brain Drain and the Main Beneficiary is China", *Time,* 21 August 2017 (online at time.com).

[22] See Michael Hsiao Hsin-Huang and Alan H Yang, "Repositioning Taiwan in Southeast Asia: Strategies to Enhance People-to-People Connectivity", The National Bureau of Asian Research, 11 January 2018 (online at nbr.org).

Yet this does not accord with the fact that a Taiwanese identity was built to a considerable degree upon the theme of repression under the KMT in the early days after World War II. It also collides with the DPP's theme of a unique Taiwanese culture that is the hallmark of the DPP's asppeal to voters but has little resonance with immigrants.[23]

Finally, Taiwan's national identity moving away from being Chinese has declined since 2016 — notwithstanding increased tension with China under Tsai and the DPP's rule. This appears counterintuitive, but it is confirmed by public opinion surveys. It may be explained in part by the fact that a Taiwanese identity peaked during the Ma presidency and/or was affected by disappointment in the Tsai administration and Beijing's increased threats combined with more carrots.[24]

Taiwan is a Democracy

President Tsai and her party's second narrative to explain tense cross-Strait relations with China is that Taiwan is a democracy and China is not, making unification presently or in the near future not only infeasible but also unthinkable. This argument took on more salience in the wake of the 2016 election.[25]

However, this theme is anything but new. Chiang Kai-shek used it in the 1950s and after to rationalise aligning with the United States and to bolster his dream of returning to China and ruling it once again. He and the KMT had more to boast about as Taiwan democratised based on Chiang and the KMT overseeing miracle economic growth that begat a middle class and their holding competitive local elections beginning in 1950 that moved up to the national level. After the DPP

---

[23] The DPP was also seen as a party hostile to Taiwan's ethnic minoriries, especially during the Chen presidency. See John F Copper, *Taiwan's Democracy on Trial: Political Change during the Chen Shui-Bian Era and Beyond*, Lanham, MD, University Press of America, 2020, pp. 59 and 75.

[24] Qi Dongtao, "Why is Taiwanese Nationalism Declining?" IPP Review, 13 February 2018 (online at ippreview.com).

[25] See, for example, J Michael Cole, *Convergence or Conflicct: The Illusion of Peace?*, London, Routledge, 2017, chapter 4.

was formed in 1986 its leaders spoke of Taiwan's democratisation as having become genuine as a result of ending the KMT's monopoly rule and party competition in elections and elsewhere. They advanced the view that Taiwan truly has become democratic beginning in the 1980s, not before.[26]

In recent years, the poll data shows that DPP leaders and voters have been more supportive (and protective) of Taiwan being a democracy than the KMT or independent voters.[27] The main reason is the DPP views Taiwan's democratic polity, including its political culture, as making it incompatible with it becoming part of China. The DPP also equates Taiwan's democracy with its right to sovereignty. In fact, these are two of President Tsai and the DPP's major talking points.[28]

However, there are a number of problems with this.

First, the United Nations and its affiliated agencies and most other international organisations, which are presumed to support self-determination (that DPP leaders espouse and link to its democracy and Taiwan's right to independence), do not in fact seriously promote democratic institutions or democratic actors in international affairs. Furthermore the UN and its related institutions and agencies do not treat Taiwan with goodwill and do not respect Taiwan being a democracy. They do not even publish economic, social or other data on Taiwan. They treat Taiwan as something between a pariah and non-existing, causing, some say, many locals in Taiwan to view themselves as the "Orphan of Asia". Taiwan under DPP governance past and present has made many appeals, directly and indirectly, to the UN — all of little or no avail.[29]

---

[26] See, for example, Joseph Wu Jaushieh, *Taiwan's Democratization: Forces Behind the New Momentum,* London, Oxford University Press, 1995.

[27] Yu Ching-hsin, "Parties, Partisans and Independents in Taiwan", in Christopher H Achen and T Y Wang (eds.), *The Taiwan Voter,* Ann Arbor, University of Michigan Press, 2017, p. 86.

[28] Steven M Goldstein, *China amd Taiwan,* Cambidge, MA, Harvard University Press, 2015, pp. 84–85.

[29] Dafydd Fell, *Government and Politics of Taiwan,* London, Routledge, 2012, p. 4.

Second, Taiwan has long sought to find and keep diplomatic allies by boasting of it being a democracy. Yet China has attracted away Taiwan's diplomatic partners because it is much bigger and more important. Even countries that are democracies and have applauded and supported Taiwan's democratisation have chosen to set up embassies in Beijing. In short, Taiwan's pitch that it is a democracy and that is important has fallen on deaf ears.

Behind this trend is the fact that most national leaders believe that diplomatic recognition should be based on the fact that a nation exists. They profess this even more if at question is an important nation. China being the largest nation in the world in population and a major world power, other countries believe that they need to have formal ties with Beijing.[30] Incidentally, due to its (and Taiwan's) one-China policy it is not possible to have ties with both, so they choose the People's Republic.

In recent years the decisions of developing countries to seek ties with Beijing have also been influenced by China's large foreign aid and foreign investments and its huge market. Taiwan could not compete. In fact by the first decade of the new millennium China had won the "aid war" with Taipei.[31] Again Taiwan being a democracy counted for little.

Taiwan now has diplomatic ties with, but a handful of countries (17 last count), and will likely find it difficult to add to this list, while it appears inevitable it will lose some of those it has. This point has been made more salient than it would be otherwise because President Tsai and her party pledged to fix Taiwan's diplomatic isolation and lack of "international space" while promoting Taiwan's democracy during the 2016 campaign.[32]

Another problem cum obstacle to Taiwan "playing the democracy card" is the fact that the appeal of democratic governance has been

---

[30] Dennis VanVranken Hickey, *Foreign Policy Making in Taiwan: From Principle to Pragmatism,* London, Routledge, 2007, p. 114.

[31] See John F Copper, *China's Foreign Aid and Investment Diplomacy, Vol II: History and Practice 1950 to the Present,* New York, Palgrave Macmillan 2016, chapter 4.

[32] John F Copper, *Taiwan at a Tipping Point,* p. 188.

declining throughout the world in recent years. That was first apparent among developing countries where the "third wave" of democratisation drew to a halt following the world recession of 2008 and 2009 (that caused the attractiveness of democracy to diminish markedly). Democracies' image and appeal also fell as popularly elected leaders in young democracies often showed they had little interest in creating solid democratic institutions while they disregarded various freedoms and economic rights. Finally, it did not help that American leaders in promoting democracy abroad were obsessed with elections and little else.[33]

Meanwhile, China benefitted measurably from democracy losing its lure in Third World countries that admired China's state capitalism model, which generated economic growth notwithstanding the global economic meltdown. Furthermore, China did not experience declining standards of living, increased poverty, public protests, rioting in the streets and so on as did Western democracies. Some pundits even suggest that the West need to copy some of China's strategies.[34]

Another problem is that Taiwan's democracy is not rated as high as what residents in Taiwan think (or as high as it probably should be). Taiwan's ranking in the Democracy Index published by the Economist Intelligence Unit is 33 in the world. It is categorised as a "flawed democracy" (the ratings are made by "experts" based on electoral processes and pluralism, civil liberties, functioning of government, political participation and political culture). As a democracy Taiwan is ranked below three African and three Latin American countries and lower than South Korea.[35]

---

[33] Joshua Kurlantzick, *Democracy in Retreat: The Revolt of the Middle Class and the Worldwide Decline of Representative Government*, New Haven, CT, Yale University Press, 2013, pp. 54–55.

[34] Joshua Kurlantzick, *Democracy in Retreat*, p. 179. See also Stefan Halper, *The Beijing Consensus: How China's Authoritarian Model Will Dominate the Twenty-First Century*, New York, Basic Books, 2010.

[35] See "Democracy Index 2017", Wikipedia, <www.wikipedia .com> (accessed 28 March 2018).

Taiwan's "low" (lower than expected in Taiwan at least) ranking may be explained in some measure by the fact that during the Ma years the government made special efforts to abide by global guidelines on governance, human rights and so on, and got virtually no applause for this. Ma also did not improve Taiwan's economic growth as he promised in 2008 and that affected residents' views on national identity and independence. Finally, he did not respond effectively to natural disasters and was seen as elitist and out of touch with voters.[36]

Following the 2016 election of a new president, Tsai Ing-wen, and a new ruling party, the DPP, both encountered a fairly severe decline in their public opinion poll ratings. This was attributed to their poor performance in generating economic growth and stalled or abortive political (generally labelled democratic) reform.[37] It was accompanied by a perception of Taiwan's democracy. Added to this was another image problem as Westerners noticed that the new administration came to power and subsequently ruled via populism, which many in the West associate with the rise of fascism and communism.[38] In short, Taiwan's democracy arguably depreciated during the Tsai administration reflecting what one author calls the four "I"s: identity, inequality information and interference.[39]

Identity politics, which had already proven to interfere with good government, helped Tsai and the DPP win the 2016 election and then govern. It then proved to contradict globalism and Taiwan's growing economic ties with China. It also inhibited effective rule and with honesty.

Inequality, mostly economic, was a central theme in Tsai and the DPP's campaign. The perception of unfairness fed populisms that were

---

[36] See Wu, "Pivot, Hedger, or Partner", in Dittmer (ed.), *Taiwan and China*, p. 209. Wu notes that Ma "deligitimised" the national identity issue by focusing on the economy in 2008 and after.

[37] John F Copper, *Taiwan at a Tipping Point*, p. 154.

[38] John F Copper, *Taiwan at a Tipping Point*, p. 119.

[39] Dhruva Jaishankar, "The Four "I"s Undermining Democracy", Brookings, 22 April 2019 (online at brookings.edu).

the DPP's forte. Youth malaise was linked. Economic populism evolved into political populism and authoritarianism.

Tsai and the DPP exploited the new information environment before, during and after the 2016 election. Digital communications increased political theatre. It created distrust in democracy as it undermined the mechanisms for deliberation and compromise. The highly publisised efforts to seize KMT funds was a good example of readjudicating an old issue that President Chen had said was resolved and which appears unconstitutional.

Finally, the Tsai administration engaged in filling the media with evidence of China interfering in Taiwan's politics. It regularly presented stories of China's political warfare activities in Taiwan and to more defections to China by Taiwan's military and intelligence personnel. Hence, it justified adding more rules that restricted travel, including using polygraph tests. Critics said this impacted personal freedoms and diminished Taiwan's democracy.[40]

China is a Bully

A third narrative the Tsai administration has employed to explain troubled cross-Strait relations is what can be described broadly as China's bullying. There is no doubt this has been and is happening; it is apparent to both citizens in Taiwan and the rest of the world. Moreover, it has increased markedly since January 2016. Chinese leaders even say they seek to punish Taiwan because of the Tsai government advocating independence and specifically because it rejected the 92 Consensus (an agreement reached in 1992 whereby both sides accepted one China with different interpretations).[41]

Thus China's statements and its actions afford an easy and credible argument that China is an oppressor and it is to blame for bad relations between Taipei and Beijing.

---

[40] "China and Taiwan", in *2017 Report to Congress of the U.S.-China Economic and Security Review Commission*, Washington, DC, US Government Printing Office, 2017, pp. 395–96.

[41] John F Copper, *Taiwan at a Tipping Point*, pp. 186–93.

On the other hand, China's bullying, or assertiveness as some call it, is simply the natural consequence of China's fast rise in economic, diplomatic and military power. Growing powers naturally exert influence on their neighbours and even beyond. China's increased sway thus can be seen as a new reality.[42]

To understand this phenomenon better, reviewing the course of China accruing its vast new power and influence is instructive.

Deng Xiaoping launched reforms in 1978, two years after Mao's death that led to China's well-known economic boom. China soon experienced "miracle" growth — double digit annual rises in its GDP. Two decades thereafter observers noted that at no time in history had a big country displayed such growth over an extended period. In fact, China went on to break the record for years of very rapid growth, 40 years, besting Taiwan's 32 years.[43] In the process, China has been transformed from a poor country to a middle level or moderately rich country (the latter certainly in terms of its foreign exchange holdings). This made China a powerful political and military power as well.[44]

Deng's models were the United States beginning in the 1800s and later Japan's and Asia's four dragons (including notably Taiwan). Deng opened up China, promoted trade and other contacts beyond its borders. This caused it to thrive economically and in other ways as it had during earlier periods of its history when it dominated its known world. The lesson to be gleaned from this is a China that is on track to becoming a great power as it once was.

Deng also decentralised political authority from the Communist Party to the government and the central government to the provincial

[42] Michael Szonyi, "Introduction", in Jennifer Rudolph and Michael Szonyi (eds.), *The China Questions: Critical Insights into a Rising Power*, Cambridge, MA, Harvard University Press, 2018, p. 1.

[43] Nicholas R Lardy, *The State Strikes Back: The End of Economic Reform in China*, Washington, DC, Peterson Institute for International Economics, 2019, p. 26.

[44] See Ezra F Vogel, *Deng Xiaoping and the Transformation of China*, Cambridge, MA, BelknapPress, 2011, especially chapters 15 and 16.

and local governments, which turned China's authoritarian cum totalitarian political system into something quite different.[45] This helped sustain China's economic modernisation.

After 9/11 the United States became bogged down by wars in Iraq and Afghanistan, trillion dollar misadventures that cost the United States dearly in terms of its global economic influence (more apparent in Asia than elsewhere). These wars were viewed both at home and throughout most of the world as failures that diminished America's national prestige and global influence. As America declines, China fills the gap.[46]

Another variable was that mid-way through the first decade of the new millennium China had developed new and advanced industries that allowed it to reduce its purchases of many advanced (and expensive) products from abroad because it now produced them at home. This, on top of its booming economy that was to a large degree driven by exports, caused China to quickly grow its foreign exchange position. This made it the world's number one country in that category. It had on hand something approaching US$4 trillion.[47]

Three or so years thereafter, in 2008–2009 China continued its fast-paced economic growth while the United States and Europe and much of the rest of the world fell into recession (Japan was already there). Since economic success in the world and the reputation gained from it are relative, China made huge gains in global influence at this time. This continued in ensuing years while America experienced the slowest recovery after an economic downturn in a long time. Giving greater resonance to what had transpired, in 2014 the International Monetary Fund reported China's GDP (using purchasing power parity) was the

---

[45] See Barry Naughton, "Deng Xiaoping: The Economist", in David Shambaugh (ed.), *Deng Xiaoping: Portrait of a Chinese Statesman,* Oxford, Clarendon Press, 1995, p. 84.

[46] Michael Mandelbaum, *Mission Failure: America and the World in the Post-Cold War Era,* New York, Oxford University Press, 2016, conclusion.

[47] China became the largest holder of foreign exchange early in the new century. By 2011 it had nearly increased threefold that of any other country in the world. See John F Copper, *China's Foreign Aid and Investment Diplomacy,* vol. 1, p. 109.

largest on earth and its economy would pass the United States early in the next decade in absolute dollars.[48]

Concurrently China also took the honour of becoming the largest manufacturing nation in the world, its foremost exporter and its biggest trading country. As a result China became the main export market for 43 countries in the world; the United States was the largest for 32 (20 years earlier China was the primary market for just two countries, compared to the United States' 44 nations).[49]

Meanwhile, in 2013, China launched a mega engineering and construction project called the Belt and Road Initiative (BRI). By 2017 BRI involved 68 countries accounting for 65% of the world's population and 40% of global GDP. Even more impressive was China's commitment of US$1 trillion for the project (compared to something just over $100 billion in current dollars the United States spent on its biggest ever project, the Marshall Plan for the recovery of Europe after World War II). Further, China projected spending US$4–8 trillion before the completion of the project.[50]

All led some observers to perceive a shift in the world's centre of gravity in what some called "Easternisation", the moving of the wellspring of global influence to the East because of China's rise. Russia had already turned from looking West to seeing the East as where its future lies. Hungary and Turkey followed. The whole world to a surprising extent was on track to refocus its attention and its foreign policy due to the magnetic-like attraction of China coinciding with its fast rise in national power status.[51]

---

[48] Ben Carter, " Is China's Economy Really the Largest in the World?" BBC News, 16 December 2014, (online at bbc.com). The United States had held that title for more than 140 years.

[49] "Dominating and Dangerous", *The Economist*, 3 October 2015 (online at economist.com).

[50] See Tom Miller, *China's Asian Dream*, London, Zed Books, 2017 for details on the project.

[51] Gideon Rachman, *Easternization: Asia's Rise and America's Decline from Obama to Trump and Beyond*, New York, Other Press, 2016.

Not only were China's present attainments startling, indicating China had become a formidable world power, but also the projections of its future power and influence further informed this. For example, China's economic influence was forecast to increase such that it would account for more than 35% of world's expected GDP growth in the next two years, double that of the United States.[52] Another indicator is the fact that China is vastly outspending the United States, the European Union and Japan in artificial intelligence and quantum computers — likely two of the best measures of future global influence.[53]

China's new global influence is generally viewed a positive thing and many welcomed it. It is instrumental in relieving global poverty and is a boon to developing countries' economic growth. However, it is also shocking and even scary to many.

Taiwan's reaction to China's rise was at once natural and dysfunctional. It was natural insofar as economic ties with China were profitable. However, it inevitably meant political ties and implied Taiwan's loss of sovereignty. Various countries, especially smaller ones (very noticeable in Southeast Asia), recognised China's influence. However, in the case of Taiwan this portends its loss of statehood. This fear was easy to play upon by one side in Taiwan's now polarised political climate and was at the heart of the growing adoption of populism on the part of anti-KMT, anti-Ma Ying-jeou candidates for office in 2014 and 2016.[54]

In fact, this became the DPP's central *leitmotif* at the time of President Ma's proposal of the Economic Cooperation Framework Agreement (ECFA) in 2010 to energise Taiwan's economy (in lieu of needed domestic reform the opposition said), making it appear that he was deliberately making Taiwan dependent on China economically.

---

[52] Jeff Desjardins, "Half of Expected World GDP: Growth in the Next 2 Years Will Come from the US and China", *Business Insider*, 5 June 2017 (online at businessinsider.com).

[53] John F Copper, "Explaining China's Fast Rise as an Innovative Country", IPP Review, 28 January 2018 (online at ippreview.com).

[54] John F Copper, *Taiwan at a Tipping Point,* p. 106 and p. 121.

This advanced a national identity in favour of Taiwanese in the debate on the "China threat" issue from then on.[55]

Since the 2016 election when Tsai Ing-wen and the DPP assumed governance this has presented a huge contradiction. Both Tsai and her party have attempted to play down the rise of China. The more radical DPP members said Taiwan could do without China economically and in all other ways. This was self-deception. Others contended that China would come around to accept the "new reality". This was unrealistic in the extreme.

The United States is Taiwan's Protector

The fourth Taiwan narrative on cross-Strait relations is US policy vis-a-vis Taiwan. The essence of this is that the United States will protect Taiwan and will guarantee its sovereignty.

Taiwan's leaders have long made the assumption that the United States would act to shield Taiwan from an invasion by China's military as it did in 1950 when President Truman dispatched the Seventh Fleet to the Taiwan Strait to block a pending assault by Mao's forces and as President Clinton did in 1996 by ordering US aircraft carriers to the vicinity when China intimidated Taiwan with missile tests close to Taiwan's shores during an election campaign.[56]

In fact, President Eisenhower formalised this role with a treaty in 1954. The US Congress did something similar in 1979 in the form of a law, the Taiwan Relations Act (TRA), to substitute for the termination of diplomatic relations and the defence treaty. The TRA was "supplemented" by three communiqués (two before and one after) and President Ronald Reagan's 1982 "six assurances". Some experts have interpreted these documents to reify what was America's "dual deterrence" policy to keep the two sides apart and prevent a conflict.[57]

---

[55] See Lin, *Taiwan's China Dilemma*, chapter 6.
[56] See John F Copper, *Playing with Fire*, chapter 1.
[57] See Richard C Bush, *At Cross Purposes: U.S. Taiwan Relations Since 1942*, Armonk, NY, M E Shaerpe, 2004, pp. 7, 235 and 239.

However, America's policy to defend Taiwan was equivocal. It declared that any effort to determine Taiwan's future by non-peaceful means is of "grave concern to the United States". Some analysts translated this to mean a firm American commitment to Taiwan; others said no. The communiqués supported the second view; Reagan's assurances bolstered the former perception.[58]

Taiwan, of course, liked (and quoted) the TRA and the assurances. China preferred the communiqués. In the United States, Republicans favoured Taiwan's stance; Democrats did less so. The Department of State liked the communiqués; Congress preferred the TRA. The upshot was that the United States had two China policies: one that emphasised America's firm commitment to Taiwan and one that did not or was unclear on the subject. This "dichotomy" was convenient for US policy-makers as it sent a mixed message regarding the United States' unquestionable commitment to Taiwan's defence. Finally it conveyed the idea that America's pledges are not to be seen as without conditions.[59]

Often heard to support Taiwan's side of the argument was that Taiwan is a democracy and that it therefore had (or should have) the right to decide its future. American officials frequently said this and concluded Taiwan was worth defending. Words in the TRA also indicate that the United States would provide Taiwan with "defensive arms" to meet its needs.

On the other side it was often mentioned that China is more important to the United States than Taiwan and is fast becoming a great world power. Furthermore, the United States' ability to defend Taiwan has been eroding in the face of China's fast improving military and America's commitments elsewhere. Finally, US opinion polls showed a shortfall of public support for "sacrificing the blood of American soldiers" to defend Taiwan.[60]

---

[58] Goldstein, *China and Taiwan*, pp. 58–59.

[59] John F Copper, *China Diplomacy: The Washington-Taipei-Beijing Triangle*, Boulder, CO, Westview Press, 1992, p. 142.

[60] The Chicago Council on Global Affairs has conducted opinion surveys on this question regularly for several years. Only around one quarter of Americans according to their polls support the employent of US military forces to defend Taiwan in the event of a conflict (see thechicagocouncil.org).

This constitutes the "theory" or basic assumptions of US Taiwan policy. What is the real US position and how does it look at the present time? Those are big questions.

US presidents have almost consistently taken a pro-Taiwan position when they campaign and sometimes early on when in office, to later shift to a more pro-China position or a policy to work with China. Explaining this phenomenon is the fact that Americans have long seen China as America's foe and disagreed with China's polity (it being a communist country). China's human rights record and more recently its trade policies are also in question. Thus taking a hard position on relations with China during an election campaign was a benefit to candidates for high office.[61] After the election, winning candidates realised it was necessary and/or advantageous to get along with China.

There are also some American precepts regarding US foreign policy that relate to its relations with Taiwan. Americans believe the United States should prevent a dictatorship from subjugating a democratic friend. Yet there is a caveat: Americans, based on the country's Civil War experience, do not see self-determination as an absolute right. They are also sceptical of promoting the expansion of democracy abroad, made more so by President George W Bush's failed efforts to do this in the Middle East.

Broadly speaking Americans have neither a hot nor cold feeling towards Asian countries in general nor US involvement there. They are friendly towards Taiwan, but they do not want to be pulled into a foreign conflict. On US national security interests, they are divided about Taiwan.[62]

Barack Obama was an exception to the pattern of pro-Taiwan sentiment that subsequently changed. When Obama became president in 2009 one of his immediate objectives was to improve relations with China. While on his first visit to China in November that year he

---

[61] See Robert G Sutter, *U.S.-Chinese Relations: Perilous Past, Pragmatic Present*, Lanham, MD, Rowman and Littlefield, 2013, pp. 2–3. The author notes this especially during the 2012 election. It was very true of the 1968 election. It was obvious in 2016.

[62] Hu Shaohua, *Foreign Policies Toward Taiwan*, London, Routledge, 2018, p. 57.

concurred with the Chinese leadership's pronouncement that Taiwan was a "core interest" (understood to mean something that China would engage its military to realise). It appeared that Obama was willing to sacrifice Taiwan for better relations with Beijing.[63]

In ensuing months Obama sent palpable signals that he planned to dump or abandon Taiwan thus fulfilling what he articulated during the campaign. He said he wanted a US foreign policy based on negotiations, not military force. Unlike his opponent, John McCain, he did not confirm that the United States had an obligation to defend Taiwan.[64]

Soon after the inauguration officials in President Obama's administration proffered talks with high-level military leaders from China and Taiwan indicating Obama did not accept at least one of President Reagan's six assurances — not to promote negotiations between the two sides. Subsequently, Obama's vice chairman of the joint chiefs stated publicly that the TRA was "outdated". This was followed by a report from the government-connected Rand Corporation opining that the United States would not be able to deploy sufficient weapons in the event of a Chinese attack on Taiwan.[65]

After this came articles in the Obama-friendly journal *Foreign Affairs* saying the United States should end its "protectorate" role vis-à-vis Taiwan. This would resolve a dangerous "flashpoint". Shortly after this the author of an article in the *New York Times* advocated America offset its $1.4 trillion debt to China via a deal to terminate arms sales to Taiwan. President Carter's national security adviser Zbigniew Brzezinski at this juncture called Taiwan an "endangered species".[66]

It appeared President Obama's China/Taiwan policy was profoundly and permanently pro-China and anti-Taiwan.

---

[63] For logic behind Obama's China diplomacy at this time, see James Mann, *The Obamians: The Struggle Inside the White House to Redefine American Power*, New York, Viking, 2013, chapter 13.

[64] John F Copper, "Will the United States Desert Taiwan?" in Wang Gungwu and Zheng Yongnian (eds.), *China: Government and Governance*, Singapore: World Scientific, 2013, p. 480.

[65] John F Copper, "Will the United States Desert Taiwan?"

[66] John F Copper, "Will the United States Desert Taiwan?" pp. 480–81.

However, it was not long before President Obama dramatically reconsidered US China policy. He came to the realisation that China had snookered him with the "core interest" idea and that Chinese leaders wished to supplant the liberal world order with the "China dream" that meant China's rise and eventual dominance in global influence. President Obama had an epiphany after which he adopted a quite hostile US China policy.[67]

Launching this *volte-face* in US China policy, Secretary of State Hillary Clinton published a piece in the magazine *Foreign Policy* using the term "Asia pivot". It embraced a plan to rally America's allies to push back against a rising and threatening China.[68]

Meanwhile, however, President Obama agreed to a budget plan called sequestration to resolve the growing US debt crisis. A major source of savings was to be a reduction in the military budget. The cuts engendered serious concerns on the part of strategic planners. Secretary of Defence Leon Panetta stated that it would make the US military a "paper tiger" and would "invite aggression". US allies, notably Asian ones, expressed deep concern.[69]

US China policy was subsequently impacted by Secretary of State Hillary Clinton's resignation and replacement by John Kerry (whose focus was on the Middle East), and the departures of several noted Asian experts from the Obama administration. Hence the pivot to Asia became viewed as a failure and by some as Obama's biggest foreign policy mistake.[70]

In the last months of the Obama presidency US-China relations had never been worse than before Richard Nixon's pursuit of rapprochement

---

[67] Wang Chi, *Obama's Challenge to China; The Pivot to Asia*, Burlington, VT, Ashgate 2015, chapter 4.

[68] Hillary Clinton, "America's Pacific Century", *Foreign Policy*, 11 October 2011 (online at foreignpolicy.com); Wang Chi, *Obama's Challenge to China*, chapter 5.

[69] Peter W Sanger, "Sequestration and What It Would Do to U.S. Military Power", *Time*, 24 September 2012 (online at time.com).

[70] John Ford, "The Pivot to Asia Was Obama's Biggest Mistake", *The Diplomat*, 21 January 2017 (online at thediplomat.org).

with China. However, Taiwan did not benefit. President Obama chose not to "play the Taiwan card". Apparently he wanted to avoid a further deterioration in relations with China at a time when he was preoccupied with the Middle East and in fear of staining his legacy as president.[71]

Thus during the Obama years Taiwan might have thought the "American shield" had been withdrawn. It chose not to. It did not believe this, or chose not to. Alternatively, it had no choice or knowing Obama would be leaving office soon it did not matter.

Conclusions

The situation of the Taiwan Strait being a high-level flashpoint persists. In fact, cross-Strait tension has increased, so has the danger of conflict since the January 2016 election. The transfer of governance to a president and political party that dislikes China and opposes unification is the main reason. Chinese leaders thus had their shackles raised by the results of that election. This was made worse by the narratives the Taiwan government adopted to explain the decline in cross-Strait relations.

The election of Donald Trump president of the United States several months thereafter added an element of uncertainty to the equation.

During the 2016 presidential election campaign Donald Trump espoused a quite critical attitude towards China focusing in particular on economic relations and the unfavourable US trade balance that Trump charged hurt American companies and workers. Trump was more condemnatory of China than previous presidential candidates had been or were. This encouraged Taiwan.

Even before he was inaugurated president, Donald Trump took a telephone call from President Tsai and subsequently declared that he

---

[71] See Lyle J Goldstein, *Meeting China Halfway: How to Difuse the Emerging U.S.-China Rivalry*, Washington, DC, Georgetown University Press, 2015, chapter 7.

did not have to adhere to America's one-China policy, all of which was music to the ears of the Tsai administration and the DPP. Some even saw Trump as a supporter of Taiwan independence.[72]

They seemed to be oblivious to the fact Trump was a negotiator president and a realist. Or that Trump's advisers told him that China is the most important country in the world to the United States and that maintaining a stable global financial system, preventing nuclear proliferation, protecting the environment and much more hinged on cordial and workable US-China relations.[73] Or that Trump appeared to have a fondness for China as reflected in the fact that his grandchildren are studying Chinese.

They also seemed to forget (or wanted to) that President Tsai had endorsed Hillary Clinton for president (a departure from Taiwan's tradition of not taking sides in a US election) and that Clinton supporters had engaged in fund raising in Taiwan. Furthermore, many members of Tsai's party were leftist progressives and many of her advisers and the pro-DPP press patently harboured ill will towards President Trump and said so with regularity.

They also ignored the fact that many important President Trump's advisers were former top military brass and they observed that Taiwan was not doing its share in helping the United States or even defending itself, expecting America to do this "free of charge". President Tsai promised to correct this and raise Taiwan's defence spending and its military preparedness but did not follow up. As a percentage of government spending the defence budget was below what it was 25 years earlier while troop levels have been cut substantially.[74]

The Tsai administration even engaged in citing what are arguably fake polls in convincing the public and the United States that its residents are willing to go to war if China seeks to force unification. Reputable polls

---

[72] John F Copper, "President Tsai's Telephone Call to President Trump", IPP Review, (online at ippreview.com).

[73] See Henry M Paulson, *Dealing with China: An Insider Unmasks the New Economic Superpower*, New York, Hachette Book Group, 2016. According to insiders in Washington President Trump heard Paulson's argument directly.

[74] "China and Taiwan", *2017 Report to Congress,* p. 389.

record that a solid majority will "wait and see", "leave the country", "hide", or "choose to surrender". The majority also supports strengthening commercial ties with China while a whopping 70% believe tensions with China under the current government will hurt Taiwan's economy in the future. Most residents say the polls, also supported cross-Strait relations under the one-China rubric, saw no necessity to declare independence, and by a huge majority (75%), did not believe Taiwan's military can defend the island against an attack by China.[75]

There is an identity issue sidebar: One of Taiwan's close friends, Steven Yates (former deputy national security adviser to Vice President Dick Cheney), challenged the poll cited by the government that most people would join in fighting a war against China's pursuit of unification. Yates stated publicly that "Taiwanese were not willing to trade their lives, assets and sacred honor" to maintain independence.[76]

This was the backdrop to the 19th Party Congress held in China the following year. Chinese leaders took stock of the serious problems facing them and charted a course for the future. By many accounts Taiwan was a top serious problem; arguably it was the most serious one. Looking forward they had to cite a solution and they did: Taiwan has to be made part of China and they set a deadline. To some observers, it looked like the "Thucydides moment" had arrived and a US-China conflict precipitated by Taiwan is much more likely.

However, the situation is more complex and indeed in some important ways different from superficial observations that led one to view was the case. There are extenuating circumstances. There are other policy drivers. Likely China's top party and government officials had to take a hard line to placate the military.[77]

---

[75] Dennis V Hickey, "Taiwan Public Opinion and National Security", China-US Focus, 4 May 2018 (online at chinausfocus.com). The author cites polls done by the Election Study Centre at the National Chengchi University in cooperation with Programme in Asian Studies Security at Duke University.

[76] Brian Hioe, "Recent Comments by Steven Yates Return to American Disrespect for Taiwanese Democracy", Bloomberg, 13 August 2017 (online at newbloomberg.net).

[77] Lawrence Chung, "China's military strength coiuld advance Taiwan unification by force, says US official", *South China Morning Post*, 16 January 2019 (online at scmp.com).

On Taiwan's part the narratives discussed earlier showed that the explanations offered by Taiwan's government were largely the product of Taiwan politics having become harshly polarised and populism having offered a solution of the day to most problems. This injected more win-lose thinking into the equation. In addition, Taiwan's leaders cum politicians had their blinders on while looking ahead to the next election. They were preoccupied with staying in power or winning. Nothing else much matters or at least nearly all issues were seen in that context.

Indeed election campaigns had become a central factor in Taiwan's democracy. Its leaders and their political parties seem always gauging and planning for the next contest, with national elections every four years and "mid-terms" (a big collection of local contests that are almost as important) positioned almost in between. Politicians and voters are nearly all of the time made aware of this. This was not a good thing as it crowds out leadership, long-range plans and rational thinking.

However, this may not be all bad. Public opinion polls have become a big wakeup call for President Tsai and the DPP notwithstanding some fake ones. It is apparent that the public often did not agree with or support the government's narratives.

There is some realisation among residents that populism and realism are at odds with each other. The former generally ignores Taiwan's security situation, claiming blindly and with emotion that the people of Taiwan will determine their future. Leaders in China and the United States as well as many scholars are well aware that small actors in international affairs do not do that. Fortunately for Taiwan the United States assumes some duty to protect Taiwan even though it is conditional. China's policy towards Taiwan shows patience to realise unification by 2049, which allows considerable time flexibility to reach a compromise and peaceful solution.

Clearly Taiwan's narratives must be seen as sensible as they relate to domestic politics but not to reality or US-China relations.

Chapter 12

A Nanyang Approach to the Belt and Road Initiative: Malaysia and Its Dilemmas

LIU Hong and LIM Guanie*

In 2013, Chinese President Xi Jinping announced a pair of initiatives to facilitate the development of economies spanning Europe and Asia. The Silk Road Economic Belt was announced in September 2013 in Kazakhstan as a programme to connect China to Europe by land, with routes interlinking relevant countries. A month thereafter in Indonesia, President Xi announced the 21st Century Maritime Silk Road, a maritime development initiative targeting the ports of Southeast Asia, South Asia, the Middle East, East Africa and the Mediterranean. These two Silk Road programmes collectively form the 'Belt and Road Initiative' (BRI). With an investment value

* LIU Hong is Tan Lark Sye Chair Professor of Public Policy and Global Affairs and Chair of School of Social Sciences, Nanyang Technological University, Singapore. LIM Guanie is Research Fellow, Nanyang Centre for Public Administration, Nanyang Technological University, Singapore. Liu Hong would like to acknowledge the funding support of the Singapore Ministry of Education AcRFTier-2 Grant (MOE2016-T2-2-087). This chapter draws some of its contents and arguments from an earlier work by the authors: Hong Liu and Lim Guanie, "The Political Economy of a Rising China in Southeast Asia: Malaysia's Response to the Belt and Road Initiative", *Journal of Contemporary China*, vol. 28, no. 116, 2019, pp. 216–231.

surpassing US$1 trillion, the BRI has become China's foremost diplomatic and economic strategy in engaging with neighbouring countries and beyond since 2013.[1]

Although BRI is a China-driven strategy unlike other national plans (such as developing the western regions or *Xibu Dakaifa*) that fall within the domestic political economy of China, its operation and success (or failure) depends fundamentally upon the engagement with and response from countries along the BRI (numbering more than 60). Existing studies on BRI have focused almost exclusively on China's interests and strategies, giving little attention to the responses of small states, such as those from Southeast Asia.[2] To bridge this gap, this chapter reaffirms the critical role that Southeast Asia plays in the BRI. It goes beyond a macro-level analysis, employing a meso-scale perspective to take into account diverse economic, political, ethnic interests and more importantly, the fluid interplay among these factors. This chapter also draws upon Professor Wang Gungwu's inspiring scholarship on Chinese overseas and Southeast Asia. Wang's bi-focalism — on the regions of China and Southeast Asia as a detached analyst as well as an involved participant — can certainly help the scholarly community better understand the BRI and its ramifications on Southeast Asia and the rest of the world.[3]

---

[1] Peter Ferdinand, "Westward Ho — The China Dream and 'One Belt, One Road': Chinese Foreign Policy under Xi Jinping", *International Affairs*, vol. 92, no. 4, 2016, pp. 941–957.

[2] See, for example, Cheng Zhangxi and Ian Taylor, *China's Aid to Africa: Does Friendship Really Matter?*, Oxford, Routledge, 2017.

[3] Hong Liu, "Wang Gengwu Jiaoshou yu haiwai huaren yanjiu: Fangfalun de chubu guancha" (Professor Wang Gungwu and the Studies of Chinese Overseas: Preliminary Observations on his Methodology), *Huaqiao huaren lishi yanjiu* (*Overseas Chinese History Studies*), no. 1, March 2003, pp. 62–69; Hong Liu and Gregor Benton, "Introduction", in *Diasporic Chinese Ventures: The Life and Work of Wang Gungwu*, Gregor Benton and Hong Liu (eds.), London, Routledge, 2004, pp. 1–9. On Wang's contribution to diplomacy and Southeast Asian studies, see Hong Liu, "Chinese Overseas and a Rising China: The Limits of a Diplomatic 'Diaspora Option'", in *China and International Relations: The Chinese View and the Contribution of Wang Gungwu*, Zheng Yongnian (ed.), Oxford, Routledge, 2010, pp. 177–199.

The Belt and Road Initiative from a Nanyang Perspective

Malaysia is a good case study to understand the BRI from a Southeast Asian perspective because firstly, it is one of the founding members of the Association of Southeast Asian Nations (ASEAN), a multilateral platform established in 1967 to promote regional integration and cooperation. Secondly, Malaysia enjoys a special relationship with China when then Prime Minister Tun Abdul Razak established diplomatic ties with Beijing in 1974. The bilateral relationship has blossomed under successive prime ministers, especially former Prime Minister Najib Razak (in office from April 2009 to May 2018).[4] Thirdly, Malaysia's ethnic Chinese minority (about 25% of the population) has long played a key role in advancing bilateral trade and investment in spite of a state-sanctioned affirmative action policy limiting the participation of ethnic Chinese in various activities.[5] Thanks to their economic success, the ethnic Chinese have often been portrayed as a bogeyman by some politicians representing the ethnic Malay population (roughly 65% of the population).[6] At a time of China rising, the financially powerful (yet politically weak) ethnic Chinese across Southeast Asia have also been viewed as a conduit in fostering China-Southeast Asia economic ties.[7] This

---

[4] Najib was defeated by the opposition bloc, captained by the evergreen Mahathir Mohamad, in the general election on 9 May 2018. Mahathir's victory at the polls means that this is his second (and likely, last) tenure as prime minister, following a first stint between 1981 and 2003. It also brought an end to one of Asia's longest ruling party — Najib's United Malays National Organisation (UMNO)-led coalition — which had ruled the country since August 1957.

[5] James Chin, "The Malaysian Chinese Dilemma: The Never Ending Policy (NEP)", *Chinese Southern Diaspora Studies,* vol. 3, 2009, pp. 167–182.

[6] Joan Nelson, "Political Challenges in Economic Upgrading: Malaysia Compared with South Korea and Taiwan", in *Malaysia's Development Challenges: Graduating from the Middle,* Hal Hill, Tham Siew Yean and Ragayah Haji Mat Zin (eds.), Oxford, Routledge, 2012, pp. 43–62.

[7] Caroline Hau, "Becoming 'Chinese' — but what 'Chinese'? — in Southeast Asia", *The Asia-Pacific Journal: Japan Focus,* vol. 10, no. 26, 2012, pp. 1–36; Hong Liu,

makes the community influential agents for deciphering whether Beijing's engagement with them represents a new mode of transnational governance.[8]

With the aforementioned as a backdrop, this chapter addresses the following questions: What are the key elements of the BRI in the context of the Southeast Asian political economy? How do business groups from China (both state-owned and private) undertake their operations in Southeast Asia (in general) and Malaysia (in particular)? Moreover, how do different forces in Malaysia (ruling coalition, opposition bloc and civil society) react to the BRI and what are their key stakes in engaging (or disengaging) with China? What implications can be drawn from Malaysia for a better understanding of the BRI, especially the huge opportunities that come with the initiative and its operational constraints? What does this mean for the country's and the region's ethnic Chinese business community? What dilemmas, if any, will Malaysia face in the context of China's growing clout in Southeast Asia?

This chapter unpacks these questions by analysing three of the most prominent BRI projects in Malaysia — East Coast Rail Link (ECRL), Bandar Malaysia and Forest City. ECRL is orchestrated by the China Communications Construction Company (CCCC), a state-owned enterprise (SOE), with strong endorsement by Najib and several chief ministers. Bandar Malaysia was jointly developed by China Railway Engineering Corporation (CREC), another SOE, and parties aligned with Najib. Forest City, on the other hand, is driven by Country Garden (a private firm), in partnership with the sultan of Johor, reflecting a rising trend of wealthy Chinese private firms venturing abroad. The chapter argues that domestic players in these projects are astute in co-opting their Chinese counterparts to advance their own goals. Their eventual success is dependent on three conditions: fulfilment of Malaysia's

"Opportunities and Anxieties for the Chinese Diaspora in Southeast Asia", *Current History: A Journal of Contemporary World Affairs*, vol. 115, no. 784, 2016, pp. 311–317.

[8] Hong Liu and Els van Dongen, "China's Diaspora Policies as a New Mode of Transnational Governance", *Journal of Contemporary China*, vol. 25, no. 102, 2016, pp. 805–821.

pro-ethnic Malay agenda, a common development goal between the state and federal authorities, and advancement of geopolitical interests for both China and Malaysia. As will be detailed later, ECRL's modest success during the Najib era (with it temporarily suspended by a resurgent Mahathir), Bandar Malaysia's failure and Forest City's arrested development underline the need to be wary of societal contestation within the BRI recipient state as well as Beijing's geopolitical goals.

Data for this chapter was obtained from personal interviews conducted from May 2016 to May 2017 with individuals who have been directly involved in China's economic engagement with Malaysia. The interviews were conducted in China, Malaysia and Singapore, focusing on two main topics — the overall business approach of the Chinese firms and their interactions with important domestic stakeholders. It was supplemented by information gathered from two public forums (March and May 2017 in Singapore) voicing views on Chinese investment in Malaysia. To enhance the robustness of the primary data, they are cross validated against newspaper essays, published reports and company websites in the English, Chinese and Malay languages. In certain cases, materials from personal blogs were retrieved to explore views candidly expressed but seldom heard, albeit with caution given their limitations. The use of these sources of information allowed for data verification and triangulation, resulting in a clearer reading of the situation from multiple perspectives. Given the sensitive nature of the issues discussed (e.g. ethnic relations and business-state interactions), all interviewees were promised confidentiality.

The subsequent section examines the literature on the internationalisation of China. It identifies the gap in knowledge, especially the lack of perspectives from Southeast Asia. The third section provides a grounded analysis by drawing upon Wang Gungwu's insights and nestling it within the context of Malaysia. The fourth section puts forth a conceptual framework hypothesising various possible outcomes to better analyse how Malaysia (and other states) respond to the BRI. It then focuses on the progress of the ECRL, Bandar Malaysia and Forest City. The chapter discusses the interconnections between key players in the BRI recipient state and unpacks the manners in which domestic stakeholders utilise Chinese capital to further their own agendas. Subsequently, the chapter analyses the progress of the three projects in the aftermath of the country's watershed general election on 9 May 2018. The last section concludes with a summary of the main arguments, with an aim to highlight the important role of Nanyang in the evolution of the BRI and the dilemmas that countries in the region face.

Approaching the Belt and Road Initiative: All about Geopolitics?

There has been a growing body of research analysing the motivations and impacts of China in its overseas expansion. Such studies tend to view actors within China as the major (if not, sole) variable behind China's foreign direct investment (FDI). Firstly, much of the debate has pinpointed the Chinese state as the primary determinant undergirding the BRI.[9] Callahan postulates that Beijing is utilising new policies and institutions related to the BRI to construct a 'new regional order', weaving specific countries into a Sino-centric 'community of shared destiny'.[10] Beeson argues that China's recent moves are presenting a formidable challenge to its immediate neighbours.[11] He contends that China is adept at exploiting rifts between key Southeast Asian countries, complicating efforts to develop a common position vis-à-vis China and successfully undermining solidarity within the region.

---

[9] See, for example, Mark Beeson, "Can ASEAN Cope with China?" *Journal of Current Southeast Asian Affairs*, vol. 35, no. 1, 2016, pp. 5–28; William Callahan, "China's 'Asia Dream': The Belt Road Initiative and the New Regional Order", *Asian Journal of Comparative Politics*, vol. 1, no. 3, 2016, pp. 226–243; Yu Hong, "Motivation behind China's 'One Belt, One Road' Initiatives and Establishment of the Asian Infrastructure Investment Bank", *Journal of Contemporary China*, vol. 26, no. 105, 2017, pp. 353–368; and Zhou Weifeng and Mario Esteban, "Beyond Balancing: China's Approach towards the Belt and Road Initiative", *Journal of Contemporary China*, vol. 27, no. 112, 2018, pp. 487–501.

[10] William Callahan, "China's 'Asia Dream'"

[11] Mark Beeson, "Can ASEAN Cope with China?"

Secondly, the state-centric perspective has been augmented by other studies on the multitude of actors shaping China's economy. They posit that the BRI is also driven by other Chinese players such as the SOEs, private firms and less well-capitalised Chinese entrepreneurs. To ensure access to overseas energy supply, Beijing has been utilising diplomatic instruments and policy banks to help its national firms — primarily the SOEs — tap into the oil and gas fields in Russia-Central Asia, Middle East-North Africa and South America.[12] In agriculture, small-scale Chinese family farms have most actively expanded westwards into Tajikistan, reacting much faster than the SOEs.[13]

These two strands of work, while insightful, tend to understand Chinese outward expansion mainly from the perspective of Chinese actors, giving little attention to the responses formulated by players in the BRI recipient states that, as will be demonstrated later, have their own agendas in their engagement (or disengagement) with China. Without a more explicit analysis of the relevant state and non-state actors from the recipient state, the reality of the initiative is likely obscure. Focusing on Chinese corporate expansion into Southeast Asia, Lim Guanie problematises the concept that the Chinese state is the most important, if not the only, variable in explaining the outward investment of Chinese firms.[14] He argues that firm strategies are influenced by a broad range of actors, especially those in the host economies, which collectively shape global production and dictate value capture. Using examples from the automobile and electronics sectors, he shows that only Chinese firms adept at managing a variety of complex factors are successful in their overseas expansion. Drawing lessons from recent

---

[12] Monique Taylor, *The Chinese State, Oil and Energy Security*, New York, Palgrave Macmillan, 2014.

[13] Irna Hofman, "Politics or Profits along the 'Silk Road': What Drives Chinese Farms in Tajikistan and Helps them Thrive?" *Eurasian Geography and Economics*, vol. 57, no. 3, 2016, pp. 457–481.

[14] Lim Guanie, "China's 'Going Out' Strategy in Southeast Asia: Case Studies of the Automobile and Electronics Sectors", *China: An International Journal*, vol. 15, no. 4, 2017, pp. 157–178.

BRI projects in Myanmar, scholars are increasingly aware of the need to pay attention to societal contestation within BRI recipient states and its potential of leading to a more contested outcome, just like how Myanmar in 2011 stunned global audiences by unilaterally suspending the construction of the Myitsone Dam, China's largest hydropower project abroad then.[15] The stakeholders — who do not normally collaborate because of competing interests — projected the construction of the Myitsone dam as the works of a common external enemy, eventually succeeding in pressuring Naypyidaw to suspend the project.[16]

Such research is sparse compared to more 'popular' literature on Chinese overseas investment under the themes of 'colonialism' and 'imperialism'. This body of literature mainly draws on case studies of Chinese firms operating in Africa and (to a lesser extent) South America. It commonly highlights Beijing's opaque state-SOE nexus, no-strings-attached stance on human rights and the poor corporate governance of Chinese firms.[17] The situation is exacerbated by these countries' weak organisational capacity of civil society and poor institutional setting.[18] Most of these works remain relatively nascent, transitioning somewhat slowly from broad-brush approaches to more critical and nuanced research.

Therefore, a perspective from Southeast Asia is imperative to decipher the on-the-ground intricacies of the BRI. Indeed, the region's political economy, socio-cultural landscapes and developmental trajectories are fairly good representatives of the developing world.[19]

---

[15] Laur Kiik, "Nationalism and Anti-Ethno-Politics: Why 'Chinese Development' Failed at Myanmar's Myitsone Dam", *Eurasian Geography and Economics*, vol. 57, no. 3, 2016, pp. 374–402.

[16] Laur Kiik, "Nationalism and Anti-Ethno-Politics".

[17] Henry Sanderson and Michael Forsythe, *China's Superbank: Debt, Oil and Influence — How China Development Bank is Rewriting the Rules of Finance*, Singapore, Wiley, 2013.

[18] Cheng Zhangxi and Ian Taylor,, *China's Aid to Africa: Does Friendship Really Matter?*

[19] Cf. Gary Hawes and Hong Liu, "Explaining the Dynamics of the Southeast Asian Political Economy: State, Society, and the Search for Economic Growth", *World Politics*, vol. 45, no. 4, 1993, pp. 629–660; and Erik Kuhonta, Dan Slater and Vu Tuong (eds.), *Southeast Asia in Political Science: Theory, Region, and Qualitative Analysis*, Stanford, Stanford University Press, 2008.

This chapter's analysis of infrastructure development in Malaysia, Southeast Asia's fourth-largest economy, aims to redress the knowledge gap pertaining to the BRI. It reveals how key domestic political actors have remoulded the initiative, thus challenging the China-centric angle that is hitherto dominant in the literature.

The Malaysian Political Economy: Ethnicity and State-Federal Contestation

Malaysia has successfully transformed its previously commodities-driven economy into a middle-income economy since independence in 1957. However, it has become less appealing in the eyes of international investors following the emergence of a newer cohort of developing economies with low labour cost advantage (such as Vietnam and Indonesia). In particular, Malaysia's decades-old affirmative action policy, significantly propelled by the controversial work of Mahathir — *The Malay Dilemma* (1970) — designed to redistribute income along ethnic lines, has become a stumbling block for investors.[20] Formally known as the New Economic Policy (NEP), which was imposed following racial riots in 1969, the policy provides preferential treatment to the *Bumiputera* (essentially Malay) population in almost all features of the economy such as employment opportunities and home ownership.[21]

Despite its lopsided nature, the NEP has arguably preserved the rule of UMNO, its chief architect and the hegemon within the ruling administration, from August 1957 to the recently concluded May 2018 general election. However, the NEP has also alienated a significant portion of the country's ethnic minorities. Its ethnocentric nature has been exploited by the pro-Malay UMNO, which frequently projects the financially powerful ethnic Chinese minority as bogeymen of the Malay community.[22] If anything, the pro-Malay agenda has strengthened in recent years, in light of the failure of the UMNO-led

---

[20] See Mahathir Mohamad, *The Malay Dilemma*, Singapore, Asia Pacific Press, 1970.
[21] James Chin, "The Malaysian Chinese Dilemma: The Never Ending Policy (NEP)".
[22] Joan Nelson, "Political Challenges in Economic Upgrading".

ruling coalition to secure its customary two-thirds parliamentary majority over the last two decades.[23] Pandering more forcefully to the ethnic Malays, UMNO's goal is to capture enough votes from the ethnic Malay-heavy rural constituencies to overcome its loss of the (predominantly non-Malay and anti-establishment) urban seats.[24]

As Malaysia finds it increasingly difficult to attract FDI from its 'traditional' sources (i.e. the industrialised Western countries, Singapore and Japan), policymakers are forced to seek alternative investments. China has thus emerged as an attractive FDI contributor, especially since the formulation of the BRI. The latest governmental statistics show that China was Malaysia's largest investor in 2017, contributing an investment totalling US$1.3 billion (equivalent to 17.7% of the country's total FDI inflow). Chinese FDI had eclipsed those from Switzerland (11.2% of inward FDI), Singapore (10.7%), the Netherlands (9.3%), Germany (7.0%) and Hong Kong (6.5%).[25] Chinese investment is especially noticeable in large-scale, capital-intensive infrastructure projects. In certain cases, Malaysian Chinese businesspeople have become useful middlemen in attracting mainland Chinese investment, mobilising their knowledge about China and the domestic market as well as their intimate relationship with the ethnic Malay-dominated state institutions and government-linked corporations (GLCs).[26]

---

[23] James Chin, "Malaysia: Heading for Sharia Domination?", *The Round Table*, vol. 105, no. 6, 2016, pp. 737–739.

[24] The party's failure to garner support from the ethnic minorities was not damaging, at least until the 2000s, as Malaysia's relatively high growth rate in the post-independence decades was sufficient to sway the opinions of a large enough portion of the citizenry (both Malays and non-Malays). However, since the early 2000s, a slowing economy and more intense competition from other developing economies have placed significant strain on this dynamic.

[25] *Annual Report 2017*, Kuala Lumpur, Malaysian Investment Development Authority, 2017.

[26] Lim Teck Ghee, "Abdullah Badawi, the NECC and the Corporate Equity Issue: View from a Personal Connection", in *Awakening: The Abdullah Badawi Years in Malaysia*, Bridget Welsh and James Chin (eds.), Petaling Jaya, Strategic Information and Research Development Centre, 2013, pp. 457–480.

However, the rosy view of the Chinese business community has to be moderated by considering the different circumstances of particular Chinese communities and the broader politico-economic reality that they are embedded in. In an interview with Laurent Malvezin, Wang acknowledges that while there is some form of intra-ethnic cooperation across borders for commercial purposes, the reality is that the ethnic Chinese 'adapt to new circumstances and thus become very different from other groups of Chinese living elsewhere'.[27] Wang's broader argument is that there exists substantial heterogeneity amongst the Chinese overseas, so it is misleading to classify them as a monolithic, undifferentiated bloc.[28] This is exemplified by recent studies detailing that Chinese capital has largely collaborated with the ethnic Malay-led GLCs rather than Malaysia's ethnic Chinese firms, particularly in the more-regulated industries (such as infrastructure and automobile manufacturing).[29] The success of Huawei and Zhongxing Telecommunication Equipment Corporation in their Malaysian ventures is not dependent on forging ties with the ethnic Chinese firms, but on strong compliance with domestic socio-political order characterised by the NEP.[30]

One also needs to consider state-federal ties. While responsibilities and revenue sources are geared strongly towards the federal government, Malaysia's 13 states still enjoy some autonomy in matters such as land use, local public services and religious affairs.[31] Nine of these states are led by ethnic Malay hereditary monarchies (also known as sultanates). Under Malaysia's unique form of constitutional monarchy, the sultans assume largely a ceremonial role, with executive power in the

---

[27] Laurent Malvezin, "The Problems with (Chinese) Diaspora: An Interview with Wang Gungwu", in *Diasporic Chinese Ventures: The Life and Work of Wang Gungwu*, pp. 49–60.
[28] Wang Gungwu, "A Single Chinese Diaspora?", in *Diasporic Chinese Ventures: The Life and Work of Wang Gungwu*, pp. 157–177.
[29] Lim Guanie, "China's Investments in Malaysia: Choosing the 'Right' Partners", *International Journal of China Studies*, vol. 6, no. 1, 2015, pp. 1–30.
[30] Ran Li and Cheong Kee-Cheok, "Huawei and ZTE in Malaysia: The Localisation of Chinese Transnational Enterprises", *Journal of Contemporary Asia*, vol. 47, no. 5, 2017, pp. 752–773.
[31] Three other smaller territories are governed directly by the federal administrators.

hands of the respective chief ministers (the heads of government).[32] While the sultans are generally popular amongst the citizenry (especially the Malays), there were some high profile instances where the sultans came up against the federal government.[33]

To illustrate the point aforementioned, one needs only to look at Johor, Malaysia's second most populous state. Johor's relationship with the federal government has been complicated by the 2006 inception of Iskandar Malaysia, a 9,300-acre special economic zone bordering Singapore. Although Johor, the country's southernmost state, stands to benefit from the success of Iskandar Malaysia, the project is viewed as an encroachment of Johor's land use, a sphere traditionally under the remit of the Johor government.[34] Furthermore, it is driven primarily by the federal government, with only limited autonomy provided to its Johorean counterpart. The dominance of the federal government vis-à-vis the Johor administration is in turn undergirded by the former's preoccupation with distributing economic growth across the country. Johor's proximity to Singapore also means that there are concerns about the shift of Malaysia's centre of gravity from Kuala Lumpur to the neighbouring city-state (and Johor, to a smaller extent).

The International Political Economy and Malaysia

Synthesising the aforementioned literature, this chapter aims to account simultaneously for the interaction of international and domestic factors by presenting a tentative framework to analyse how Malaysian actors respond to China (see Table 1). The constructs are

---

[32] The sultans are known to exercise their influence on the state administration, sometimes incurring the wrath of the politicians. See David Seth Jones, "Resolving the Constitutional Question of the Malaysian King and Rulers", *Asian Journal of Political Science*, vol. 3, no. 1, 1995, pp. 13–31.

[33] David Seth Jones, "Resolving the Constitutional Question of the Malaysian King and Rulers".

[34] Ng Keng Khoon and Lim Guanie, "Beneath the Veneer: The Political Economy of Housing in Iskandar Malaysia, Johor", *Trends in Southeast Asia*, vol. 3, no. 12, 2017, pp. 1–28.

Table 1:   Alignments of Interests between China and BRI Recipient States

Project/Analytical Dimension	Intertwining of Domestic Ethno-Political Agenda with Chinese Objectives	State-Federal Contestation	Convergence of China-Malaysia Geopolitical Goals
East Coast Rail Link	High	Low	High
Bandar Malaysia	Moderate	Low	Low
Forest City	Low	High	Low

Source: Compiled by the authors.

theoretical ideal-types and serve primarily as heuristic devices, yet they potentially contribute to a better understanding of how domestic actors engage with their Chinese counterparts. Examining the interplay of domestic ethno-political goals and Chinese interests, state-federal contestation and convergence of geopolitical goals, Table 1 isolates and examines *three* of the *most crucial variables* undergirding the BRI. It is *only* when these *three variables* are *properly addressed* can the projects *be rolled out successfully*. This *three-tiered analysis* is useful for incorporating motivations from multiple interest groups, particularly in countries operating on a federal government structure (such as Malaysia), with political power often apportioned unevenly between the central and local administrative units.

As detailed previously, ECRL, Bandar Malaysia and Forest City are chosen because they are three of the most important BRI projects in the country. In addition to their massive capital outlay, these three projects are selected because of the differing characteristics of their proponents and the power relations involved. ECRL and Bandar Malaysia are to be constructed by large Chinese SOEs, with the support of Beijing and Putrajaya (especially Najib). Country Garden, a private firm, has instead cooperated with the sultan of Johor. Due to the pervasive influence of the sultan, Forest City cannot be classified as a traditional private-private collaboration. Table 1 hypothesises that ECRL has been implemented expeditiously during the Najib era because it simultaneously fulfils the NEP directive, minimises state-federal contestation, and advances the geopolitical aims of both China and Malaysia. By contrast, the collapse of Bandar Malaysia, even in the absence of state-federal conflict, is attributable to its moderate conformance to the NEP and the lack of convergence between Chinese and Malaysian geopolitical goals. Notwithstanding the clout of the sultan, Forest City has failed to make a lasting impact because it neither promotes noticeable pro-Malay policies nor the geopolitical ambitions of both China and Malaysia. Johor's thorny ties with the federal government have also undermined the Forest City project.

China in Malaysia: Three Case Studies

East Coast Rail Link: Remoulding regional geopolitics

With state-owned CCCC as the main contractor and with 85% of the construction cost financed by soft loans from Beijing, ECRL was lauded by Najib for its potential to better connect the relatively backward east coast states (Pahang [Najib's home state], Terengganu and Kelantan) to Selangor, the country's most prosperous state. The improved connectivity (for passengers and freight) was expected to bridge the economic divide between both regions, a chronic issue since the British colonial era. Valued at a sum of US$18.2 billion, ECRL had been fast-tracked by the government to commence construction in July 2017 rather than in late 2017 as initially expected.[35] ECRL had also been given top priority by CCCC. The SOE believed that ECRL, the largest railway project in Southeast Asia, would create demonstration effects that would advance its business prospects in Southeast Asia as well as other countries involved in the BRI.[36]

---

[35] Lin Say Tee, "Flushed with Construction Jobs", *The Star*, 11 March 2017, <https://www.thestar.com.my/business/business-news/2017/03/11/flushed-with-construction-jobs/> (accessed 10 January 2018).

[36] "Malaixiya Donghaiantielu Xiangmukaigong Zhilichengwei Shifangongcheng" (East Coast Rail Link to Become a Model Project), *Xinhua Silk Road*, 14 August 2017, <http://silkroad.news.cn/Company/Cases/ppjs/45238.shtml> (accessed 10 January 2018).

The 600km mega project boasted a strong pro-Malay undertone as almost the entire stretch of the railway would pass through the three ethnic Malay-heavy states of Pahang, Terengganu and Kelantan. Their importance to UMNO increased further following UMNO's concerted attempt to promote an even stronger ethnic Malay agenda (vis-à-vis other ethnic groups).[37] One of UMNO's major moves was to forge an alliance with the Malaysian Islamic Party (PAS), its traditional rival in the rural east coast states. To attract more votes from ethnic Malays (especially those from the rural constituencies), both parties have come together to advance a more hardline version of the already biased NEP.

In the ground-breaking ceremony of ECRL, Najib, flanked by the chief ministers of the three east coast states, argued that ECRL was a 'game changer' and 'mindset changer' for the people along the railway route. He also promised that the economies of UMNO- and PAS-governed Pahang, Terengganu and Kelantan would experience a spike in annual growth of 1.5% when the project is completed as high value-added economic activities in sectors such as agriculture and tourism will be stimulated.[38] The Terengganu Chief Minister Ahmad Razif Abdul Rahman was especially bullish about the project, stating that it would 'speed up the modernisation of the state' and 'transform Terengganu towards a first-class region to work and live in'.[39] His focus, as well as that of Najib, on the potential economic benefits of ECRL was reflective of Malaysian politics. UMNO, as the dominant party of the governing coalition, has traditionally relied on its ability to develop the economy in securing its political legitimacy. The chief minister of opposition-governed Selangor was not present at this function, though the overall mood of Selangor is not to oppose ECRL, but to pressure the federal

---

[37] James Chin, "Malaysia: Heading for Sharia Domination?"

[38] Abdul Halim Hadi, "ECRL Bawa Limpahan Ekonomi Menyeluruh" (ECRL to Bring in Widespread Economic Benefits), Utusan Online, 17 November 2017, <http://www.utusan.com.my/berita/nasional/ecrl-bawa-limpahan-ekonomi-menyeluruh-1.554274> (accessed 21 January 2018).

[39] Adrian David, "ECRL Set to Boost Terengganu Transformation Plan", *New Straits Times*, 10 August 2017, <https://www.nst.com.my/news/nation/2017/08/266293/ecrl-set-boost-terengganu-transformation-plan> (accessed 10 January 2018).

government to be more forthcoming with the project's cost and financing. Nevertheless, Selangor is the smallest beneficiary of ECRL as only about 17km of the railway is planned within its territory.[40]

Another notable aspect of ECRL was its geopolitical dimension. Upon completion, it will connect Pahang's Kuantan Port (jointly managed by a Malaysian conglomerate and Guangxi Beibu Gulf International Port Group, an SOE) to the bustling Port Klang on the west coast. This potential land bridge could provide a 'significant resolution' to China's over-reliance on the Strait of Malacca, what it calls the 'Malacca Dilemma'.[41] To put things into perspective, about 80% of current Chinese energy needs pass through this narrow waterway. This new network will create alternative trade routes, but with significant Chinese involvement as China now has a direct interest in both the Kuantan Port and ECRL itself. The project could also negatively impact Singapore's stature as the leading shipping and commercial centre of Southeast Asia. While a combined sea and land route via Kuantan Port and ECRL is estimated to cost more (in bulk cargo per tonne) than the existing sea route via Singapore, the travel time can be shortened by 30 hours (18% reduction from current levels).[42] The shorter travel time is useful for the movement of time-sensitive goods such as exotic food and biomedical products.

Bandar Malaysia: Merging state capital with state capital

The second case illustrates intriguing linkages between a Chinese SOE and 1MDB, a Malaysian centrally controlled-GLC. Bandar Malaysia was a 197-hectare mixed development project in the heart of Kuala

---

[40] "Three Questionable Areas of East Coast Rail Line (ECRL)", Blog Page of Yeo Bee Yin, last modified 2 April 2017, <http://www.yeobeeyin.com/2017/04/three-questionable-areas-of-east-coast.html> (accessed 10 January 2018).

[41] Leslie Lopez, "Malaysia's East Coast Rail Line Touted as a Game Changer", *The Straits Times*, 22 December 2016, <http://www.straitstimes.com/asia/se-asia/malaysias-east-coast-rail-line-touted-as-a-game-changer (accessed 10 January 2018).

[42] Leslie Lopez, "Malaysia's East Coast Rail Line Touted as a Game Changer".

Lumpur, encompassing both residential and commercial properties. Its main proponent was 1MDB, a GLC associated with Najib.[43] Bandar Malaysia's most important selling point was its strategic location and transit-oriented outlook. It was to serve as Southeast Asia's premier transportation hub, housing the terminus of the proposed Kuala Lumpur-Singapore high-speed rail (HSR) project and providing railway linkage to several major airports in the region. Additionally, Bandar Malaysia would link up with the ambitious Pan-ASEAN Rail Transit to Bangkok and beyond. The entire project was expected to attract a total investment of US$53 billion over 20 to 25 years.[44]

As Kuala Lumpur is governed directly by the federal government and 1MDB is a centrally controlled GLC, there is no necessity to navigate the complicated interests between different layers of governments, unlike the two other China-Malaysia projects. For 1MDB, it roped in a China-Malaysia consortium in December 2015, selling 60% of its stake in Bandar Malaysia to the latter.[45] The consortium is in turn 60%-owned by CREC, one of China's largest SOEs, with Malaysia's Iskandar Waterfront Holdings (IWH) holding the remaining 40% equity.[46] Notably, CREC's investment in the venture took place merely months after the *Wall Street Journal* reported that nearly US$700 million was deposited into what are allegedly the personal bank accounts of Najib.[47] The money is alleged to have moved through government agencies, banks and companies linked

---

[43] William Case, "Stress Testing Leadership in Malaysia: The 1MDB Scandal and Najib Tun Razak", *The Pacific Review*, vol. 30, no. 5, 2017, pp. 633–654.

[44] Trinna Leong, "Chinese Govt Firm to Invest $2.7b in Bandar Malaysia", *The Straits Times*, 22 March 2016, <http://www.straitstimes.com/asia/chinese-govt-firm-to-invest-27b-in-bandar-malaysia> (accessed 10 January 2018).

[45] Trinna Leong, "Chinese Govt Firm to Invest $2.7b in Bandar Malaysia".

[46] IWH, in which low profile ethnic Chinese businessman Lim Kang Hoo owns 60% of its equity and another GLC the remaining 40%, is one of Malaysia's more successful examples of public-private partnership in recent times.

[47] Tom Wright and Simon Clark, "Investigators Believe Money Flowed to Malaysian Leader Najib's Accounts amid 1MDB Probe", *Wall Street Journal*, 2 July 2015, https://www.wsj.com/articles/SB10130211234592774869404581083700187014570 (accessed 26 March 2018).

to 1MDB before ending up in Najib's personal accounts. Najib had served as chairman of 1MDB's Board of Advisers until the entire board was dissolved in May 2016. A comprehensive report was tabled after a probe into alleged graft and mismanagement at the 1MDB. In January 2016, the newly installed Attorney General of Malaysia cleared Najib of corruption charges pertaining to such allegations. For CREC, this seemingly risky decision went against conventional economic rationale. Its partner, IWH, was quick to highlight Bandar Malaysia as the latest example of how the BRI generates mutual benefits for both countries. According to IWH, Bandar Malaysia could serve as a platform for aspiring Chinese firms to enter the Malaysian as well as the wider Southeast Asian markets. IWH also stated that Malaysian firms, especially the small and medium enterprises (SMEs), stand to benefit from the potential influx of Chinese capital and technology.

Nevertheless, the investment drew immediate flak from the public. Liew Chin Tiong, a vocal member of the opposition bloc at the time, argued that CREC's investment was tantamount to bailing out the beleaguered 1MDB.[48] Implying that bailouts usually come with conditions, Liew even wagered that a China-led consortium would be awarded the proposed Kuala Lumpur-Singapore HSR. Liew asked if such a bailout would lead to a compromise in the country's long-held neutrality in the face of China-US rivalry in Southeast Asia. While 1MDB was quick to stress that CREC's involvement in the project was not in any way linked to the eventual award of the Kuala Lumpur-Singapore HSR, several reports have seemingly nullified its claim. For instance, a report notes the 'many differences in the detailed terms' between officers from China and Malaysia.[49] One of the largest stumbling blocks is a China pressuring Malaysia that it 'must try its

---

[48] "DAP MP: China Firms Sure to Win KL-Singapore Rail Job after Role in 1MDB Turnaround", Malay Mail Online, 1 January 2016, <http://www.themalaymailonline.com/malaysia/article/dap-mp-china-firms-sure-to-win-kl-singapore-rail-job-after-role-in-1mdb-tur> (accessed 26 March 2018).

[49] Ho Wah Foon, "Rescue Bandar Malaysia or Face Fallout", The Star, 5 May 2017, <http://www.thestar.com.my/news/nation/2017/05/05/rescue-bandar-malaysia-or-face-fallout-buyers-of-project-failed-to-meet-payment-obligations-says-fin/> (accessed 10 January 2018).

best' to help China win the proposed HSR project, in which Japanese firms are also interested. Other major disagreements centred on the ownership and operation of the HSR terminus, and the design and concept of Bandar Malaysia.[50] According to Ho Wah Foon, Malaysians 'could not agree to proposals that the HSR terminus be owned by China', as this will be 'against national interest'.[51]

These discrepancies weaken 1MDB's promise to further Malaysian interest. They especially jeopardise the livelihood of the ethnic Malay populace that GLCs like 1MDB are supposed to protect. Facing such pressures, 1MDB had to abort the deal with the CREC consortium. Indeed, it was withdrawn a few days before Najib was due to attend the inaugural BRI summit in Beijing in May 2017. As if to underline his stance, Najib courted Dalian Wanda, one of China's largest private firms, as a replacement for the consortium during the same visit. While Dalian Wanda eventually pulled out of the project because of financial difficulties and some political pressure from Beijing, Bandar Malaysia remains popular amongst other investors. At least two Japanese conglomerates, Mitsui and Daiwa, had submitted bids to take over the project.[52] Najib's bold move, while primarily driven by 1MDB's lack of relevance to ethnic Malays as well as the geopolitical complications of excessive Chinese influence in Bandar Malaysia, was also buttressed by the (at least threefold) appreciation in value of the land beneath Bandar Malaysia and the project itself. The appreciation was largely due to a radically restructured 1MDB, clearer masterplan and already-formalised tax incentive package for Bandar Malaysia.[53]

---

[50] Sumisha Naidu, "Capital Controls, High-Speed Rail behind Collapse of Bandar Malaysia Deal?" Channel NewsAsia, 6 May 2017, <http://www.channelnewsasia.com/news/business/capital-controls-high-speed-rail-behind-collapse-of-bandar-8823716> (accessed 25 March 2018).

[51] Ho Wah Foon, "Rescue Bandar Malaysia or Face Fallout". The new federal administration has suspended the HSR project in late May 2018, citing cost concerns.

[52] "Tokyo Joins Beijing in Race for Bandar Malaysia Development", *Today*, 20 July 2017, at <http://www.todayonline.com/world/asia/tokyo-joins-beijing-race-bandar-malaysia-development> (accessed 25 June 2018).

[53] Public forum, Singapore, 25 May 2017.

Forest City: Embedding transnational Chinese capital into local politics

The third example is Forest City, a mega project driven by Country Garden. The firm was listed on the Hong Kong Stock Exchange in 2007 and worth US$20 billion as of May 2017. While the firm has also invested in other foreign economies, Malaysia remains its most important market.[54] Located near the Malaysia-Singapore Second Link, Forest City is the project closest to Singapore within Iskandar Malaysia. While still at an early phase of development, it eventually will take the form of four manmade islands sprawled over 1,386 hectares of land. With a projected total investment of US$58 billion, it is envisioned to house 700,000 people over the next 20 years.[55]

Country Garden has established a 60/40 joint venture for the development of Forest City. It owns 60% stake in the project while Esplanade Danga 88 Private Limited holds the remaining 40%. The parties behind Esplanade Danga 88 are the sultan of Johor (64.4% stake), the Johor state government investment arm (20% stake) and Daing Malek Daing Rahman, a member of the Royal Court of Advisers to the Johor Royal Court (15.6%).[56] Country Garden's choice of joint venture partner is within expectations, considering the receptive outlook of the Johor royalty towards business.[57] The sultan has endorsed the increasing presence of Chinese FDI in Johor: "The Chinese investors have the confidence and foresight to believe that their money is well spent... If the Chinese are prepared to invest here, why should it be an issue?"[58]

---

[54] Country Garden, *2016 Annual Report*, Hong Kong, Country Garden, 2017.

[55] A planned population increase of 700,000 (mostly from China) is almost equivalent to 20% of the entire population of Johor in 2016 (3.6 million).

[56] Nigel Aw, "Royal Businesses — Who is Daing A Malek?", Malaysiakini, 18 July 2014, <http://www.malaysiakini.com/news/269133> (accessed 26 June 2018).

[57] "10 Things to Know about the Sultan of Johor", *The Straits Times*, 20 March 2015, <http://www.straitstimes.com/asia/se-asia/10-things-to-know-about-the-sultan-of-johor> (accessed 26 June 2018).

[58] Wong Chun Wai and Nelson Benjamin, "Johor Sultan: Singaporeans will Live in Johor and Work in Singapore", AsiaOne, 19 March 2015, <http://www.asiaone.com/singapore/johor-sultan-singaporeans-will-live-johor-and-work-singapore> (accessed 26 June 2018).

The sultan is widely acknowledged to enjoy a good relationship with Yeung Kwok Keung, Country Garden's founder and chairman. In March 2017, Yeung was conferred by the former as a Dato (a traditional ethnic Malay honorific title commonly used in Malaysia). According to Country Garden, Yeung was conferred the title for his 'outstanding contribution to the economic development of Johor and industrial collaboration between China and Malaysia'.[59] The sultan viewed the development of Forest City as a watershed event: "Today, the state's history has entered a new phase. At this special occasion, let us join hands to witness and promote the great friendship between Malaysia and China".[60] More specifically, Country Garden asserts that Forest City's 'informal diplomacy' has facilitated communication between Chinese and Malaysian firms, underlining its commitment to the BRI. *People's Daily* also reports the conferment event 'as an award to the BRI project'.[61]

Forest City's scale has not gone unnoticed and has become a contentious political issue. Mahathir, as leader of the opposition bloc, had openly criticised the development. Mahathir harped on two interrelated issues — the outflow of capital and jobs to Chinese firms and the influx of Chinese immigrants. Mahathir's outcry over the potentially large numbers of Chinese immigrants into Forest City had become

---

[59] Country Garden, "Country Garden's IECs Reopened after Upgrading", PR Newswire, 20 March 2017, <http://www.prnewswire.com/news-releases/country-gardens-iecs-reopened-after-upgrading-300426007.html> (accessed 8 June 2017).

[60] "Country Garden's IECs Reopened after Upgrading", PR Newswire; "China-Based Property Developer Country Garden Inks Agreement for Pacificview's New Project Forest City in Malaysia", PR Newswire, 15 March 2017, <http://www.prnewswire.com/news-releases/china-based-property-developer-country-garden-inks-agreement-for-pacificviews-new-project-forest-city-in-malaysia-300423871.html> (accessed 8 June 2017).

[61] "Yidaiyilu' Xiangmu Huo Baojiang: Biguiyuan Senlinchengshi Chancheng Ronghe Erciqianyue" (Belt and Road' Project Praised: Country Garden Inks Second Phase Agreement for Forest City), *People's Daily*, 13 March 2017, <http://house.people.com.cn/n1/2017/0313/c164220-29141345.html> (accessed 5 December 2017). This view of linking the Forest City project with the BRI emerged repeatedly in the authors' interviews with the key management personnel of the project (Singapore, May and July 2016; Beijing, September 2016).

a nationwide political issue. On 6 January 2017, in his widely read blog, Chedet, Mahathir claimed that '[w]e cannot allow thousands of acres to be owned, developed and settled by foreigners. If we do that literally they would become foreign enclaves… We are going to see large chunks of Malaysia being developed by the foreign buyers and being occupied by them'. He also tapped into Malaysia's decades-old ethnocentric politics by alleging that Chinese citizens brought in through Forest City would be given identity cards, enabling them to vote in general elections and reshape Malaysia's political setting.[62]

Mahathir's politicisation of Forest City has been driven by the political agenda of his newly established Parti Pribumi Bersatu Malaysia (known simply as Bersatu).[63] Like the long-ruling UMNO, its electoral strategy depends largely on securing votes from the ethnic Malay populace, especially those from the rural heartlands. Mahathir's attacks on Forest City and its Chinese investors (and the sultan of Johor, by extension) were seen as a tool to gain traction with these voters as the primarily conservative rural ethnic Malay remain wary of ethnic Chinese Malaysians and their links (whether real or imagined) with a rising China.[64]

For Mahathir, Johor is of crucial significance as the state has been chosen as the base of Bersatu. By campaigning against the 'Chineseness' of Forest City and categorising those involved as 'selling out the Malays', the party was hoping to win elections in Johor, the birthplace and stronghold of UMNO.[65] Indeed, merely days after the blog

---

[62] "Johor Sultan Slams Dr Mahathir for Playing 'Politics of Fear and Race'", *Today*, 16 January 2017, <http://www.todayonline.com/world/asia/johor-sultan-says-had-enough-dr-mahathirs-fearmongering-over-chinese-investors> (accessed 26 June 2018).

[63] Mustafa Izzuddin, "The Real Reason Malaysia's Mahathir is Taking on the Sultan of Johor", *South China Morning Post*, 22 January 2017, <http://www.scmp.com/week-asia/politics/article/2064002/real-reason-malaysias-mahathir-taking-sultan-johor> (accessed 26 June 2018).

[64] Mustafa Izzuddin, "The Real Reason Malaysia's Mahathir is Taking on the Sultan of Johor".

[65] Bhavan Jaipragas, "Mahathir versus the Sultan: How Chinese Investment could Sway Malaysian Election", *South China Morning Post*, 18 January 2017, <http://www.scmp.com/week-asia/politics/article/2063111/mahathir-versus-sultan-how-chinese-investment-could-sway> (accessed 25 June 2018).

posting, the sultan of Johor, in an interview, responded: '…Mahathir has gone too far with his twisting of the issue… creating fear, using race, just to fulfil his political motives'.[66] The sultan explained that Johor cannot be choosy with whom it does business with. As if to underline the sultan's stand, Forest City was then hit by China's latest round of capital controls, implemented in March 2017 to directly curb the outflow of funds and to stabilise the exchange rate of the Chinese Yuan (CNY). According to *Global Times*, an influential Beijing-controlled newspaper, capital controls are necessary to stop Chinese companies from irrational foreign investment.[67] The sectors most scrutinised are real estate, cultural and entertainment, implying that projects such as Forest City are no longer encouraged by Beijing. To further stem capital outflows, the Chinese government banned its citizens from converting CNY into other currencies for overseas property purchases. For Country Garden, it has since closed down all its Forest City sales centres in China and pledged to refund buyers who made down-payments on properties at Forest City but are no longer able to transfer the rest of the payment out of China.[68]

To prop up its hitherto China-heavy consumer base, Forest City has been forced to market the project to clients from other economies. Sales galleries have been launched (or are being launched) in the Philippines, Indonesia, Vietnam, Thailand, Taiwan and Dubai.[69] Nevertheless, a senior executive revealed that Country Garden faces substantial difficulties in marketing to non-Chinese consumers as its sales staff are only experienced in selling to buyers from China.

---

[66] Wong Chun Wai and Nelson Benjamin, "Johor Ruler Slams Dr M over Chinese Investment Comments", *The Star*, 16 January 2017, at http://www.thestar.com.my/news/nation/2017/01/16/political-spin-angers-sultan-johor-ruler-slams-dr-m-over-chinese-investment-comments/ (accessed 25 June 2018).

[67] Wang Cong, "'Irrational' Overseas Investments Stop", *Global Times*, 31 July 2017, <http://www.globaltimes.cn/content/1058921.shtml> (accessed 10 January 2018).

[68] "Laporan: Pemaju Forest City Tutup Pusat Jualan di China" (Report: Forest City Developer Closes Sale Centers in China), Malaysiakini, 10 March 2017, <https://www.malaysiakini.com/news/375209> (accessed 21 January 2018).

[69] Malaysiakini, "Laporan: Pemaju Forest City Tutup Pusat Jualan di China",

They have hardly sold to overseas buyers and can only converse in the Mandarin language, limiting their utility. It is also revealed that their sales plan retains its *zhongguo* flavour (China-centric), with little attention paid to the aspirations of the other targeted consumers.[70]

In short, the confluence of Malaysia's political struggle and China's financial curbs caught Country Garden by surprise, hampering Forest City's construction and sales efforts. In the meantime, a poll in Johor indicated that 29% of the respondents were unhappy with the influx of Chinese investment which was blamed for the rising property prices in the state. The intertwining of politics and business through the example of Country Garden, therefore, highlights the precarious challenges of Chinese investments in a politically charged, multi-ethnic society such as Malaysia.[71]

Discussion: Politics (with Nanyang Characteristics) in Command

The CCCC, CREC and Country Garden cases reveal several points. Firstly, the decades-old NEP remains a key variable. Despite some criticisms from opposition lawmakers, ECRL was viewed positively by the leadership of the three ethnic Malay-dominated states of Pahang, Terengganu and Kelantan. Its proposed linkage to several hitherto economically backward towns and villages dovetailed well with UMNO's strategy of aggressively capturing votes from ethnic Malays, especially those from the rural constituencies. The pro-Malay agenda is not too evident in Bandar Malaysia and Forest City. While CREC joined forces with two formidable domestic partners in IWH (40%-owned by a GLC) and 1MDB (a GLC), the reality is that 1MDB (and Najib) has been dogged by a series of high-profile controversies,

---

[70] Interview, Johor Bahru, 7 May 2017.

[71] Chan Kok Leong, "*Tak Percaya, Tak Rasa Kesan Buat Penduduk Johor Tolak China, Raikan Singapura*" (Distrust, Disconnect Cause Johoreans to Spurn China, Embrace Singapore) *The Malaysian Insight*, 23 February 2018, <https://www.themalaysianinsight.com/bahasa/s/39338/> (accessed 26 February 2018).

diminishing the appeal of Bandar Malaysia to the citizenry (especially the ethnic Malays).

For Forest City, it is essentially a private venture undertaken by the Johor sultan in conjunction with Country Garden, another private firm. While Country Garden also labelled Forest City as a BRI-related project, it is *not* a project driven by the Chinese and/or Malaysian authorities, albeit the ready endorsement evidenced by the site visits of Najib and the Chinese ambassador to Malaysia on two separate occasions. Forest City does not emphasise very strongly any pro-Malay policies as it is envisioned to welcome foreign capital and expertise. Therefore, it had come under heavy criticisms from several quarters, especially Mahathir. His strategy of targeting ethnic Malay votes from the Malay heartlands of Johor, a traditional UMNO stronghold, further necessitated the need to heighten the 'Chinese-ness' of Forest City and associate Chinese property investors with the domestic ethnic Chinese populace. Mahathir's moves were designed to tap into the fears of the conservative ethnic Malays who often view Malaysians of ethnic Chinese descent as a 'fifth wheel'.

The contrasting fates of the three China-Malaysia projects show that the NEP has intertwined itself with China's interests. Thus, projects without a clear conformance to the NEP (whether real or imagined) are unlikely to receive mass support. For the ethnic Chinese business community of Malaysia in general, they have not been offered opportunities to take part in high profile projects such as ECRL and Forest City. In the event that they are, they are expected to function as a 'bridesmaid' to the GLCs and even the political elites, much like how IWH had behaved in Bandar Malaysia. This finding both strengthens and weakens Caroline Hau's and Liu Hong's assessment of the ethnic Chinese.[72] On one hand, the ethnic Chinese are appreciated for their

---

[72] Caroline Hau, "Becoming 'Chinese' — but what 'Chinese'? — in Southeast Asia"; Hong Liu, "Opportunities and Anxieties for the Chinese Diaspora in Southeast Asia". See also Hong Liu and Zhou Yishu, "New Chinese Capitalism and the ASEAN Economic Community", in *The Sociology of Chinese Capitalism in Southeast Asia,* Yos Santasombat (ed.), New York, Palgrave Macmillan, 2019, pp. 55–73.

business know-how and ties to Chinese firms, the GLCs and politically powerful ethnic Malay politicians. Nevertheless, Malaysia's political nuances mean that ethnic Chinese firms such as IWH have to incorporate the wishes of their ethnic Malay partners and those of the Chinese investors into the BRI projects, in addition to their own commercial calculus. While they want to take part in the BRI, they are not as well-endowed as the GLCs because the latter enjoys state patronage and access to favoured projects. Notwithstanding the collapse of Bandar Malaysia, interviews with other prominent ethnic Chinese businessmen suggest that ethnic Chinese firms are aware of the delicate situation that they are in and have since readjusted their business models and broadened their political networks to better accommodate the new political economic situation. If anything, their tentative optimism, captured in the excited tone of the chairman of a prominent ethnic Chinese firm, on the prospect of more BRI projects entering Malaysia underscores their sensitivity to the ever-changing dynamics between both countries.[73]

Secondly, it is important to analyse the state-federal contestation undergirding these projects. For the ECRL, this contestation was mostly subdued across the four states (three on the east coast and one on the west) it was to traverse through. While these states enjoy some autonomy, especially on land matters, their governments have not opposed ECRL, except that of opposition-governed Selangor. As illustrated in the previous section, the Selangor chief minister is relatively receptive to the project, notwithstanding some of his colleagues' concerns on its cost and financing terms. Indeed, the chief ministers of the three east coast states have welcomed the project as most of the railway will be located in their states. While it helps the then federal government that the three chief ministers were either UMNO members (Pahang and Terengganu) or were aligned to it (Kelantan), another key factor was the manner in which Najib, in his capacity as the head of the federal government, had projected ECRL as a crucial cog in the development trajectory of both Malaysia and the east coast states.

---

[73] Interview, Beijing, 31 October 2016.

In particular, he had promised to more forcefully reduce the socioeconomic gap between the east coast and the wealthier west coast of Peninsular Malaysia.

For Bandar Malaysia, state-federal contestation was absent as the project was located exclusively in Kuala Lumpur, the country's de facto economic capital. While not needing to consult governments at the state level was helpful in advancing the project, this factor per se was insufficient to sustain Bandar Malaysia, as the next paragraph will illustrate (in addition to the previous paragraph's argument). State-federal rivalry was most obvious for Forest City. Its extreme south location seems to have exacerbated the already uneasy ties between Johor and Putrajaya. The federal government, cognisant of the need to spread out economic growth across all of its states, has traditionally been wary of the southward movement of the country's economic clout. Forest City's emergence, coupled with the vibrancy of the rest of Iskandar Malaysia, could lead to a situation where the tail (Forest City and Johor) wags the dog (the entire country). More broadly, it reflects the lack of cohesive institutions to mediate differences between the federal government and the local ones.

Thirdly, the geopolitical dimension of these BRI projects is most clearly reflected in ECRL. Connecting the Kuantan Port on the east coast of Peninsular Malaysia to the bustling Port Klang on the west coast could resolve China's perennial 'Malacca Dilemma'. The new routes opened up by ECRL will also offer Malaysia a window of opportunity to bypass Singapore. The geopolitical undertone for Bandar Malaysia was just as salient. CREC had seemingly forwarded its interest as well as that of the Chinese state by securing a stake in one of Malaysia's largest infrastructure projects in recent years. In addition, Bandar Malaysia was considered a prized BRI project because of its position as the terminus of the proposed Kuala Lumpur-Singapore HSR and a key node of the mooted Pan-ASEAN Rail Transit network, both of which were poised to be landmark infrastructure projects within Southeast Asia. Yet, subsequent reports show that the terms demanded by the Chinese (such as the request for a leeway in the bidding of the HSR project) were not acceptable to the Malaysian bureaucracy. The timing of the project's abortion, merely days before the inaugural BRI Summit in Beijing in May 2017, also implies that the Malaysian leadership was in no mood to 'save China's face'. Indeed, Najib, buoyed by at least a tripling of Bandar Malaysia's original value, attempted to secure a new partner in the form of Dalian Wanda during the BRI Summit.

Forest City's status as a private venture means that it is mostly devoid of geopolitical power. Despite claims of Forest City fostering China-Malaysia ties in its 'informal diplomacy' and the sultan's cordial ties with Country Garden, the reality is that Malaysia's bilateral relationship is the purview of the federal government. Country Garden's alliance with the sultan of Johor does not negate the fact that he remains a ceremonial figure, albeit with some degree of political influence. For Beijing, Forest City represents the type of 'irrational investment' that it is curbing through capital controls. It is thus unlikely for Country Garden to receive concrete support from Beijing, at least in the near to medium term.

The geopolitical agenda of the three China-Malaysia projects can be interpreted along two interrelated dimensions. The first dimension relates to the capability of small states (such as Malaysia) in attracting and even rejecting (or at least, circumscribing) Chinese capital to meet domestic geopolitical expectations. Malaysia's experience underlines the relative inability of China in imposing its will on its BRI partners. Yet, there is also a justified concern that Malaysia is creeping towards China's sphere of influence, especially with regard to ECRL. While it is too early to label it a 'new regional order' or a new Sino-centric 'community of shared destiny', this finding does demonstrate China's capacity in exploiting the weaknesses of various Southeast Asian countries through a series of diplomacy moves combined with aid and investment packages.

The Re-Emergence of Mahathir: Reshuffling State-Business Ties

UMNO and its allies were voted out in the general election on 9 May 2018. The UMNO-led coalition lost power not only at the federal level, but also in several important states, including Johor, its birthplace and traditional vote bank. While there were several reasons leading to its rejection, the disquiet surrounding the Najib administration's management of the BRI ranked as one of the more prominent factors.[74] Although Mahathir has stopped short of cooling ties with Beijing since assuming prime ministership for the second time, it must be noted that he actively critiqued large-scale projects like Forest City and the Kuala Lumpur-Singapore HSR.[75]

Mahathir's success at mobilising electoral support further underlined how the debates and controversies surrounding the BRI had meshed with Malaysia's complex, multi-layered politics, indirectly inducing regime change. This further reinforces our argument that the BRI recipient countries have their own political and economic goals that may not be in-line with BRI objectives and when divergence emerges, the former tends to assume a bigger role in determining the outcome, a view that has also been keenly put forth by Wang Gungwu. When asked whether China was spreading its influence in an eventual attempt to control the Malaysian economy in a prescient newspaper interview conducted 10 months before the election, Wang responded: "How could China do that? Malaysia is a sovereign state with its own government, leaders and national interests… *China cannot force itself on Malaysia*. China can make an offer and *you can always say no*. You take the investment because you calculate it and think *it suits your national interest*" (emphasis added).[76]

---

[74] See also Bridget Welsh, "'Saviour' Politics and Malaysia's 2018 Electoral Democratic Breakthrough: Rethinking Explanatory Narratives and Implicatons", *Journal of Current Southeast Asian Affairs*, vol. 37, no. 3, 2018, pp. 85–108.

[75] Notwithstanding his sharp wit and famed oratory skills, it would be a mistake to label him 'anti-China' or 'anti-BRI'. When asked during an interview with British Broadcasting Corporation (BBC) whether China was 'bringing about a new form of colonialism with their One Belt, One Road infrastructure projects', Mahathir nonchalantly responded: "No, no, no, not at all. One Belt, One Road is okay". This interview can be found online at <https://www.youtube.com/watch?v=0HhlYkz3Sag> (accessed 18 January 2019).

[76] Tho Xin Yi, "China can Make an Offer and You can Always Say No", *The Star*, 23 July 2017, at <https://www.thestar.com.my/news/nation/2017/07/23/china-can-make-an-offer-and-you-can-always-say-no/> (accessed 25 January 2019).

Indeed, during his official visit to China in August 2018, Mahathir announced that ECRL would be 'deferred until such time we can afford, and maybe we can reduce the cost also if we do it differently'.[77] Mahathir's decision to shelf ECRL (and the HSR) is widely interpreted as a cost-cutting measure, but probably its more important goal is to shrink (or at least, delegitimise) the economic base of the Najib clique. More practically, ECRL's shelving (or de facto renegotiation) does not negate the fact that despite losing Putrajaya, UMNO and PAS have reinforced their grip on the state assemblies of the three east coast states, in addition to defeating most of Mahathir's allies vying for federal seats there. To preserve his legitimacy, Mahathir cannot afford to alienate voters from these states. Mahathir must have also realised that the expeditiousness in which the previous federal and state authorities implemented the project implies that some segments of the Malay-heavy constituencies can (and have already) tap into ECRL's spillover effects. This can be seen in the determination of the new administration in persisting with the ECRL. It has been renegotiating the terms of the deal with CCCC since August 2018, seeking to reduce the ECRL's cost and to include more local products and services into the project. As of 22 January 2019, negotiation is still ongoing, but the new administration has seemingly terminated the original contract to CCCC while seeking a new contractor who can offer more favourable terms.[78]

Notwithstanding its strategic location at the heart of Kuala Lumpur and the increase in land value, Bandar Malaysia is not likely to enjoy a revival, at least not in the near to medium term. Any hopes of revival will largely hinge on the verdict behind the top echelons of 1MDB, especially Najib himself. Following his fall from grace, Najib's

---

[77] Goh Sui Noi, "East Coast Rail Link and Pipeline Projects with China to be Deferred: Malaysian PM Mahathir", *The Straits Times*, 21 August 2018, <https://www.straitstimes.com/asia/se-asia/east-coast-rail-link-and-pipeline-projects-with-china-cancelled-says-malaysian-pm> (accessed 22 August 2018).

[78] Trinna Leong, "Malaysia Cancels Deal with China Company, Seeks New Contractor for East Coast Rail Link", *The Straits Times*, 22 January 2019, <https://www.straitstimes.com/asia/se-asia/malaysia-cancels-deal-with-china-company-seeks-new-contractor-for-east-coast-rail-link> (accessed 25 January 2019).

involvement in 1MDB has been reinvestigated by the new administration. As of 25 October 2018, he had been charged with six counts of criminal breach of trust involving US$1.59 billion of government funds, in addition to another 32 charges for money laundering and graft.[79] Furthermore, the financial scandal involving 1MDB seems to have taken on a life of its own, with probes related to it taking place in at least 10 countries. The exact figure misappropriated has been reported to amount to at least US$4.2 billion.[80] Apart from Najib, some of the alleged parties involved in the scheme include prominent investment banks and western celebrities. The complexity of the 1MDB case means that a settlement is unlikely to be reached anytime soon. Any potential new bidders for Bandar Malaysia will have to navigate the situation cautiously before taking on the project.[81]

Lastly, Mahathir's re-ascension to the prime ministership did not see him take on a more conciliatory stance with Country Garden and its allies. Almost immediately after returning from his work visit to China, Mahathir proclaimed on 27 August 2018 that Malaysia will not allow foreigners to buy residential units in Forest City. He justified his stance, claiming that '[o]ur objection is because it was built for foreigners, not built for Malaysians. Most Malaysians are unable to buy those flats'.[82] This strongly worded statement, while consistent with his pre-election campaigning, piled further misery on Country Garden. Mahathir's

[79] "Najib, Ex-Treasury Chief Charged with Criminal Breach of Trust involving RM6.6 Billion", Channel NewsAsia, 25 October 2018, <https://www.channelnewsasia.com/news/asia/najib-razak-irwan-serigar-charged-cbt-malaysia-treasury-10862066> (accessed 25 January 2019).

[80] Shamim Adam, Laurence Arnold and Yudith Ho, "How Malaysia's 1MDB Scandal Shook the Financial World", Bloomberg, 10 January 2019, <https://www.bloomberg.com/news/articles/2019-01-09/how-malaysia-s-1mdb-scandal-shook-the-financial-world-quicktake> (accessed 25 January 2019).

[81] Tom Wright and Bradley Hope, *Billion Dollar Whale: The Man Who Fooled Wall Street, Hollywood, and the World*, New York, Hachette Books, 2018. Wright and Hope were amongst the first people who investigated and broke the news about the 1MDB.

[82] "Dr M: Foreigners cannot Buy Residential Units in Forest City", *The Star*, 27 August 2018, <https://www.thestar.com.my/business/business-news/2018/08/27/malaysia-says-forest-city-project-off-limits-to-foreign-buyers/> (accessed 25 January 2019).

broadside also caught the firm by surprise, especially when Yeung (the patron of Country Garden) had paid a personal visit to Mahathir at the latter's office in the national Parliament on 16 August 2018. After their 40-minute meeting, Yeung released a press statement endorsing the new administration: "I am confident that Malaysia, under the leadership of [Prime Minister] Tun Dr Mahathir Mohamad, will continue to welcome foreign businesses and investors. Therefore, I intend to invest more in Malaysia in the coming years, potentially in the area of modern agriculture and robotics industry, as per the country's law and regulations".[83] It was only after slightly more than a week that Mahathir clarified the situation, this time explaining that '[t]hey can buy the property, but we won't give them visa to come and live here".[84] In addition to Mahathir's public airing of his displeasure against the project, Forest City has been placed under scrutiny by a committee set up by the new Housing and Local Government Minister Zuraida Kamaruddin. Taking a cue from Mahathir, Zuraida stressed that the review was to ensure locals, in particular Johoreans, would not be sidelined from buying homes there.[85]

Conclusion: Malaysia's New Dilemmas

In *The Malay Dilemma*, Mahathir — prior to taking up his first term of prime ministership — highlighted the economic disparities between the Malays as the indigenous people and the ethnic Chinese, calling for

---

[83] "Country Garden Considers Increasing Investments in Malaysia", *EdgeProp*, 24 August 2018, <https://www.edgeprop.my/content/1417418/country-garden-considers-increasing-investments-malaysia> (accessed 25 January 2019).

[84] "In Abrupt U-Turn, Mahathir says Foreigners can Buy Forest City Properties but no Visas will be Given", *Today*, 5 September 2018, <https://www.todayonline.com/world/foreigners-can-buy-forest-city-properties-no-visa-dr-m-reiterates> (accessed 25 January 2019).

[85] "Malaysia to Review Foreigner Quota for Forest City, Tighter Restriction Foreseeable: Minister", *Today*, 6 September 2018, <https://www.todayonline.com/world/malaysia-review-foreigner-quota-forest-city-tighter-restriction-foreseeable-minister> (accessed 25 January 2019).

affirmative actions by the government to offer protection for the Malays. The implementation of the NEP since 1969 has significantly reduced the gaps between the two major ethnic groups and helped bring about a reasonably large Malay middle class, with some of them emerging as key players in politics and the economy. While the dilemmas faced by the Malays initially identified by Mahathir might have largely faded away half a century later, the country has faced new sets of dilemmas that go far beyond racial politics and are deeply embedded in the domestic political economy within a fast changing region symbolised by the rise of China. Malaysia's policy choices are increasingly shaped through a complex process of (re)negotiations among different stakeholders, both internally and externally. The domestication of external political economy has played a much bigger role than the case of the early 1970s when the dilemmas were first elaborated.

This chapter has demonstrated the complicated manners in which the BRI has taken shape in Malaysia. Despite their wealth and technical expertise, Chinese firms cannot forge ahead without understanding the aspiration of the Malaysian stakeholders. In short, BRI projects require the cooperation (or at the very least, non-hindrance) of these players. The chapter has underlined the value of looking beyond large-scale geopolitical shifts and conventional literature that depict the BRI under sweeping, uncritical themes. ECRL's partial success, Bandar Malaysia's collapse and Forest City's arrested development show that the BRI's success (or failure) in Malaysia is dependent on three key conditions: fulfilment of Malaysia's longstanding pro-ethnic Malay policy, a mutual vision between the state and federal authorities, and advancement of geopolitical interests for both China and Malaysia.

What then are the region-wide implications of these case studies? Thus far, Malaysian actors have seemingly captured economic benefits from China while preserving some level of independence in the face of gigantic BRI projects. This position is first illustrated by Najib, then Mahathir. In particular, Mahathir's stature as one of the world's eldest statesmen has even given him 'moral authority' to seemingly reassert his country's position vis-à-vis China. The point here is that the BRI is still relatively nascent and smaller states in the region certainly possess sufficient autonomy to hold and even bolster their stance. It is hoped that the framework put forth in this chapter as well as its arguments will contribute to the further explorations of the ways through which other states — not least those from Southeast Asia on which we have a great deal to gain from Professor Wang Gungwu's rich experience and perceptive insights — have responded to the BRI and the latter's intertwining with the local political economy.

Chapter 13

Beijing's New Policy towards the Chinese Overseas: Some Reflections

Leo SURYADINATA*

Professor Wang Gungwu has been studying Chinese overseas for many decades and produced numerous articles and books on the subject. Although I am not his student, I benefitted significantly from his writings. Some of the points that I raised in this chapter have been inspired by his writings and I would like to acknowledge my indebtedness to him.

The focus of my chapter is about Beijing's new policy towards the Chinese overseas after the rise of China. Is the policy new? Had there been such a policy in China's history? What are the factors contributing to the change? What is the content of this policy? What conclusion can be drawn from this study? Let us look at China's policy towards the Chinese overseas from the historical perspective, first with an examination of the term Chinese overseas and their number.

Chinese Overseas: Terms and Number

The Chinese overseas is coined by Professor Wang Gungwu to refer to Chinese outside China, regardless of their citizenship.[1] It is different

* Leo SURYADINATA is Visiting Senior Fellow at the ISEAS-Yusof Ishak Institute and Professor (adjunct) at the S Rajaratnam School of International Studies, Nanyang Technological University.

[1] Wang's books which used "Chinese Overseas" rather than "Overseas Chinese" as their titles: Wang Gungwu, *China and the Chinese Overseas,* Singapore, Times Academic Press,

from the term Overseas Chinese which refers to Chinese nationals overseas. Although the term is still China-centric, in this chapter I would use "Chinese overseas" rather than "Overseas Chinese". The term "ethnic Chinese" is used when I refer to foreign citizens of Chinese descent.

In China itself, the terms *huaqiao*, *huaren* and *huayi* are used to refer to the Chinese overseas. *Huaqiao* refers to Chinese nationals who are overseas; *huaren* refers to foreigners of Chinese descent and *huayi* means "of Chinese descent", which is similar to *huaren*. However, some use the term to refer to foreign nationals of Chinese descent who have lost their Chinese culture. I do not think that *huayi* indicates the cultural background of the Chinese; it simply means the person is of Chinese descent.

Chinese migration has a long history and the number of Chinese overseas is also large. Moreover, it is difficult to define "Chinese" outside China. Due to the complexity of the issue and lack of official statistics on the Chinese in Southeast Asia, what we have now is only an estimate of the number of "Chinese overseas". The figures given are between 40 million to 60 million. Top leaders in China often used the latter figure (60 million) when referring to the overseas Chinese or *huaqiao-huaren*. The Chinese overseas are not only large in number but also strong economically. China leaders noted that overseas Chinese businessmen are rich and "command US$5,000 million capital".[2] Not surprisingly, the Chinese overseas have now become the wooing target of the Chinese government.

There was a misleading assumption that the Chinese overseas are a homogeneous group and are willing to identify themselves with China. They are always oriented towards China and would cooperate with the government of China when requested. The Chinese authorities seem to have overlooked the heterogeneity of this group.

1991; Wang Gungwu, *The Chinese Overseas: From Earthbound China to the Quest of Autonomy*, Cambridge, Massachusetts, Harvard University Press, 2000.

[2] Leo Suryadinata, *The Rise of China and Chinese Overseas: A Study of Beijing's Changing Policy in Southeast Asia and Beyond*, ISEAS, 2017, p. 156.

Traditional Policy

Understandably, China has not always been concerned with the Chinese overseas. During the Qing dynasty up to the 18th century, the Chinese overseas were not in the good books of the Chinese authorities. The most often cited example as the attitude of the Qing government towards the Chinese overseas was its response to the 1740 massacre in Batavia (now Jakarta).[3] The Chinese arrived in Java long before the Dutch. When the Dutch arrived the Chinese were persuaded to stay and help build Batavia. However, prior to 1740 the Dutch East Indies encountered an economic crisis and there were rumours that the Chinese would be expelled from colonial Indonesia. There were also rumours that the Chinese outside the castle were prepared for a rebellion. The decision of the Dutch governor to get rid of the Chinese eventually led to the notorious Angke (Red River) Affair where approximately 10,000 Chinese were slaughtered. Many were women and children. When the massacre was reported to the Qing court, high officials in the Qing government noted that "the Han Chinese who were killed, had been living in the barbaric land for a long time.....they abandoned the civilized life...now they suffered, this is their own fault".[4]

When the Dutch envoy wanted to apologise, Emperor Qian Long was quoted as having said, "They were forsaken people from the Heavenly Kingdom; they had left their ancestral cemetery for making profits overseas, the Qing Court would not want to know about them".[5]

---

[3] The best study on the 1740 massacre is a dissertation written by Johannes Theodorus Vermuelen, De Chineezen te Batavia en de Troebelen van 1740. The English translation was done by Tan Yeok Seong and published in the *Journal of South Seas Society*, vol. IX, Part 1, June 1953, pp. 1–68.

[4] "Qing wenxian tongkao" (Comprehensive Investigations on the Qing Dynasty Documents), Cited in Zhuang Guotu, *Zhongguo fengjian zhengfu de huaqiao zhengce* (Overseas Chinese Policies of China's Feudal Governments), Xianmen, Xiamen University press, 1989, pp. 98 and 122.

[5] Li Changfu, Zhongguo Zhimin Shih, Taiwan Shangwu, 1976, p. 71.

This non-protectionist policy was amended during the second half of the 19th century when the Qing Court realised the economic value of the Chinese overseas. Consul-General Huang Zunxian was one of the well-known examples cited to show the concern of Qing officials for the overseas Chinese. Towards the end of the Qing rule, the Qing Court welcomed the investment of overseas Chinese and sold official titles to them in order to gain profits. Some rich overseas Chinese indeed invested in China, even built railroad in their home province and many purchased official titles from the Qing Court, signifying that the overseas Chinese were still affiliated with China. It was also towards the end of the Qing Dynasty that the first Chinese Nationality Law (1909) was promulgated.

The Nationality Law was based on the principle of *jus sanguinis* (blood ties) rather than *jus soli* (birthplace). It stipulated that all Chinese, regardless of their birthplace, were the nationals of China. One would only lose one's Chinese citizenship with the permission of the Chinese government.[6] It is difficult, if not impossible, to gain such a permission. Therefore many overseas Chinese who were born overseas and obtained the nationality (or subject-ship) of other countries became persons with dual nationality status.

Less than three years after the announcement of this nationality law, the Qing government was overthrown by the revolutionaries led by Sun Yat Sen. The newly established Republic of China soon issued a new nationality law in 1912, which was revised slightly in 1914, bearing little difference with the Qing Nationality Law. The dual nationality status of the overseas Chinese therefore stayed but of little consequence as China would not be able to intervene when the Chinese overseas were not within the territory of China. The dual nationality status became relevant only when an overseas Chinese was in China and Chinese law could be applied to him/her. The case in point was a

---

[6] For a discussion of various China's nationality laws and their implications, see Leo Suryadinata, "China's Citizenship Laws and Southeast Asian Chinese", in Leo Suryadinata, *The Making of Southeast Asian Nations: State, Ethnicity, Indigenism and Citizenship*, Singapore, World Scientific, 2015, pp. 85–99.

Chinese economic offender (Oen Keng Hian, a Dutch subject by the Dutch East Indies law) escaped from Java to take refuge in Shanghai in 1926. He was not extradited but was tried in Shanghai in accordance with the Chinese law.[7]

In 1927 Chiang Kai Shek led the expedition to the north, defeated the warlords and re-established himself as the leader of China. In 1929 the Republic of China issued another revised nationality law which had little difference in its contents. Notably, Kuo Min Tang's (KMT's) China under Chiang Kai Shek regarded the overseas Chinese as China's nationals and expected them to be patriotic and loyal to China. Overseas Chinese nationalism (Chinese transnationalism) was encouraged.

On the KMT's China policy towards Chinese overseas, Professor Wang Gungwu argued that "government and party officials in China assumed that all sojourners [huaqiao] were equally willing to identify with whatever cause was dominant in China.….the calls for loyalty to China did not take into account the very different conditions under which the various sojourners communities lived. Patriotism and China's salvation were seen as absolute concepts and, unless they were drummed into the sojourners who were living far away from home, it was feared that the message would not be heard. Such tactics were very damaging for the Chinese overseas, who were seen as potentially dis-loyal subjects in the countries in which they lived. It would take decades of effort to dispel the picture of every Chinese as someone always loyal to China and never fully attached to his or her adopted home".[8]

The Policy of the People's Republic of China

When the People's Republic of China (PRC, known in the West as "Communist China") was established in 1949, no new nationality law was issued, implying that the KMT nationality law was still effective. Nevertheless, many non-communist and anti-communist countries in

---

[7] Leo Suryadinata, *The Making of Southeast Asian Nations*, p. 88.
[8] Wang Gungwu, *The Chinese Overseas*, p. 80.

Southeast Asia were suspicious of China and overseas Chinese. With the exception of Indonesia and Myanmar that established diplomatic relations with the PRC in 1950, other states did not do so until the 1970s. Even Jakarta also broke ties with Beijing in 1967 and only restored ties in 1990. Singapore established diplomatic ties with China in the same year of 1990, a few months after Indonesia did so.

China was eager to receive recognition from Southeast Asian countries. In September 1954 at the People's Congress, it decided to solve the "overseas Chinese problem" by settling the dual nationality issues with any country, starting with which China had diplomatic ties.[9] In 1955 during the Asian-African Conference in Bandung, China succeeded in signing the settlement of dual citizenship agreement with Indonesia.

Prime Minister Zhou Enlai even encouraged Indonesian Chinese to adopt Indonesian citizenship and integrate themselves into local society. Apparently, China wanted to get rid of its "historical burden" and cultivate friendly relationships with Southeast Asian states.[10] When China later established diplomatic relations with Southeast Asian countries, in their joint communiques, there was always a standard clause that states that Chinese who have opted for local citizenship ceased to be China's nationals.

After the demise of Chairman Mao, Deng Xiaoping re-emerged as the leader of the PRC in 1977 and began to introduce four-modernisation programme to modernise China in various fields. In 1978 Deng visited some Southeast Asian states and discovered that many ethnic Chinese leaders refused to identify themselves with China. Perhaps the encounter between Deng with Lee Kuan Yew in 1978 was a turning point in Deng's thinking of overseas Chinese. At the dinner in honour of Deng, Lee Kuan Yew made a speech that the ethnic Chinese in Southeast Asia are linked to Southeast Asia and do not

---

[9] Stephen FitzGerald, *China and the Overseas Chinese: A Study of Peking's Changing Policy*, 1949–1970, Cambridge University Press, 1972, pp. 102–103.

[10] Stephen FitzGerald, *China and the Overseas Chinese*, p. 152.

expect China to sacrifice for them and neither should China expect Southeast Asian Chinese to sacrifice for China.[11]

It was after Deng's return from Southeast Asia that China promulgated the 1980 Nationality Law based on the will of the individual. Any Chinese overseas who obtained foreign citizenship on his/her free will automatically ceases to be a Chinese national. This has made the legal status of ethnic Chinese in Southeast Asia and beyond clear; they only have single nationality.

In 1996 there was an amendment to the 1980 Nationality Law which stipulated that it does not apply to the Chinese in Hong Kong. Foreign nationals of Chinese descent who were born either in mainland China or Hong Kong would remain as Chinese citizens if they reside and work in Hong Kong.[12]

A New Policy

The situation began to change after the rise of China as a world economic power. The single nationality policy that was introduced in 1980 when China was still relatively weak were questioned by some new migrants and mainland Chinese politicians at the end of 20th century and the beginning of the 21st century, coinciding with the rise of China. There was a proposal for a dual nationality law for overseas Chinese, but the proposal was not accepted.

Nevertheless, the encouragement of overseas Chinese to opt for local citizenship and integrate themselves into local society has been quietly abandoned for a number of reasons: First is the exodus of new Chinese migrants to the West. Now China has a large number of new Chinese migrants overseas. A large number are believed to have adopted foreign nationality; second is the need for Chinese overseas as its social capital.

Since the turn of the 21st century, Beijing's leadership seems to have assessed that the Chinese overseas are no longer a liability but an asset

---

[11] "Our Future in S-E Asia — Lee", *The Straits Times*, 13 November 1978.

[12] Leo Suryadinata, *The Rise of China and Chinese Overseas*, pp. 33–34.

for China. Beijing considers the Chinese in Southeast Asia and beyond as members of the "Chinese Nation" that could support China both economically and politically, especially in China's quest for a super-power status.

When China was weak and underdeveloped, its attraction was minimal for the Chinese overseas. It was also not strong enough to exercise an assertive policy with regard to the Chinese overseas. However, China's economic strength today has enhanced Beijing's capability in the foreign policy arena and it wants to show its influence to Asians, if not to the rest of the world. China's new foreign policy stance has been reflected in various events in recent years.

First, Beijing began to relax the distinction between *huaqiao* and *huaren* from 2001,[13] when it revived the semi-official organisation *Zhongguo guiqiao lianhehui* or the Federation of Returned Overseas Chinese Associations (*Qiaolian* for short). The government of the PRC invited *huaren* throughout the world to be its "advisers" and "overseas committee members". In the same year, Overseas Chinese Affairs Office (OCAO) organised a meeting of the World Federation of *Huaqiao Huaren* Associations (*Shijie huaqiao huaren shetuan lianyihui*), inviting the participation of both Chinese citizens overseas and foreign citizens of Chinese descent.

In 2004, China established Han Ban or the Executive Body of the Chinese Language Council International to promote the teaching of the Chinese language (or the Han language, as it is known in mainland China) and culture through the establishment of educational institutions known as Confucius Institutes in Southeast Asia and beyond.

In 2006, during an outbreak of anti-Chinese violence in the Solomon Islands, China began to repatriate all affected Chinese,

---

[13] James Jiann Hua To, citing an article published in China's *People Daily* on 8 January 2001, stated that "...when referring to qiaowu [overseas Chinese affairs], the terms "foreign nationals of Chinese descent", "foreigners of Chinese origin", and "people of Chinese origin residing abroad" are often used interchangeably with "Chinese nationals overseas". See James Jiann Hua To, *Qiaowu: Extra-Territorial Policies for the Overseas Chinese*, 2014, p. 112.

regardless of their nationality, to Guangdong and Hong Kong.[14] In May 2008, when a massive earthquake struck Wenchuan county in Sichuan, Beijing appealed to *huaqiao* and *huaren* to show their solidarity with China by making contributions.[15] In the same year, Beijing again appealed to all Chinese overseas, regardless of their citizenship, to help China ensure the success of the Beijing Olympic Games and to participate as volunteers during the occasion.[16] Beijing emphasised that the Chinese overseas were still members of Chinese nation (*Zhonghua Minzu*), thus promoting Chinese transnationalism.

In 2011 or even earlier, China introduced a Great Overseas Chinese Affairs Policy (*Da qiaowu zhengce*), emphasising the inclusion of *huaren* within its "Overseas Chinese Affairs" programme. It is clear that the change in China's overseas Chinese policy — blurring the distinction between *huaqiao* and *huaren*, using overseas Chinese as social capital — has started long before Xi Jinping came to power. It coincided with the rise of China as the economic power, beginning from the end of Jiang Zemin's term, developed during Hu Jintao's presidency and further developed by Xi Jinping when he assumed presidency in 2013.

The Xi Jinping Era

One of the indicators that the overseas Chinese has become an important tool for China's transnational expansion was the revival of "Five Overseas Chinese Institutions Mechanism" (*Wu Qiao Jizhi*) during Xi Jinping's presidency. These *Wu Qiao* (five overseas Chinese institutions) consist of three levels, namely, national, provincial and

---

[14] For a short discussion of the Solomon Islands affair, see Grace Chew Chye Lay, "The April 2006 Riots in the Solomon Islands ", *CHC Bulletin,* Issues 7 and 8 (May and November 2006), pp. 11–21.

[15] Yang Bao'an, "Zhongguo younan, huaren zhiyuan" (When China Is in Trouble, Ethnic Chinese Come to Her Rescue), *Zaobao Xingqitian,* 8 June 2008.

[16] For a brief discussion of this topic, see Leo Suryadinata, "A New Orientation in China's Policy towards Chinese Overseas? Beijing Olympic Games Fervour as a Case Study", *CHC Bulletin*, Issue 12, November 2008, pp. 1–6.

township.[17] These five institutions mechanism coordinating meeting started in 1983 during Deng Xiaoping's era, but slipped temporarily into a dormant state and revived during Hu Jintao's presidency. When Xi Jinping became president, it was revitalised. In 2014, it held the 32nd coordinating conference to implement the overseas Chinese policy.[18] It has become clear that through the Wu Qiao mechanism, overseas Chinese has become central to China's foreign policy.[19]

In 2014, President Xi Jinping, made a speech at the Conference of World Federation of Huaqiao Huaren Associations where he referred to the overseas Chinese as members of "Zhonghua big family" (*Zhonghua da jiating*). When he addressed the meeting, he used the term "*haiwai qiaobao*" (overseas compatriots) rather than "*haiwai huaren*" (Chinese overseas).[20] Although the occasion was the world *huaqiao* and *huaren* conference, Xi only used the term *qiaobao* and completely ignored the distinction between *huaqiao* and *huaren*. This policy became clearer in the following year when President Xi proposed the "One Belt, One Road" strategy (OBOR, and thereafter renamed Belt and Road Initiative or BRI) in which the Chinese overseas were envisaged to play a part.

In early July 2015, the first World Huaqiao Huaren Entrepreneurs Conference (WHHEC, *Shijie huaqiao huaren gongshang dahui*) was

---

[17] These five institutions are Overseas Chinese Affairs Office (OCAO, also known as Qiao Ban), the Federation of Returned Overseas Chinese, (also known as Qiaolian), Zhi Gong Dang, Overseas Chinese Committee in People's Representatives Congress and the Hong Kong, Macao and Taiwan Compatriots Committee, available at <http://www.npc.gov.cn/npc/bmzz/llyjh/2016-06/06/content_1991120.htm> (accessed 16 May 2018).

[18] <http://www.npc.gov.cn/npc/bmzz/llyjh/2016-06/06/content_1991120.htm> (accessed 16 May 2018).

[19] There is also an article on this Wu Qiao seen as a mode of transnational governnance, see Liu Hong and Els van Dongen, "China's Diaspora Policies as a New Mode of Transnational Governance", *Journal of Contemporary China*, vol. 25, no. 102, pp. 805–821.

[20] <http://pic.people.com.cn/n/2014/0607/c1016–25116878.html> (accessed 23 July 2015).

held in Beijing. Top leadership of China, namely, Premier Li Keqiang and chairperson Qiu Yuanping made speeches to urge *huaqiao huaren* to support Xi Jinping's BRI to ensure its success. Premier Li Keqiang even recognised these Chinese entrepreneurs as the new effective force of China's economic transformation. They serve as a bridge between China and foreign countries and project the new image of "Chinese entrepreneurs".[21] In fact, there is an ethnic Chinese-initiated "World Chinese Entrepreneurs Convention" (WCEC, *Shijie huashang dahui*), which has been held periodically since its launch in Singapore in 1991. However, as the WCEC is not initiated and controlled by Beijing, it therefore established a rival one in order to serve its national interest. The second WHHEC conference was held in 2017, urging Chinese entrepreneurs to help in the China economic offensive and BRI, as well as the unification of Taiwan and the Mainland.[22]

Participants of the WHHEC consist of both *huaqiao* and *huaren*, with the majority *huaren* rather than *huaqiao*. To ask foreign nationals to serve the interest of China would appear to be unreasonable and would also put some participants in an awkward position.

In 2015, after hosting the first WHHEC conference, a new proposal to woo foreign citizens of Chinese descent, known as the Huayi Ka (*Huayi* Card) system was introduced.

Huayi Card

On 5 December 2015, *Ming Bao*, a major Chinese language daily in Hong Kong, reported that on 27 November 2015 Guo Hong, the director of the management committee of the Zhong Guan Cun (known as the "Silicon Valley of China", located in Beijing), had made an unexpected announcement of a pilot project known as the *Huayi*

---

[21] <www.sznewscom/content/2015-07/07/content_11861357.htm> (accessed 10 July 2015).

[22] <http://www.chinareform.org.cn/open/view/201706/t20170613_266502.htm> (accessed 26 July 2018).

Card system.[23] According to the announcement, the card would be issued to any qualified person of Chinese origin so that he/she could stay in China as a permanent resident and enjoy almost all the privileges of a Chinese citizen. Unlike dual nationality status, the cardholder does not have voting rights in China.[24]

The project aims to recruit more professionals for high technology and economic development. The idea came from the Indian practice of issuing two types of identity cards for Indians overseas known as Persons of Indian Origin (PIOs) cards and Overseas Citizens of India (OCI) cards.[25]

In reality, China already has the green card system which was introduced roughly 10 years ago. While the Green Card system is ethnicity-blind, the *Huayi* Card is based on Chinese ethnicity. Beijing aims to get ethnic Chinese professionals/entrepreneurs to work and live in China.

The announcement has caused a lot of confusion. Some thought the *Huayi* Card idea was confirmed but the authorities said that it would only be a pilot and would be tried out in 2016. Presumably, the

---

[23] See Zhongguo shixing huayi ka, zhenshi chengren shuangchong guoji (China Begins to Test the *Huayi* Card That Shows the Recognition of Dual Nationality Status), available at <www.mingpaocanada.com/tor/htm/News/20151205/taa1_r.htm> (accessed 10 December 2015). The discussion in this section is mainly based on this report.

[24] For a discussion of the *Huayi* Card, see Leo Suryadinata, *The Rise of China and Chinese Overseas*, pp. 217–221.

[25] For Chinese studies on PIO and OCI, see Zhang Yinglong and Huang Chaohui, Yindu qiaomin zhengce yanjiu (A Study of the Policy on Indian Citizens Overseas), in Zhou Nanjing (ed), *jingwai huaren guoji wenti taolunji* (Citizenship Issues of the Chinese outside China: A Collection of Papers) Hong Kong, 2005, pp. 290–311; Qiu Li Ben, "Yindu Guoji yimin yu qiaowu gongzuo de lishi yu xianzhuang (The History and Present Situation of Indian International Migrants and Overseas Indian Affairs), *Huaqiao huaren lishi yanjiu* (Overseas Chinese History Studies), no. 1, March 2012, pp. 24–35. According to these studies, the Indian government introduced the PIO card in March 1999 and the OCI card in January 2003. Both cards have a common feature, namely, card holders do not have political rights in India. The PIO card was merged into the OCI card on 9 January 2015. See announcement by the Indian Ministry of Home, available at <http://mha1.nic.in/pdfs/Merge_PIO_OCI.pdf> (accessed 5 February 2016).

system would be tested on a small group of foreign Chinese first and if the result proves promising, it would then be implemented on a larger scale.

The *Huayi* Card system was criticised by many observers who are conversant with the Chinese overseas situation, especially in Southeast Asia. In China, Professor Liang Yingming of Peking University commented on its shortcomings and the risks associated with adopting the ethnic principle in issuing permanent residency rights.[26] The Chinese press in Singapore also published reports that were unflattering to the *Huayi* Card.[27] Probably because of such criticisms, OCAO had second thoughts about introducing the system at the moment. It is also possible that the system cannot be implemented due to strong domestic opposition. Many domestic Chinese disagreed to grant special status and social benefits to foreign citizens of Chinese descent.

The director of OCAO, Qiu Yuanping, announced on 8 March 2016 that the report concerning the *Huayi* Card was untrue.[28] Thereafter, there was a similar report which quoted her as saying that OCAO did not have any plans to issue *Huayi* Cards. However, OCAO would amend the existing regulations to make it easier for foreigners of Chinese descent (*waiji huaren*) to receive the permanent resident status and enjoy other facilities in China.[29] In other words, the scheme has been shelved for the time being.

---

[26] "Beida jiaoshou liang yingming: zhongguo yao lizhi kandai haiwai huaren lichang" (Professor Liang Yingming of Peking University: China Should Look at the Stand of Overseas Chinese Seriously), *Lianhe Zaobao*, 22 February 2016.

[27] For instance, "Bendi xuezhe: mohu huaqiao huaren jiexian" (Local Scholar: Blurring the Boundary between Huaqiao and Huaren) *Lianhe Zaobao*, 19 February 2016.

[28] "Qiu Yuanping huiying qiaojie guanzhu redian: Huayika baodao bushushi" (Qiu Yuanping Responded to the Hot Issue among the Overseas Chinese: The Report on the *Huayi* Card Is Untrue), available at <www.chinanews.com/gn2016/03-10/7792404> (accessed 20 April 2016).

[29] "Guowuyuan qiaoban zhuren Qiu Yuanping: muqian hai wei kaolv chutao huayika" (Qiu Yuanping of the OCAO, the State Council: Currently There Is No Intention of Issuing the

However, in January 2018, the *South China Morning Post* reported that China would introduce a five-year multi-entry visa for foreigners of Chinese origin starting from February 2018. The purpose was to allow foreigners of Chinese descent to participate in "China's economic development".[30] Some saw this as a substitute of the *Huayi* Card as this is given based on ethnicity. Nevertheless, the privileges offered differ from those of the *Huayi* Card system.

The Single Nationality Law and *Hukou*

While Beijing introduced new policies for Chinese overseas, including the blurring of the distinction between *huaqiao* and *huaren*, welcoming overseas Chinese talents to serve China and using Chinese overseas as social capital, it has also continued to stick to the 1980 Nationality Law, that is, to ensure that foreign citizens of Chinese descent are not entitled to the Household Registration (alias *hukou*) in China as it entails social benefits which are only enjoyed by citizens.

In fact, many Chinese migrants who have become foreign citizens were reluctant to give up their *hukou*. Recently there was a sketchy report that the Chinese government wanted to continue to eradicate foreigners' *hukou*. It was reported that between 2013 and June 2014, the government of China succeeded in deregistering 1.06 million foreign citizens of Chinese descent.[31] The same report also noted that in early 2018, the government and Chinese embassy in Canada warned foreign citizens of Chinese descent to voluntarily de-register their *hukou*. If discovered, they would not be allowed to leave China until they have completed the de-registration.[32]

Huayi Card), available at <http://cn.chinadaily.com.cn/2016lianghui/2016-03/13/content_23844522.htm> (accessed 20 April 2016).

[30] <https://www.scmp.com/news/china/society/article/2131030/ethnic-chinese-and-want-live-china-find-out-if-you-qualify-new> (accessed 26 July 2018).

[31] <http://news.sina.com.cn/o/2018-02-19/doc-ifyrqwkc8254692.shtml> (accessed 26 July 2018).

[32] <http://news.sina.com.cn/o/2018-02-19/doc-ifyrqwkc8254692.shtml> (accessed 26 July 2018).

It is not known how many new Chinese migrants (known as *xin yimin*) have repudiated China's citizenship and how many have their *hukou* deregistered. The *Huayi* Card system which offers the returned *huaren* talents a special status enjoyed by Chinese citizens minus voting rights has certain similarities with *hukou*, a possible reason why it was eventually scrapped.

Conclusion

The new Beijing policy towards the Chinese overseas is not entirely new. During the KMT era, China introduced a policy to include Chinese overseas as Chinese nationals along with their loyalty to China. The government promoted patriotism and Chinese nationalism among the Chinese overseas that caused problems for them. However, the difference is that the KMT China was weak and was unable to implement the policy while Xi Jinping's China is economically strong enough to implement such a policy.

Initially, post-KMT China followed the KMT policy towards the Chinese and subsequently changed the policy to encourage overseas Chinese to be integrated with local society where they lived. It even promulgated the single nationality law. However, with the exodus of the Chinese and the rise of China, the government has reassessed the importance of the Chinese overseas and eventually adopted a new policy.

Nevertheless, the policy is clearly directed at wealthy Chinese and Chinese professionals. Despite this new policy, the 1980 Nationality Law (which was amended in 1996 for Hong Kong residents) remains. Therefore an argument can be raised that Beijing is practising a dual policy for Chinese overseas: on the one hand, it blurs the distinction between *huaqiao* and *huaren*, and on the other, it does not change its single nationality law to dual nationality law. Obviously, the present single nationality law is still beneficial for the PRC's national interest.

As a superpower, China needs to maintain cordial relations with its neighbours. It should be sensitive in its policy formulation for Chinese overseas, especially those who have opted for non-Chinese nationality. They should be respected for their choice.

China has also introduced a protection policy towards overseas Chinese who were persecuted. Ships and planes were sent to save migrants in distress, regardless of their citizenship as in the cases of the South Pacific, the Middle East and Africa.[33] However, these rescue works were done when the interest of these Chinese coincide with the national interest of the PRC.

This policy is likely to have negative responses from other countries that have a large number of ethnic Chinese population. It is natural that a country wants to protect its nationals, but is unnatural if a country is also attempting to "protect" the people who are no longer their nationals. In countries where ethnic Chinese issues are still sensitive, China's new policy is controversial to say the least.

---

[33] For a study on these events, see Leo Suryadinata, *The Rise of China and Chinese Overseas*, pp. 69–94.

Chapter 14

China's rise, Globalisation 4.0 and Innovative Global Governance

WANG Huiyao*

Introduction

Globalisation has fuelled economic growth for hundreds of years. The global movement of goods and services has defined eras and set agendas, exposing power dynamics and structures, breaking and making relationships on the way. China as a nation has played a role in globalisation processes over the centuries. Recently, however, China has seen economic growth at unprecedented levels, elevating the nation to become the world's second largest economy and a key player in global trade. The economic transition of China has made waves the world over, with many seeking to theorise and predict how the new economic power will present itself on the international stage. China occupies a unique position at present; it faces many challenges, but also enjoys incredible opportunities. The path and strategy that it adopts will impact not only its own population but have regional and global significance.

* WANG Huiyao is President of the Centre for China and Globalisation and Dean of the Institute of Development Studies of China Southwestern University of Finance and Economics.

Historical Context: Globalisation 1.0, 2.0, 3.0 and now 4.0

It is commonly accepted among economists and academics that there are defining phases in the processes which constitute globalisation. These eras, while primarily describing the mode of globalisation, are shaped by a range of conditions which impact the direction, manner and often the means of globalisation processes. The current phase, globalisation 4.0, exhibits further intensified processes of global trade, down to the personal level, and is often coupled with Industry 4.0 or the "Fourth Industrial Revolution". For a deeper understanding of the present condition of globalisation, especially in relation to China and its development, it is necessary to briefly explain preceding iterations of the process. Globalisation can loosely be defined as the expansion and intensification of networks and processes which enable trade and exchange over transnational distances. Networks that function as a mediator between actors separated by vast geographical distances have been in existence for millennia and are not the focus of this chapter. However, it is these networks that delineate the four generally recognised phases of globalisation.

Firstly, Globalisation 1.0 describes the initial wave of concerted efforts to expand global trade networks which occurred at the beginning of the 20th century. Largely propelled by the British Empire, this push for increased trade depended on new forms of mechanical power, such as steam, which made it possible and economical to consume goods made far away. The globalisation that preceded the outbreak of the two World Wars (WW) was characterised by extreme laissez-faire capitalism, without global governance and the sharing of benefits of global trade.

The end of WWII marked the beginning of Globalisation 2.0, which saw the forging of an international community brought together by the horrors of war. It is in this period that the notion of global governance took hold and the Marshall Plan was implemented. Economically, this came in the form of the World Bank, International Monetary Fund and the formulation of the General Agreement on

Tariffs and Trade (GATT). These institutions were governed in part internally, but were a result of global governance mechanisms such as the United Nations (UN). It was the establishment of these systems which defined this period. Technological, logistical and social advances such as electricity and assembly-line production made during the wars boosted manufacturing and production, reigniting trade networks and driving the much-needed economic activities.

Globalisation 3.0 came into fruition towards the end of the 20th century, with not only increased flows of goods and personnel, but also high-tech goods manufactured in locations with low wages becoming increasingly common. It is in this era that the GATT morphed into the World Trade Organisation (WTO), further enhancing trade dispute and tariff mechanisms to better suit new patterns of global trade. China began to engage in global economic systems with the introduction of the reform and opening-up process beginning in 1978. As China looked to expand its knowledge base and grow its economy, while manufacturers were looking to move their operations worldwide, opportunities abounded for both sides. There was an overlap of China's economic reforms and the elements which defined the processes of Globalisation 3.0, and China's current economic status compared with the beginning of economic reforms in 1978. The success achieved by China during this period defines, in large part, China's support for globalisation and free trade today, and informs its desire to contribute to and maintain the future direction of integrated global trade systems.

In terms of production, Globalisation 4.0 mirrors the concepts of Industry 4.0 or "the Fourth Industrial Revolution". Both describe the development of the means of production in four steps, from mechanisation and steam/water power to mass production and electricity to computer and automation to "fourth generation" technology such as advanced automation, cyber-physical systems and the Internet of Things. These trends are converging at a time of unprecedented change and growth occurring at an exponential rate across almost all regions and nations, affecting systems of production, management and governance.[1] Globalisation 4.0 has come at a crucial moment in global economic governance. China has solidified its position as the world's second largest economy and looks set to become the world's largest within the next two decades. National initiatives such as "Made in China 2025" seek to address the shift in manufacturing and production, aiming to place China as a leading figure in automation and high-tech manufacturing.[2] Chinese technology companies are among world leaders in advanced network systems, mobile technology, robotics and artificial intelligence. China leads the world in the scale and passenger volume of its high-speed rail network and logistics systems. Internally, innovative local and municipal Chinese governments are using technology in their governance and providing services that are creating some truly "smart" cities.

New Global Challenges: Protectionism and "the Two Traps"

Having reaped immense benefits from globalisation, China has stood out and remained a key backer of deeper economic globalisation and freer international trade. However, this has not come without criticism and opposing policies by some nations. The number of nations which have moved to limit engagement and withdraw from the international stage has increased. This can be seen in the recent uptick of protectionist trade policies. Throughout history, people have often sought to simplify reality into an easy-to-comprehend narrative involving only two forces battling it out for supremacy. China-US relations are no exception. Theories pertaining to a rising power challenging an existing dominant power have been regularly applied to China-US relations, though many question the utility or accuracy of such comparisons.

---

[1] Schwab Klaus, "The Fourth Industrial Revolution: What It Means, How to Respond", World Economic Forum, 14 January 2016, <https://www.weforum.org/agenda/2016/01/the-fourth-industrial-revolution-what-it-means-and-how-to-responn/> (accessed 15 January 2019).

[2] <http://english.xiongan.gov.cn/2018-04/14/c_129850585.htm> (accessed 15 January 2019).

Protectionism

Countries including the United States and some European nations have adopted protectionist policies to revive economic structures, largely in manufacturing and other industries. Protectionist policies in this context have gained popularity, as have populist politics aimed at rejuvenating perceived national characteristics and restoring a certain image of the nation.

The presidency of Donald Trump is the most representative of this trend. An elected president running on the slogan of "America First", President Trump has implemented numerous protectionist economic policies targeting international trade. These included the reworking of the North American Free Trade Agreement (NAFTA) to its new form, the United States Mexico Canada Agreement (USMCA), imposing tariffs on a variety of goods produced outside the United States such as steel, aluminium, solar panels and washing machines, and an array of targeted tariffs on Chinese-produced goods which ignited the China-US trade war.

The United Kingdom's (UK) decision to leave the European Union (EU) has also been put forward as a hallmark of rising protectionist sentiment across Europe. The referendum result, referred to as "Brexit", was won on the back of a campaign which emphasised control over immigration, independence from EU bureaucracy and British identity. With the UK's withdrawal from the EU yet to be realised, it is not clear what direction the UK will take following its exit and what effect this will have on other EU member states flirting with populist politics.

The Thucydides and Kindleberger traps

China's position as a proponent of free trade and economic reform stands in contrast to US protectionist sentiments. This reason, as well as the fact that China is fast surpassing the United States as the world's largest economy, has raised the popularity of theories regarding the fate of these two countries. The most commonly adopted theory that describes potential conflict between the United States and China is the Thucydides Trap. It posits that when a rising power rivals a ruling power, it will inevitably challenge the existing hegemon. Former director of the Belfer Centre for Science and International Affairs and professor at the John F Kennedy School of Government at Harvard, Graham Allison, was the first to use the Greek historian's concept in reference to the future path of China-US relations. His team's analysis of past cases in which a rising power had confronted an established power found that 12 out of 16 had resulted in conflict, often causing severe harm to both powers.[3] Whilst this theory has a certain historical credibility, even according to its leading proponent, Professor Allison, conflict between China and the United States is not guaranteed and can be avoided.

The second trap that is used to describe the rise of China and the repercussions for the United States is the Kindleberger Trap. Originating from the late economic historian Charles Kindleberger, the term was coined by Harvard Professor Joseph Nye. The concept, like the Thucydides Trap, describes a shift in power but places impetus on the rising power to contribute to the international system it is inheriting through its production of global public goods.[4] The United States' inclination for protectionism is seemingly showing the retreat of the United States from a position of global leadership; if China is to take up the mantle, this concept dictates it must assume international responsibilities accorded to such a position. China would also need to have significant international presence if it were to overtake the United States, providing foreign aid and strengthening soft power capabilities.

Building an Asian Community

In view of Trump's unilateral America First policy, many Asian countries (often traditional allies and partners of the United States) have gradually turned towards China. At the same time, it appears that efforts for

---

[3] "The Thucydides Trap: Are the U.S. and China Headed for War?" *The Atlantic*, 24 September 2015, <https://www.theatlantic.com/international/archive/2015/09/united-states-china-war-thucydides-trap/406756/> (accessed 15 January 2019).
[4] <https://www.cfr.org/blog/four-traps-china-may-fall> (accessed 15 January 2019).

Asian regional integration have gained momentum. This is evident in the revival of relations between China and India, China and Japan, and China and the ROK (Republic of Korea or South Korea), as well as the reboot of the China-Japan-ROK trilateral summit. This is representative of a need for further integration and the increasing willingness of Asian nations to seek out Asian counterparts when dealing with regional issues. This trend can also be seen to be connected to Asia's strengthening economic might and confidence in international engagement.

There have long been talks of establishing a wider Asian community built on the back of shared values. A system of Asian values was advocated by Malaysian Prime Minister Mahathir Mohamad and former Singaporean Prime Minister Lee Kuan Yew to define elements of society, culture and history common to nations of Southeast and East Asia. This notion of Asian values gained traction in China, Malaysia, Singapore, Indonesia and Japan.

Lee maintained that, more than economics or politics, a nation's culture would determine its fate. From such a standpoint, nations with common cultural elements are well-placed to assist each other in achieving mutually beneficial goals.[5] This mirrors Japanese sentiment of "Ideals of the East", which was embraced by some nationalist circles as it challenged the West and offered the possibility of Japanese leadership in a new Asia.[6] The reality of such beliefs was explored with the rise of the "Asian Tigers" (Singapore, Hong Kong, South Korea and Taiwan) beginning in the 1950s, where some attributed the economic success of East and Southeast Asian countries to "Asian values". Whilst it is extremely difficult to pin down and analyse what "Asian values" are, there is no doubt cultural affinity between many Asian communities and nations which could be used to further integrate people and economies in East and Southeast Asia in the future.

---

[5] Zakaria Fareed, "A Conversation with Lee Kuan Yew", *Foreign Affairs*, 31 August 2017, <https://www.foreignaffairs.com/.../conversation-lee-kuan-yew> (accessed 15 January 2019).

[6] Okakura Kakuzo, *The Ideals of the East*, London, J Murray, 1903.

Renowned Professor Zheng Yongnian pointed out that both Western and Chinese civilisations retain their unique characteristics and that one cannot replace or copy the other. In his many works, Professor Zheng notes that while Asian nations should be free to utilise Western theories and systems as tools to achieve economic success and social development, Asian values should always form the ballast of Asian countries' social and economic transformation, as blindly following or completely embracing Westernisation will cause severe issues for the nation. Acknowledging the wealth of diversity in the region, he also emphasised that China only represents part of Asia's values and there is a need to integrate China's outlook with the philosophies of other Asian countries, such as India and Japan, as well as Western civilisations, to construct a comprehensive picture of Asian values.

Overseas Chinese communities

Overseas Chinese communities can be found in almost all corners of the globe. With this community a stereotype proven to be factually true also emerges: the disproportionate involvement of Chinese communities in business.

Professor Wang Gungwu explores the historical context to this phenomenon in his book, *The Chinese Overseas*. He delves into the 2,000-year history of Chinese attempts to venture abroad and the underlying values affecting Chinese overseas migration. China in the past prohibited its citizens ("earthbound Chinese") from leaving the land and travelling and settling overseas; however, with time, first traders, then peasants and workers eventually found new livelihoods abroad. Through his analysis of Chinese migrants, Professor Wang uncovers some major themes of global history: the coming together of Asian and European civilisations, the ambiguities of ethnicity and diaspora consciousness, and the tension between maintaining one's culture and assimilation.[7]

---

[7] Wang, Gungwu, *The Chinese Overseas: From Earthbound China to the Quest for Autonomy*, Harvard University Press, 2002.

There are about 60 million overseas Chinese in different parts of the world. The majority, over 50 million, live in Southeast Asia, with around 6.5 million in North America.[8] Overseas Chinese reportedly hold between US$200 billion and US$300 billion in assets.[9] On a per capita basis, Singapore has the highest proportion of overseas Chinese outside Greater China, while Australia has the highest proportion outside Asia.[10] The overseas Chinese in Southeast Asia not only dominate trading and services, but also are big players in banking and property. As a matter of fact, the overseas Chinese communities including those hailing from China, Taiwan and Hong Kong form such a strong economic network that if you do business in East and Southeast Asia outside of Japan and Korea, you more often than not will end up doing business with people of Chinese heritage. The overseas Chinese are themselves a natural link between China and the rest of the world, in part due to their cultural similarities with mainland Chinese and the social and economic relations with their adopted homes. Overseas Chinese communities can play an important bridging role in enhancing mutual understanding between China and countries around the world, specifically in East and Southeast Asia. Notably, these communities could play a more significant role as China's position grows globally.

China's Belt and Road Initiative

China's Belt and Road Initiative (BRI) seeks to promote regional and continental integration. The project was launched by President Xi in 2013 and with the successful completion of numerous projects, an international BRI community is being forged along the routes of the initiative. The BRI, with its global nature and involvement of a vast array of diverse nations, has already garnered many international

---

[8] <https://en.wikipedia.org/wiki/Overseas_Chinese> (accessed 15 January 2019).
[9] Centre for China and Globalisation, *2016 Report on Development of World Overseas Chinese Entrepreneurs*, November 2016, <http://en.ccg.org.cn/2016-report-on-development-of-world-overseas-chinese-entrepreneurs/> (accessed 15 January 2019).
[10] <https://en.wikipedia.org/wiki/Overseas_Chinese> (accessed 15 January 2019).

partners; China signed an MOU (Memorandum of Understanding) in 2016 with the United Nations Development Programme (UNDP) to cooperate on the initiative.[11] As the vast initiative continues there will be a need for deeper integration of the BRI into existing world systems.

As both developing and developed countries are welcomed to join the BRI, a community of shared interests has been created. China is enhancing relations between the BRI and existing multilateral intitutions such as the WTO, World Bank and IMF. This will aid the progression of BRI projects and the general direction of BRI-related trade, investment and infrastructure. By deepening cooperation with the UN, the BRI could advocate for the establishment of a new UN institution or department for BRI affairs, building on the China-UNDP MOU on BRI cooperation signed on the margins of the 71st United Nations General Assembly.

China's New Role in Global Governance

China's global governance strategy is formulated according to the aforementioned unique situation. Its rising global position, as seen in the above "trap" concepts, is often set against the United States rescinding the leading role it has held in the world. Whilst it is unclear or inaccurate to draw this type of conclusion, there is no doubt that China will continue to develop and progress according to its specific conditions and ever-changing external factors. China faces many challenges and incredible opportunities regarding global governance at present. The impact of the way in which China deals with such problems and what opportunities it decides to grasp will be felt around the world.

China and Global Governance 2.0

China has been one of the biggest beneficiaries of the US-led world order, gaining immensely from globalisation and world trade. It has

---

[11] <http://www.undp.org/content/undp/en/home/presscenter/pressreleases/2016/09/19/undp-and-china-to-cooperate-on-belt-and-road-initiative.html> (accessed 15 January 2019).

repeatedly emphasised that it is not setting out to change the incumbent world order and is prepared to uphold and improve it together with other countries, especially through cooperation with the United States. Yet, China also has great potential to innovate global governance by actively engaging and promoting new international institutions.

Regionally, the desire for increased integration between Asian nations, especially East and Southeast Asian countries, is evident not only at the Boao Forum for Asia, ASEAN and APEC, but also in the increase in free trade initiatives in the region. The Regional Comprehensive Economic Partnership (RCEP), Free Trade Area of Asia Pacific (FTAAP) and Comprehensive and Progressive Agreement for Trans-Pacific Partnership (CPTPP, formerly TPP) have emerged over the past decade as potential platforms for China to lead in the development and establishment of new trade systems. Whilst China's involvement in these agreements has been limited, there are huge opportunities for China to further promote globalisation in these forums.

China-US global governance

China's promotion of free trade has signalled to the world that it is open to engagement through economic systems; this is especially true for China's engagement with the United States. The two nations are tightly bound, with their economies heavily dependent on one another; relations between the two nations have truly global implications. Whilst there may be some merit to the Thucydides and Kindleberger traps and potentially disastrous global consequences could result if wrong steps are taken, it seems more likely that China and the United States will seek to find a balance in their approaches to global governance.

On the Thucydides Trap, many experts believe that due to the enmeshed nature of the global economy and processes of global trade, of which the United States and China are major stakeholders, the two nations will choose or be forced to choose to cooperate instead of resorting to conflict. Historian Niall Ferguson coined the term *Chimerica* to represent the great new geopolitical reality — that the 21st century will be dominated by China and America.[12] Even with some friction in China-US ties in recent years, the future of the relationship is generally expected to be one of peaceful cooperation because of their deep inter-dependence. A complete breakdown of the relationship, harking back to the days of the Cold War, would come at extremely high cost to both China and the United States. Professor Chu Yun-Han, a distinguished China-US expert, has commented that despite tension in China-US relations, there are still many opportunities for mutual accommodation and cooperation in defusing geopolitical flashpoints and tackling global issues. Many existing multilateral arrangements still tie the United States and China together and compel them to engage regularly and seek common ground to move forward.

China has also sought to ease concerns highlighted by the Kindleberger Trap. As China has developed economically, it has estab-lished itself as a contributor of global public goods. The BRI is a prime example of a grand initiative which aims to provide public goods to nations involved in its multitude of projects. However, China has also become increasingly involved in existing global governance structures, for example, as an active member of the UN Security Council and deepening its work with other UN bodies. Through greater engage-ment on top of its vast economic activity, China anchors its global strategy on the emerging multi-polar world, in which no superpower can unilaterally dictate norms and rules. It is also a strong advocate of multilateralism, which is the only viable path to sustaining an open, invigorated and inclusive global economy and coping with challenges to the sustainability of global community. Recent anti-globalisation tendencies do not change the fact that globalisation is irreversible. The ups and downs of China-US trade tensions are similar to the rough patch in the China-US relationship experienced in 2009 and 2010 following the financial crisis. With China taking a more active and responsible international role, it can avoid both the Thucydides Trap

---

[12] "Niall Ferguson Says U.S.-China Cooperation Is Critical to Global Economic Health", *Washington Post*, 17 November 2008, <http://www.washingtonpost.com/wp-dyn/content/article/2008/11/16/AR2008111601736.html> (accessed 12 January 2019).

and the Kindleberger Trap, help upgrade the global governance system and maintain a delicate balance with the United States.

Global governance suggestions for China

As China continues to adapt and establish its grand strategy of global governance, it should take into consideration areas where it can play an impactful role not only in existing institutions, but also through newer organisations which will shape the path of Globalisation 4.0.

Following US withdrawal from the TPP, China could seek to join its new incarnation, the CPTPP, in order be on the ground level of what will become the third largest free trade zone after USMCA and the EU. With the approval of the governments of Japan, Australia, Mexico, Singapore, New Zealand and Canada, CPTPP came into effect at the end of 2018. This ushered in the formal establishment of a multilateral trading system which accounts for 13.2% of the global economy and 15% of total world trade volume.[13] Connecting markets boasting an overall population of over 500 million, CPTPP is the largest free trade agreement in the Asia-Pacific region.[14] If China were to join CPTPP, this would be in accordance with China's national policy of promoting greater economic openness and the "going global" development path of Chinese industry and enterprises. China's accession to CPTPP could also prove conducive to providing a long-term settlement mechanism for China-US trade disputes, as well as helping advance international cooperation on the BRI.

Another platform for China to reinforce free trade is the proposal for a FTAAP as a way to overcome the "noodle bowl" effect created by overlapping and conflicting elements of numerous free trade agreements (FTAs) in the region. The FTAAP, more ambitious in scope than the Doha round, would create a free trade zone that would considerably

---

[13] Centre for China and Globalisation, *CPTPP, An Opportunity for China in Future Free Trade*, January 2019 <http://en.ccg.org.cn/cptpp-new-opportunities-for-china-in-future-free-trade/> (accessed 15 January 2019).

[14] <https://www.mfat.govt.nz/en/trade/free-trade-agreements/free-trade-agreements-in-force/cptpp/cptpp-overview> (accessed 15 January 2019).

expand commerce and economic growth in the region. An equally ambitious proposal is the RCEP, first proposed by ASEAN leaders and with similar aims as the FTAAP.[15] Seeking to remove trade barriers and lower tariffs between member nations with corresponding free trade agreements, the 16 participating countries account for almost half of the world's population, over 30% of global GDP and over a quarter of world exports.[16] However, since the rise of CPTPP, RCEP and FTAAP negotiations have stalled. As the desire for a comprehensive system to set guidelines and benchmarks for all the entangled FTAs that span Asia Pacific exists, it would just require a nation with significant clout — like China — to reignite these talks.

Geographical proximity, cultural similarity and shared values of Asian countries are a good starting point to realise the BRI. The initiative can build on the success of China's positive bilateral relations in Asia or regional FTAs already in place to provide impetus for the progression of the aforementioned comprehensive FTA mechanisms. Meanwhile, if China were to engage in a multilateral trade agreement in line with BRI it could be helpful to attracting Western countries to further cooperate with China in global affairs or, if possible, even join the BRI. Establishing a BRI rule-based governance system for the initiative would help to create an official BRI management organisation which can facilitate multilateral communication and coordination of BRI affairs. This would require the establishment of a standing committee or a standing secretariat to deal with routine responsibilities and host regular activities like annual events, without which the initiative may struggle to achieve its goals.

In addition to changing dynamics in global governance and finance mechanisms, as well as developments in the global economy as seen in the changes brought about by the "Fourth Industrial Revolution", there is a need to create new organisations and initiatives in these areas.

---

[15] <https://asean.org/?static_post=rcep-regional-comprehensive-economic-partnership> (accessed 15 January 2019).

[16] <https://dfat.gov.au/trade/agreements/negotiations/rcep/Pages/regional-comprehensive-economic-partnership.aspx> (accessed 15 January 2019).

China is uniquely placed to perform a central role in leading the international community in many of these issues. One of these is E-commerce, where China leads the world in a number of online sales platforms, in supporting technology and in infrastructure. Chinese companies could provide significant insight and share experience with other nations.

Conclusion

The remarkable progress made by China since the launch of reform and opening-up shows the strength and resilience of the nation and its people. The ever-changing dynamics of global trade and world political systems call for China to play a bigger role. Joining CPTPP and rekindling negotiations for RCEP and FTAAP would provide a steady economic foundation for China to achieve this goal. It would also aid in easing economic relations with the United States and enable the progression and internationalisation of the BRI.

How China's rise will impact the world remains to be seen. Can China be compared with the United States after the end of WWII? Can the BRI be seen as an equivalent to the United States' Marshall Plan? Or is this the beginning of a more multipolar world system? How do nodes of power and networks of economic activity span the globe? While answers to these questions remain uncertain, China's global governance strategy without a doubt will be a crucial factor in future globalisation efforts and global politics.

Index